D0084798

The World Gas Trade

About the Book and Editor

The proximity of vast reserves of natural gas to the great energy-consuming markets of the world, the relative environmental harmlessness of gas, and its competitive price make the use of gas increasingly attractive to an energy-hungry world. Within the next two decades we will see the use of gas and gas-related technologies expand in industrialized nations as well as among developing countries.

An international group of authorities on the political economy of natural gas analyzes the key factors influencing present gas supplies and uses and looks to the future, when new logistic systems and technological advances will affect both producers and consumers. The basic political, economic, and security considerations of energy will undergo a concomitant change in response to the increased availability and affordability of gas. In most markets, government monopolies direct the gas trade; in North America there will be a renewed role for private enterprise. Japan may also find its position greatly altered; although there are at present no pipeline connections to suppliers, and Japan is currently dependent on far-away sources of liquified natural gas, the contributors predict that future gas links to East Asia are highly likely.

The World Gas Trade explores the growing gas trade, anticipating that within the next several decades the foundation will have been laid for gas-fueled economies to displace oil-based economies in the world system.

Melvin A. Conant is president of Conant and Associates, Ltd., in Washington, D.C., and publisher of the international monthly Geopolitics of Energy. He is the editor (with commentary) of Oil Strategy and Politics, 1941-1981 (Westview, 1982), the selected papers of Walter J. Levy.

The World Gas Trade

A Resource for the Future

edited by Melvin A. Conant

Westview Press / Boulder and London

Dedicated to Theresa G. McConnell
whose good spirits and unstinting efforts
have made so much possible

Westview Special Studies in Natural Resources and Energy Management

Copyright © 1986 by Westview Press, Inc.

Published in 1986 in the United States of America by Westview Press, Inc.; Frederick A. Praeger, Publisher; 5500 Central Avenue, Boulder, Colorado 80301

Library of Congress Cataloging-in-Publication Data
The world gas trade.
    (Westview special studies in natural resources and energy management)
    Bibliography: p.
    Contents: Overview / Melvin A. Conant -- International gas trade / Jonathan P. Stern -- International gas contracts / Gerald B. Greenwald -- [etc.]
    1. Gas industry--Addresses, essays, lectures.
I. Conant, Melvin. II. Series.
HD9581.A2W67 1986   382'.42285   86-1711
ISBN 0-8133-7185-6

Composition for this book was provided by the editor.
This book was produced without formal editing by the publisher.

Printed and bound in the United States of America

The paper used in this publication meets the requirements of the American National Standard for Permanence of Paper for Printed Library Materials Z39.48-1984.

6   5   4   3   2   1

Contents

• gas pricing principles and practices • Netherlands • Algeria • Norway • Soviet Union • level of prices
• political limits • differences in
U.S. and European views • security
and transmission • gas in larger context of international relations

Norwegian shelf resources • markets:
United Kingdom and the Continent •
Germany • political factor in German-
Soviet relations • France • Belgium •
Italy • security of supply: the Nor-
wegian interest • role of Norwegian
gas in future West European demand •
Norwegian trade and gas policies •
factor of time and competition in
Norway's gas future

• Gas growth in Eastern Europe reserves • production • exploration •
self-sufficiency? • consumption patterns • imports from U.S.S.R. • pipelines • joint construction projects:
contractual and financial aspects •
gas pricing and prices

• Natural gas in the U.S.S.R. • reserves • development • production
achievements • role of Western Siberia: progress and problems • Soviet
internal gas supply system • investments • infrastructure • issues in
coordination of assignments and performance • vital importance of energy
progress: critiques of First Secretary M.S. Gorbachev • technology

U.S. market • logistics • effect of
changes in U.S. market and gas import
policies

Canadian reserves • domestic demand •
export record • changes in U.S. gas
regulations (1978) • Canadian gas
becomes non-competitive • changes
since 1983 in U.S. gas market regulations • question of price competition

Structure of Canada's gas industry •
companies • logistics • regulation
and pricing • change in Canadian domestic and export policies and practices • deregulation: the New Agreement of 1985 on pricing and taxation
• domestic sales • exports • implications of deregulation

Link between oil and gas • Mexican
gas policy • Reforma discoveries •
economic developments • debts •
question of gas exports to United
States • negotiations begin in 1977
and collapse • pricing of Mexican gas
competitive with Canada

Domestic political, economic and financial pressures (1980-84) • Mexican debt burden and negotiations •
energy policies • loss of U.S. market

Growth in gas reserves • technological advance • greater availability • industrial and developing nations • economies of scale • base-
load priorities • premium use • role
of government: the public/private

Preface

INTRODUCTION

This volume of essays by international authorities deals with the role of natural gas in the great energy markets of the world. The common theme throughout is the current and prospective importance of gas supplies in fueling the residential, commercial, and industrial energy requirements of an increasing number of nations. It is a subject which would have been given scant attention only two decades ago. The introduction of natural gas in its various forms, transported from often distant sources, has precipitated another great change in fuels. Through the different backgrounds and perspectives of the authors, the reader is invited to appreciate the complexities and the prospects which will affect our economies increasingly in coming decades.

The versatility of natural gas, its ease in processing and handling, its cleanliness as a fuel, and its comparatively lower cost gives it undeniable advantages over all other sources of primary energy -- except, eventually, those of solar origins.

Opinions differ as to the likely importance of natural gas' share of energy markets in decades to come. But it is the view of the Editor, shared only by some, that in societies near to already known vast gas reserves, this fuel will challenge and quite possibly surpass the role of oil and of coal in all of their uses. For this to happen, natural gas at the "burner tip," or with the end user, will first and foremost have to be price competitive. If this is demonstrable by suppliers over the short to long term, and if the continuous supply of contracted volumes is understood to be a necessary condition, the large investments required to bring gas to the markets will then be forthcoming, and the potential for natural gas will be realizable. The introduction of increasing gas volumes into energy markets marks the beginning of another great energy revolution.

* * *

Units of measurement in this book are:

for reserves or resources: trillion cubic feet (TCF)

for production, supply and demand: billion cubic feet per day (BCF/D)

for LNG (when expressed in millions of tons):
1 MMT = 1.4 billion cubic meters (BCM)

for converting BCM to BCF/D:
1 BCM = 35.3 BCF divided by 365 = BCF/D

for converting BCM to TCF:
1 BCM = .04 TCF

for converting terajoules (10^{12}) to BTU:
1555 joules = 1 BTU (see Table 6.5)

Note that throughout the text there will be differences in calculations of reserves, supplies and demand in many situations. These differences are often irreconcilable. Gas data (like all energy data) are best considered to be approximates of truth.

Melvin A. Conant

1

Overview

Melvin A. Conant

Essential to one's appreciation of gas issues
and options is an understanding of the general
history, supply, and demand for this fuel.

The advent of the Industrial Revolution depended on the availability and low cost of a fuel
alternative to wood. The answer was found in coal.
Its unique advantage lay in its higher BTU content,
its burning qualities and its ready availability
within most industrializing nations. While wood
could and did fuel steam boilers, wood could not,
for example, by itself have made the steam engine
as vital and ubiquitous as it so quickly became.
For that, a different fuel was required, and it was
coal. Nevertheless, as late as 1860, fuel wood
constituted 85 percent of U.S. energy consumption
and coal represented 15 percent. By the mid-1880s,
coal had 50 percent of the U.S. market; by 1920,
coal provided nearly 80 percent of U.S. energy
consumption. Then came petroleum. By the end of
the 1940s, oil was the leading U.S. commercial
fuel; twenty five years later, oil was the leading
commercial fuel of the world.

Oil was less costly to bring to market, easier
to stock, and cleaner to burn than coal. Its
singular disadvantage of being found in comparatively few very large fields, distant from market
centers, was overcome through the efforts of private sector oil companies which created an international system for its dependable supply nearly
anywhere. It is a wild guess as to how much longer
it can keep its lead position. While today's
surplus in crude producing capacities leads many

1

to assume oil will always be available when needed, the consequential retort may be that outside the Soviet Union and the Middle East the greatest discoveries of giant oil fields occurred mainly before 1950, despite subsequent advances in our knowledge of oil geology and of the technology to explore. Poor finding rates outside the Middle East warn that the world may deplete its oil capital at an ever-increasing rate.[1]

The most likely successful challenge to oil is natural gas for all of the same but even greater competitive advantages ascribed to the earlier greater attraction of oil over coal. Natural gas has become in many situations the preferred fuel source for all economic sectors except, perhaps, in heavy industry. It is conventional wisdom which tells us that the growing worldwide need for liquid transport fuels insures a major, continuing market for gasoline and diesel. Yet, even in this requirement, gas is making inroads. It is altogether possible that gas will in time, in many transport areas, displace current conventional fuels; in industrial countries and in those experiencing rapid development, the use of gas in transport is no longer novel or primitive but an accepted fuel whose greater use is an object of national energy policy.

What, then, is "natural gas"? Its origin is believed to be similar to those of oil which is also a product of decayed vegetable matters in different conditions of heat and pressure; hence gas and oil together comprise what is referred to as petroleum. It is a naturally occurring fuel and is differentiated from manufactured or "town gas," obtained mainly from coal or small gas reserves, whose particular use over many years lay mainly in lighting and residential heating. Beginning early in this century, the increasing availability of natural gas reduced the importance of manufactured gas. Research into coal conversion technologies remains of high energy priority. If conversion processes prove some day to be cost-competitive with natural gas supplies, coal-derived gas could be a supplemental and valuable source of additional gas. But the time when this might happen, on a scale large enough to be meaningful, is not until the next century.

Natural gas is often produced simultaneously with oil for they are often found together. In such situations the gas is termed "associated" and has to be separated. In years past or even still today when there is no market need for such gas, it is either flared or recycled back into the field where it adds to the pressure forcing oil to the surface. When found separately, in fields of its own, the gas is described as "non-associated." In either case, the gas is stripped of its natural gas liquids such as propane and butane -- used for liquefied petroleum gas supplied to smaller volume gas users -- and pentane (a blending agent for gasoline and for petrochemical purposes). A "dry" gas is left: Methane (upward to 75 percent) for residential, commercial, and industrial fuel needs plus petrochemical requirements as well; some ethane is also left for chemical feedstocks. It is the methane which is the key fuel, transported mainly through pipelines; a small proportion will be shipped by tankers under very low temperature in the form of liquefied natural gas (LNG).

LIQUEFIED NATURAL GAS

LNG -- the supply of natural gas through ocean trades began in 1969 with a volume of about 0.2 BCF/D. Ten years later, the total supply had reached 3.4 BCF/D and by 1984 the volume was nearly 5 BCF/D. This swift increase in an expensive form of gas, requiring advanced technology and specially designed and operated carriers and terminals is, in effect, an acknowledgment of the attractiveness of natural gas. Yet LNG trade in gas ranks far below that of international pipeline deliveries. While world LNG trade grew from 0.5 BCF/D to 5 BCF/D in the years 1969-84, world trade pipeline deliveries rose from some 3.2 BCF/D to about 15 BCF/D in the same period.

LNG trade is mainly between Abu Dhabi, Alaska, Brunei, Indonesia, and Malaysia to Japan; Japan received 3.5 BCF/D of LNG in 1984 or nearly 70 percent of the total world LNG trade. This very large share is a reminder of Japan's current lack of pipeline link to supplies, a unique circumstance in the community of industrial nations. LNG moves also to Europe and a very marginal volume to

the United States. Its front-end capital costs
have always served to limit LNG to special situations. Of all the forms in which gas is traded,
LNG may have the smallest prospects. Great advances in the technology and laying of undersea gas
pipelines now allows for the linking of supplies
and markets thus rendering LNG trade even less
attractive.

LIQUEFIED PETROLEUM GAS (LPG)

Best known for its convenient fuel storage
tanks for single dwellings and light consumer
production (and now appearing as an alternative to
gasoline/diesel transport fuels), LPG is still a
small percentage share of free world gas consumption: 10 percent. It is an expensive gas, compared
to gas delivered to consumers by pipeline, hence
its greater market seems limited to situations --
such as Japan and a number of developing nations -
- for whom LPG is the only gas source currently
available, except for LNG. Since 1970, its growth
in production has been from about 62 MMT to approximately 94 MMT in 1984. The largest consumer has
been by far the United States but the greatest
growth in consumption is seen in Africa, the Middle
East and Latin America.

Where are natural gas reserves located?[2] The
largest deposits lie within the Soviet Union --
some 1450 trillion cubic feet (TCF) or nearly 43
percent of the world's proved reserves. Next, the
Middle East in which Iran leads (at 475 TCF), then
Qatar with at least 150 TCF and Saudi Arabia at 123
TCF. These gas reserves are likely to be rated
larger with subsequent greater knowledge of the
fields.

North America ranks third in the regional
scale with the United States at 198 TCF and Canada
with 92 TCF for a total of 290 TCF. Next in order
comes Algeria (109 TCF), Norway (89 TCF) and Mexico
(77 TCF); then the Netherlands with proved reserves of 68 TCF; Kuwait, Venezuela, Malaysia,
Indonesia, Nigeria, Iraq, and the United Kingdom
possess proved gas reserves in the range of 55-26
TCF.

These constitute the principal reserves although there are many more nations with smaller gas assets scattered worldwide.

We have to be aware of the "life" of these proved reserves based on current annual production. In some cases, those nations which rank among the possessors of the largest reserves have a current depletion rate which sharply reduces their life expectancy as a consequence of high volume production. The most critical example is that of the United States.

Table 1.1

World Natural Gas Reserves (TCF),
Production (BCF/D) and Years Remaining
(as of end 1984)

Country	Proved Reserves (TCF)	Production* (BCF/D)	Years Remaining
U.S.S.R.	1450	58	60
Iran	479	.8	100+
U.S.A.	198	50	10
Qatar	150	–	100+
Saudi Arabia	123	1	100+
Algeria	109	2	100+
Canada	92	7	31
Norway	89	3	75
Mexico	77	3.5	55
Netherlands	68	7	25

World Total 3400

*Excluding gas flared or recycled -- not supplied to energy markets.

It should also be noted that world reserves/production ratios and the years remaining at the then current production level have increased. (See Table 1.2).

Table 1.2

"Life" of Gas Reserves

Date	Years Remaining
1974	43
1975	51
1980	51
1984	60

It is these proved reserves (3400 TCF) and potential estimates of additional volumes of more than 3000 TCF which support the view there is a large opportunity in major energy markets for ever-increasing volumes of natural gas and of increasing market shares.

Current forecasts of demand do not, by and large, support this thesis:[3]

Table 1.3

Potential Word Gas Demand As a
Percent of Primary Energy
(In circumstances of moderate rise
in oil prices)

Country/Region	1990	2000
U.S.S.R. (and East Europe)	30	34
West Europe	18	17
North America	24	23
JANZ[4]	14	13
Middle East	33	48
Latin America	15	15

But none of these estimates fully reflect the as-yet-largely-untapped gas resources near to these markets -- they appear, in effect, to discount the likelihood these gas assets will be developed. This apparent exclusion of the impact of very large additional supplies on energy markets has to be reexamined in light of the proposition that natural gas imports will be price competitive with alternative fuels. The object lesson of Algeria in this respect has to be thought about: this great potential supplier to the West European market, possessing 109 TCF of proved reserves, has so far lost out by refusing to acknowledge the importance of a gas price competitive with other fuels, and by acting in ways as to raise doubts among importers about Algeria's assured delivery of contracted volumes at acceptable prices.

In 1984 natural gas had about 19 percent of world energy markets. In the year 2000, the market share of gas is forecast to be 21 percent and afterward demand could rise by a further one percent annually. These conventional estimates of market share will be proven wrong in the great European and Soviet markets as proximate supplies from the Middle East (and the U.S.S.R.) move to Europe. By the year 20 30 it should not be at all surprising to find gas has overtaken oil and is 50 percent of Eur-Asian commercial energy needs.

Since the great bulk of gas production serves domestic and/or proximate markets, a fuller appreciation of what gas prospects could mean requires rearranging conventional tables to reveal the comparative gas wealth of regions (measured in total 1984 proved and possible additional volumes yet-to-be-discovered) against estimated production for the year 2000.

Table 1.4 is of utmost significance. It highlights the greater concentration of gas resources in or near two of the largest gas markets of the world: Western Europe and the Soviet Union. The very magnitude of these gas volumes makes clear both the loci of the future largest gas markets and the geopolitical importance of their gas links. It is this picture which has caused the United States to make clear the depth of its political and defense concerns should West Europe (whose own indigenous gas supplies have to be supplemented from proximate suppliers) become too dependent on a single source -- namely, the Soviet Union. For what is emerging is a wholly different energy prospect -- one in which a vast continent's fuel needs are met increasingly not by the logistics of oil but by supply systems moving natural gas, very

Table 1.4

Region	Total of Proved & Possible Reserves (TCF)	Production in 1984 (BCF/D)	Potential Supply in 2010 (BCF/D)
No.America (incl. Mexico)	1200	60	70-80
EurAsia (incl. West Europe, North Africa, USSR, and Middle East)	6000	81	180

largely by pipelines, from the U.S.S.R. east and west; from the Middle East to Europe and to Japan; from North Africa to Europe, and from Norway to western and central Europe.

Thus, to the advantages which these EurAsian natural gas reserves in particular bring to energy markets (assuming its longer-term price competitiveness with alternative fuels), the geopolitical dimension must be added. A nation's, or a region's, dependence on large-scale fuel imports raises questions about political relationships and security implications. Natural gas is no exception.

This will be true for North America, far into the next century, as the United States becomes more dependent on Canadian, and possibly Mexican supplies, and perhaps on Venezuelan LNG. For reasons of lower gas demand and industry's unsuccessful pursuit of some form of U.S. government price and volume support, further consideration of construction of the 4,500 mile Alaskan Natural Gas Transportation System to the Lower 48 states has been postponed. The cost of such a system was thought (in the late 1970s) to approach $45 billion, and the gas itself would have been expensive. Nevertheless, there remains a geopolitical interest in being able to tap Alaskan gas avoiding ocean routes and an even greater dependence on foreign suppliers.

The geopolitical factor holds for the West European region also as it becomes increasingly dependent not only on Soviet but Algerian gas (a dependence on these sources which will grow if Norwegian gas is not forthcoming), including the probability of supplies piped from the Middle East (Iran; Lower Arab Gulf). Japan has these geopolitical gas trade concerns as well and these will be wide-ranging and continuous, mitigated somewhat as Australian, and possibly Canadian, sources are drawn on but in the form of LNG: Unless and until Soviet piped supply reaches Japan, Japanese interests will be in oceanic gas transport. Eventually, Japan will be linked, however, to the EurAsian gas system.

PIPELINES AND WORLD TRADE

The increase in natural gas flowing through pipelines reflects the growing significance of this trade between Canada and the United States; between Norway and Northwest Europe, between the U.S.S.R. and Eastern and Western Europe, and from Algeria to Europe. Marginal volumes flow from Mexico, Bolivia, and Afghanistan.

The most extensive gas pipeline system is in the United States; that of the Soviet Union is currently second with Europe ranking third.

Nevertheless, in spite of the larger role of pipelines for internationally traded gas, and the increase in LNG volumes, only 10 percent of the total gas consumed is foreign-sourced. If and when European and United States domestic gas reserves become depleted, that 10 percent share of gas consumed which now moves internationally is certain to increase.

One final comment: Gas trades are competing more forcefully for energy market shares. This is true everywhere. As traditional, commercial practices become greatly altered, largely as a consequence of changing government policies, competition intensifies, gas should do much more than hold its own in energy market shares. Meanwhile, and probably for many years, gas markets are in turmoil generally. This is an altogether positive development, one in which gas will be freer to compete with alternative fuels.

With these political/economic, resource and demand factors in mind, we turn to more detailed considerations of gas markets. The authors of the following chapters will not agree with all of these introductory thoughts as they relate to the situations and prospects with which they are familiar. But all of us agree the subject of gas is of increasing importance, worldwide.

NOTES

[1]Consult World Petroleum Resources: A Perspective, Charles D. Masters, U.S. Geological Survey, Reston, Virginia, 1985. For the United States alone, see U.S. Conventional Oil and Gas Production: Prospects to the Year 2000, Joseph P. Riva, Jr., John J. Schanz, Jr., John G. Ellis, Westview Press, Boulder, CO, 1985.

[2]The BP Review of World Gas (August 1985), issued by BP Gas, London, is an indispensable source of data. Consult also World Petroleum Resources and Reserves, Joseph P. Riva, Jr., Westview Press, Boulder, CO, 1982 for an authoritative and lucid exposition of the known and probable locations of gas (and oil).

[3]"Gas Energy Review," American Gas Association, Washington, D.C., September 1985. Also see the chapters in this book by Jonathan P. Stern and Simon A. Blakey.

[4]For reasons totally mystifying, Japan, Australia, and New Zealand gas demand is combined. Japan is far and away the largest consumer -- and likely to remain so.

2

International Gas Trade:
The Three Major Markets

Jonathan P. Stern

COMMENTARY

We begin the description of the world gas trade by directing our attention to those great markets which are served by the overwhelming bulk of natural gas moving internationally: the United States, Western Europe and Japan. In subsequent chapters we look more specifically at the domestic aspects of these markets. But now we are to consider the sources and conditions affecting supply in three different situations, each very remote from the others. If the first great market for gas imports was the United States, the second was Western Europe. The third and most special case of all -- Japan -- remains totally dependent on ocean transport for its gas although Western Europe was an earlier opportunity for LNG supplies from North Africa.

Jonathan P. Stern emphasizes the distinctions to be drawn between gas and other forms of energy as the latter -- coal, oil -- move toward short-term market prices and the former, gas, still depends on long-term relationships between suppliers and consumers, largely for reasons of the high cost of gas logistics. Even this distinction may be fading as the United States, for example, acts to emphasize policies which directly encourage greater competition, both within its domestic market and between its foreign suppliers and domestic gas interests, such as to induce suppliers, pipeline companies, and consumers to depart from long-term contractual links. The same policy direction may be less evident in Europe and is irrelevant in the unique circumstances of Japan except where encouragement of competition between LNG suppliers offers a parallel to the U.S. experience.

Of course -- and it is vital to remember this point -- reference to market forces or increased competition for gas markets is easier in time of gas surplus. When supply gets tighter as is likely to happen first in the United States, the temptation for a return to government price and market regulations is probably inevitable. But neither in the case of Europe, nor or Japan, is there an early prospect of tight supplies either of piped natural gas or of LNG. We mention this because Mr. Stern emphasizes the gas price factor in defining the future for gas in the industrial community.

-- Editor --

INTRODUCTION

There are three major international gas trade markets: Western Europe (including the Nordic countries) -- which, apart from trade between countries, currently embraces imports from North Africa and the U.S.S.R.; North America -- where the United States is the importer, with Canada and Mexico as exporters, plus a small quantity of LNG from Algeria; Asia -- where Japan is presently the sole importer (although soon to be joined by South Korea and others), taking supplies from Southeast Asia, the Middle East, and Alaska.[1] Trade in more than marginal volumes of natural gas has only grown up over the past quarter of a century. Although the dimensions of the trade -- equivalent to some 4 million barrels per day oil equivalent -- remain small in comparision to oil, both world gas reserves and trade projects currently under study, have the potential to raise this figure by several orders of magnitude. The aim of this essay is not principally to estimate the potential for natural gas trade in the future (although I shall make some predictions in this respect), but to indicate the nature of the obstacles which stand in the way of much larger volumes of natural gas than are presently contemplated moving in international gas trade to the three major markets up to the end of the century.

For students and chroniclers of international gas trade, one of the most frustrating features of the subject is that it does not lend itself to generalizations.[2] It is extremely difficult to make broad judgments on the behavior of importers and exporters, even within the major markets, let alone across the trade groupings. Even seemingly uncontroversial statements such as: Exporters are looking for the highest price and importers for the lowest, require careful scrutiny. Although it is correct to stress the essential diversity of the markets, they share a number of joint concerns about the trading relationship between importer and exporter. The ways in which they have chosen, and will choose to deal with these problems, center on the present status of international gas trade contracts and the status and robustness of those contractual relationships in the future.

For the past two decades, the element which has set gas trade apart from trade in other fuels, specifically oil and coal, is the contractual relationship.[3] Natural gas has become the last bastion of long-term -- by which is meant twenty to twenty five years -- contractual relationships, in an energy world which is increasingly dominated by spot markets, market out clauses and force majeure claims. An important issue for the future is whether natural gas can decisively move away from long-term contracts and whether it will prosper by so doing. The elements of the contractual rela-tionship which are under particular scrutiny are: The relationship of gas prices to the prices of other fuels; the take or pay clause; flexibility of the terms of the contract regarding the frequency, speed and latitude of contractual changes over the term of the trade. It is in the differences in attitude toward these factors that the markets have taken different directions in the 1980s and some actors, particularly in the U.S. market, have parted company from the norms which have deter-mined the trading relationships hitherto.

The reason that natural gas trade contracts evolved differently from other energy trade rela-tionships relates to the difficulty in transport-ing the fuel and the volume of investment which needs to be advanced for the construction of a pipeline or a liquefied natural gas project, in advance of any gas being traded. In almost every gas trade project, contracts have to be signed covering sales of gas prior to any investment being made in the transmission system.[4] A production/ transmission system typically requires a multi-billion dollar investment, with a construction period of not less than three years and perhaps as long as a decade. The investment is then amortized over a period of years when the gas begins to flow. It goes without saying that if the trade should be interrupted, for whatever reason, in the early years of the contract once the investment in the transmission facilities has been sunk, but before the monies have been amortized, both parties stand to lose a great deal of money. Both importer and exporter therefore try to ensure that they are absolutely sure of the sincerity of their partner, the backing of the relevant governments, the technical ability of their engineering contractor and the feasibility of their designs before they go forward. Resolution of these problems, plus the negotiation of the actual terms of the contract, usually requires a period of several years prior to contracts being signed. This is followed by the construction period, and the term of the contract. In the majority of natural gas trades, the time span from the start of negotiations to the end of the contract term generally exceeds thirty years.

WESTERN EUROPE

Large scale natural gas trade in Western Europe was made possible by the discovery, in 1959, of the Groningen field in the Netherlands, which started the "gas revolution" on the Continent. Dutch gas exports commenced in the 1960s and were followed by the first liquefied natural gas (LNG) trades from Algeria, which were small in volume but for the first time enabled gas to be moved across water by ship, rather than the familiar pipeline. In the late 1960s and early 1970s the Soviet Union began to export gas to Western Europe by means of long distance pipeline networks, and later in the 1970s, the pipeline gas from the Norwegian North Sea fields reached Continental Europe and the United Kingdom (U.K.). Finally, in the early 1980s, pipeline gas from Algeria reached Italy (through Tunisia and Sicily), completing the major external connections to the Continental gas grid.

(See Table 2.1). Discoveries in the U.K. sector of the North Sea, in the 1960s, had separated that country from the rest of the Continent and, with the single exception of the link to the Norwegian shelf, the U.K. remains an island in terms of gas supplies.[5]

In the 1980s, Western Europe is experiencing a combination of two developments: Indigenous reserves in the major importing countries are beginning to run down; the first gas trade contracts signed in the 1960s are beginning to expire and require renegotiation or replacement by others.[6] This, in turn leads to two following considerations: Countries in Western Europe can begin to see a time when they will become dependent upon imports from outside the region for more than one half their total supplies.[7] At the same time, they have amassed more than two decades of experience in this trade and can begin to formulate the terms that they would like to see in force over the coming decades when their dependence on foreign sources will be greater than hitherto.

The countries which export gas to Western Europe also have long experience and can begin to evaluate where their interests lie in the future. In most cases, gas trade began as a marginal export venture with no great promise of a very large return. Only in the case of the Netherlands, was it clear that the size of the field which had been discovered, relative to anticipated domestic demand, and the large volumes which were marketed at the outset, would make natural gas an immensely important export commodity. In the case of other exporters, such as the U.S.S.R., this only became clear in the mid-1970s as the dimensions of the Siberian resource base were uncovered; and in the Norwegian case only in the late 1970s with the discovery of the Troll field.

Both Norway and the U.S.S.R. have the potential to increase exports considerably, with enormous volumes of gas surplus to domestic requirements and Algeria could certainly increase its export volumes, although not to the same extent as the other two countries. Moreover, improvements in transportation technology make possible the notion of pipeline and liquefied gas exports from as far away as West Africa and the Middle East. The

Table 2.1
European Gas Trade 1984
(billion cubic feet per day)

Exporter Importer	Algeria	Libya	Netherlands	Norway	USSR	FRG	Total***
Austria					0.41		0.41
Belgium	0.16		0.58	0.20			0.93
Denmark							negl
Finland					0.08	negl	0.08
France	0.81		0.78	0.22	0.45		2.26
Italy	0.66	0.04	0.46		0.76		1.92
Luxembourg			0.04				0.04
Netherlands				0.30			0.30
Spain	0.13	0.07					0.20
Switzerland			0.05			0.11	0.16
U.K.				1.36			1.36*
West Germany			1.82	0.55	1.27		3.65
Yugoslavia					0.36		0.36
Total Western Europe***	1.76	0.11	3.73	2.62	3.33	0.11	11.67
East							
European 6					3.28		3.30**
Total Europe							14.98

* includes 0.01 BCF/D from Denmark

** includes 0.2 BCF/D export from Romania to Hungary

*** totals may not add due to rounding

Source: Cedigaz, Le Gaz naturel Dans Le Monde en 1984, (Paris: 1984).

feeling in the mid-1980s, therefore, was that Western European importers might be facing an embarrassment of choice over the next two decades. The more difficult question concerns the way in which the trading relationship in West Europe will evolve up to the end of the century.

Over the past twenty five years, these relationships have generally held together very satisfactorily in an atmosphere which has been commercially profitable for both sides. This is not to say that all actors are satisfied with every aspect of their involvement, or believe that they struck the best deal that they possibly could, or did not consider the possibility of trying to radically change the terms of the trade due to adverse conditions. The most obvious example being the Netherlands during the 1970s, when Gasunie was of the view that Dutch gas prices were too cheap compared with other fuels. Furthermore, in the mid-1980s, it is clear that Dutch imports of Norwegian gas are surplus to requirements and that it would be in the interest of the Netherlands to break this contract. However, there has never been a question that the Netherlands would act in this way, although in 1980, the country demanded forced renegotiations with its gas customers at a time when other gas exporters were achieving significantly better terms with those countries.

The exporter which has not adhered to contractual conditions and refused to renegotiate these in an orderly and acceptable manner is Algeria. In the French and Belgian LNG contracts and the Italian contract for gas from the trans-Mediterranean pipeline, the Algerian side used the threat and practice of embargo, or refusal to commence trade, in order to force through higher prices than originally agreed in the contracts. These actions, and other examples from the trade with the United States, have produced the impression that Algeria is not a reliable supplier and this has greatly affected European perceptions of the desirability of imports from this source.

In fairness, one must note a number of more positive points about the Algerian situation: first, the country carried out its contractual obligations with the United Kingdom in an LNG trade which ran its full fifteen-year term with goodwill and good experience on both sides. Second, Algeria served as the pioneer of LNG trade and in that capacity suffered a great deal as enormous capital investments were made, sometimes in equipment and plant which failed to live up to specifications.[8] This partly accounts for the switch of emphasis from LNG to pipeline gas as a mode of export in the 1980s. Third, in its experience with the Spanish LNG contract, the initial fault appears to have been on the side of the importer, with the trade never reaching more than 30 percent of contractual volumes due to a failure to construct the pipelines to bring gas to Spanish cities.

The other major way in which the trading relationship has been affected, but not disrupted, is by the growing perception of the importance of security of supply, which has brought governments much more into decision making on natural gas trade in the 1980s. It was inevitable that, as imported supplies began to constitute an increasingly large share of total gas supplies, the question of dependence upon non-European supplies would become a more important issue in the trading relationship in Western Europe. While in the view of utilities, the most difficult problem centered on the commercial unreliability of Algeria, in the governmental arena, attention centered on the U.S.S.R. The dispute between the Reagan administration and West European governments over the desirability of importing additional gas from the U.S.S.R., occupied the better part of two years, 1980-82, and gravely strained international trade and foreign policy relationships between the Allies.

An uneasy truce had been signed within the framework of a May 1983 International Energy Agency (IEA) Ministerial Communique, stressing the virtue of member states "avoiding undue dependence upon" a single source of supply.[9] In plain language, this was interpreted to mean that no important West European country (West Germany, France, Italy), should import more than one third of its total supply from the U.S.S.R. The report was backed by a gas security study by the IEA, which came to the conclusion that the position of member countries was satisfactory up to 1990, as far as the possibility of a crisis stemming from an interruption from any one source of supply was concerned; after 1990, this situation should be reviewed. It was, however, quite clear that neither the Reagan administration nor any other government was concerned with any natural gas security problems other than those relating to the U.S.S.R. Indeed the American side greatly weakened their case by encouraging West European utilities to import gas from the very North African countries which were, at that time, causing the utilities immense problems.[10] In terms of previous experience the position that Soviet gas was "insecure" and all other gas was "secure" had no foundation in anything other than the ideological mindset of its protagonists. The lasting effect of the dispute, aside from the possibility of its recurrence, has been to bring governments into the arena of natural gas supply decisions and to cast supplies not in terms of secure versus insecure sources, but rather in terms of Soviet and non-Soviet sources. By 1985, the dispute had been shelved, but not solved, and with the second Reagan administration safely enscounced in the White House, it is an issue in trans-Atlantic relations which could be reopened.

One of the few positive results of this episode was the discussion on the logistics of gas supply and the ability to move volumes around the West European grid in response to supply crises. Attention came to focus on these arrangements at the time of the concern over the security of Soviet gas supplies. Dutch flexibility was said to be such that sales could be doubled, in comparison to average volumes, if the situation should warrant this.[11] At this time, 1981-82, the thinking was that European importers could "rent" gas storage space in the Groningen field, paying a regular fee for the privilege of being able to call on gas at short notice when they had been let down by their "insecure" suppliers. While this was a logistical possibility, it was commercially impractical since it required importers to pay potentially large sums to secure gas that they might never use, and at the same time precluded the Dutch from committing this gas to firm contracts sales, in case it should be needed for emergencies. Moreover, such speculation erred in being fixated on security of Soviet supplies, for which Dutch supplies would be the only alternative, while it neglected to consider the possibility that in a situation where Algerian supplies were the subject of interruption, countries might well turn to Soviet supplies before all others.

The Dutch have naturally preferred to sell additional quantities of gas on a firm basis. By mid-1985, Gasunie had agreed to ten year extensions for almost all of its present export contracts.[12] The renegotiation, or extension, of contracts where the facilities have been amortized, thus greatly enhances the flexibility of the terms on which the gas can be sold. The same effect can be achieved by constructing facilities with a larger capacity than required under contractual arrangements. In both cases, there may be greater flexibility in delivery capabilities over short periods of time than would generally be associated with firm contracts.

With the passing of immediate concern about Soviet gas supplies in the mid-1980s, and a change in the perception of the market situation from relative scarcity to relative abundance, the issue of short-term commercial contracts, outside any question of gas security, has been brought to the fore and centers on Soviet capability. Throughout the entire trans-Atlantic pipeline dispute, the Soviets were relegated to the status of spectators. However, the expansion of the capacity of the Soviet gas transmission infrastructure has created a new situation which could conceivably have a considerable effect on the gas trading relationship within Western Europe. With Soviet transmission capacity entering Western Europe currently exceeding, by some margin, that necessary to fulfill firm contracts, the Soviets therefore have two options if they are not to allow this capacity to remain idle. They can fill up the capacity by sending more gas to their East European allies or they can try to sell gas to West European countries on short-term contracts, outside the long-term, firm sales. It has already been announced that, in the period 1986-90, a pipeline will be constructed from the Yamburg field in Siberia to supply Eastern Europe with additional quantities of Soviet gas. The Soviets seem keen to separate the transmission structure which serves Eastern Europe, from that delivering gas to West

European customers. This is of course not wholly possible due to the fact that pipes to Western Europe must cross either Czechoslovkia or Hungary.

As far as short-term or "spot" sales to West European countries are concerned, there have been a number of rumors of spot sales -- or at least offers of such sales -- in the trade press. Firm contracts for only around 2.7 BCF/D from the new export pipeline would give a total export to Western Europe of just over 5 BCF/D in 1990 and would leave spare capacity in existing Soviet pipelines to Western Europe in the order of 1-1.5 BCF/D. It is therefore correct to look toward a two-track Soviet gas export policy: Long-term contract gas in the order of 5 BCF/D versus gas supplies sold outside long-term contracts, which may be called "spot gas," (although this is simply a convenient shorthand and is an unsatisfactory term), which may reflect sales over a period from three months to three years. The point is that the U.S.S.R., with its huge resources, great flexibility and non-market economic system, is in a unique position to take advantage of such developments, offering short-term volume contracts at attractive prices. The offer made to Belgium in 1984, although seeming to have been more of a negotiating weapon for the importer to use against its regular supplier, was a pointer to the future in this regard.[13]

Speculation has been raised by the successive rounds of contract renegotiations between Soyuzgazexport and the West European buyers that in the future, the Soviets will be prepared to offer large volumes of gas at prices well below, what one might loosely term, "the going rate." This suggestion seems to me to be misplaced. At the time that the contracts were signed, the buyers -- and particularly Ruhrgas -- made it clear that they expected the price to reflect conditions in the end use sectors where the gas would be competing. Prices of competing fuels in those sectors fell in the period 1981-84 and it is therefore perfectly consistent that gas export prices should be renegotiated downward.[14] In any event, it is unlikely that the Soviets would be interested in offering large scale supplies at much lower prices or that the importing utilities would be willing to take

the risk of accepting assurances that such prices
would hold in the longer-term. As a Ruhrgas
executive noted, "....it would on the one hand seem
improbable for the Soviet Union...to undercut its
current export prices and thus to put its current
overall export price level at risk. On the other
hand, buyers in Continental Europe would not give
priority to new Soviet gas offered under these
conditions...".[15]

    While the West European gas trading relation-
ship is therefore unlikely to include the Soviets
offering large volumes of gas at very low prices,
it could well see a proportion of annual Soviet gas
sales -- perhaps as much as 10-20 percent -- being
offered on short-term contracts. It is important
to say that the West European gas market has not yet
shown that it is sufficiently flexible to accommodate transactions of this kind which involve significant volumes. Nevertheless, this is a radical
departure from past contractual practice which is
being actively considered and may become very much
more significant in future West European gas
trade. The only country which is well placed to
take advantage of such flexibility is the U.S.S.R.
The Netherlands could certainly operate in this
way, but as mentioned before, the Dutch contemplated spot gas sales commanding a premium price
over firm contracts, rather than a lower, bargain,
price. It remains to be seen whether they are
prepared to change their view on this subject.

ASIA-PACIFIC

    Japan came to natural gas trade only in the
late 1960s and early 1970s as a response to two
developments, one domestic and one international.
From the domestic standpoint, the country required
clean sources of energy which could meet the increasingly stringent pollution standards being
introduced in the major cities. Internationally,
the first oil crisis highlighted the vulnerability
to interruptions in the supply and price of oil,
virtually all of which is imported. Diversification away from oil, and specifically away from
Middle East oil, became a priority of considerable
proportions and natural gas was admirably placed
to perform this function.

Natural gas trade in Japan was characterized by two additional features which marked it out from the way in which business was conducted in other OECD countries. The electric utilities have dominated the trade, which accounts for around three quarters of total consumption of the fuel. It is commonly said that the gas business in Japan is really the electric power business, and although that does a disservice to the gas utilities which are rapidly expanding their fields of operation in both the residential and commercial sectors, it correctly identifies the sector which introduced the fuel to Japan and where the really large markets are still to be found. Internationally, Japan had no option other than to import gas in liquefied form and, with the waning of enthusiasm for this mode of trade in other parts of the world, rapidly became the leading world importer of LNG and the target of any country located between the Pacific Basin and the Middle East, where any exportable surplus of natural gas was discovered.

In the Japanese LNG trades, contractual relationships were even more important than in the other two major markets. Not only did LNG trades typically require much higher investments per unit compared with pipeline trade, but they were being entered into, specifically in order to lessen Japanese dependence on insecure, imported oil. The length of contracts portended stability with the inference that stability meant security. The way in which Japanese LNG importers handled their trading partners reflected the seriousness with which both Japanese commercial parties and successive Japanese governments regarded the security of supply aspects of the trade, both in the selection of their partners and in the management of commercial changes in contractual conditions.

Parity with crude oil -- a concept hotly disputed in gas trade negotiations in Western Europe and the United States and never achieved by exporting countries to those markets -- was accepted as a rough guiding principle in the Japanese market in the latter part of the 1970s, and formalized in 1980 with the renegotiation of the Abu Dhabi price, with seemingly very little public discussion.[16] The reasons why Japanese utilities accepted even this limited principle of parity

with the delivered price of crude oil, with so
little apparent resistance, are not entirely
clear. It may be significant that the intial
introduction of the concept came in the first
Indonesian contract, negotiated in the wake of the
first oil crisis when decisions would have been
influenced by the panic over oil supplies which
swept the industrial world and particularly Japan,
with its huge vulnerability to interruptions in
imported oil supplies. In addition, Japanese
utilities were burning crude oil in power plants,
so that it may have seemed entirely reasonable to
the electric utilities to pay the same price for
gas as for oil. Thirdly, it was evident that the
utilities were prepared to pay a premium for pollution-free fuels in order to meet increasingly
stringent air quality restrictions. Fourthly,
utilities may well have seen long-term LNG contracts as being more secure than oil and therefore
were willing to pay premium over existing prices.
While prices do not tell the whole story (in some
contracts, Japanese financing for the initial investment was taken into account in the commodity
price), in the period 1977-79 the Indonesian contracts commanded a price of 50 cents to a dollar per
MMBTU higher than the other three contracts which
tracked each other fairly closely. Indeed the
Alaska and Brunei contract prices have never been
more than a few cents apart since the mid-1970s.[17]
    By the beginning of 1980, the utilities in-
volved in the other three contracts felt themselves compelled to accede to the demands of the
other exporters, particularly Abu Dhabi, to renegotiate prices along the lines of the Indonesian
example. The utilities involved could have claimed, with every justification, that they had not
agreed to a crude oil parity formula in original
contracts. There is no public evidence that the
other LNG suppliers exerted undue pressure on the
utilities, certainly not to the point of threaten-
ing to cut off supplies. Three possible reasons
suggest themselves: first, it may have seemed to
the Japanese utilities that crude oil parity, in
some form, was to become the standard pricing
formula in world gas trade. This was the period
when Algeria was attempting to introduce the principle into the trade with Western Europe and the

United States. Second, in the wake of the 1978-79 oil price rise and further uncertainty surrounding Gulf oil supplies, the attraction of LNG may have been growing steadily greater. Third, the trades with the U.S. (Alaska) and Brunei had been in operation for ten and seven years respectively, with excellent experience in both cases. With receiving facilities largely amortized and the general success of the trades, importers may not have wished to jeopardize these operations, even to the point of conceding a considerable price increase.

In their actions, the importing utilities were determined to do nothing that would jeopardize the future of LNG trade and, having nurtured the projects in the early stages, they were prepared, even if not delighted, to make concessions in the commercial terms in order that the trade should continue unhindered. The success of the initial LNG ventures was due in no small measure to the financial assistance extended by the Japanese partners. The Indonesian LNG project was financed indirectly by the buyers of the gas and the Japanese government. The utilities (led by a trading house) borrowed funds from the Export-Import Bank of Japan and commercial banks and reloaned them to Pertamina. Repayment was made by the counterpurchase of LNG against the loans which had been extended. The Japan National Oil Corporation (the state oil company of Japan) guaranteed 60 percent of the total Japanese credit and the Japanese buyers provided a guarantee of payment of the balance. A government-to-government loan was extended through the Japanese Overseas Economic Cooperation Fund to cover Indonesian infrastructure costs. Overall, Japanese financing provided more than $1.4 billion, or 86 percent of the total Indonesian project cost, but a rather smaller percentage in the cases of both Brunei and Malaysia.[18]

In a wider perspective, throughout the 1970s, Japan maintained a position of considerable importance as a trade partner for all the Association of South East Asian Nations (ASEAN) countries. For all countries (with the exception of Brunei where the figure is greater than 50 percent), Japan represents around a quarter to a third of their trade turnover, with a number of countries running substantial trade deficits with Tokyo. The exceptions to this are Indonesia and Brunei where Japanese imports of oil and gas far outweigh the value of exports. For Japan, ASEAN countries accounted for around 10 percent of exports and 15 percent of imports in the early 1980s, but the resource element in the trade is extremely significant.[19] Quite aside from resources and commerce, Japanese security concerns in Southeast Asia are focused not only on regional stability of political systems and relations between neighboring states, but also on the maintenance of secure transit routes, specifically sea lanes. ASEAN countries -- Indonesia, Malaysia, and Singapore -- command the vital waterways through which nearly the totality of Japanese oil and LNG (to say nothing of other commodities) have to pass.

Overall, it is not exaggerating to say that LNG trades have greatly aided Japanese foreign trade and foreign policy initiatives in Southeast Asia during the 1970s. While similar commercial concessions were extended to the United States and Abu Dhabi, these projects were minor, in volume terms, in comparison with the Southeast Asian trades. Despite the fact that concessions made to LNG exporters over the past fifteen years, may well have been necessary and beneficial, in the context of Japanese energy vulnerability and wider commercial, political, and security reasons, these developments have given rise to some problems which will need to be addressed if LNG is to make further advances in the Japanese market.

By 1985, Japanese LNG electricity and gas utilities were importing LNG from a diversified group of countries in Southeast Asia, the Middle East, and the United States. Another contract was about to be signed with Australia and utilities had already been considering for a number of years projects with: Canada, the U.S.S.R., Qatar, Thailand, and many others (see Table 2.2). Far from the perceptions of shortage and vulnerability of the 1970s, Japanese LNG importers in the 1980s are beginning to realize that they are facing a considerable number of potential sellers who have no near-term, alternative export market. Despite the large number of apparent choices in the 1980s and

Table 2.2

Japanese LNG Imports 1985-2005
(billion cubic feet per day)

Source	Contracted 1985	Expiry Date	Import Projections		
			1990	1995	2005
Alaska	0.13	1989	0.13	0.13	--
Brunei	0.72	1992	0.72	0.70	0.30
Abu Dhabi	0.29	1997	0.29	0.40	0.40
Indonesia	2.10	1997-2004	2.10	2.10	2.10
Malaysia	0.84	2003	0.84	0.84	0.84
Australia		2010	0.28	0.82	0.82
	4.08		4.36	4.99	4.46
1983 Government demand forecasts:*			5.11	5.60	6.3-7.0

Possible Contracts			Quantity of LNG Imports not yet contracted		
Canada	0.41	)			
USSR (Sakhalin)	0.42	)			
Thailand	0.35	)	0.75	0.61	1.8-2.5
Qatar	0.84	)			

*1990 and 1995 only; 2005 is author's demand projection.

Source: Stern, Op. Cit. 1985, Table 10.1

the excellent record of the projects which were already operational, utilities are cautious in signing future contracts, partly because of uncertainty over demand and partly because of perception that the terms of the trading relationships which have evolved thus far, will have to change, if the fuel is to expand its role in the Japanese energy balance. The attempt to combine a changing, more competitive trading relationship with politically acceptable sources of supply, is a task which will occupy the Japanese utilities increasingly in the late 1980s and beyond.

The problem, simply stated, is that Japanese LNG import contracts were designed for, and have succeeded in maintaining, stability in the rapidly changing energy world of insecure and unstable oil supplies and prices. However, as the world has moved from perceived energy "crisis" to perceived energy "glut," with stagnant demand and falling (real) prices for most energy commodities, the advantages of stability have become the disadvantages of immobility and inflexibility. These disadvantages center on two main aspects, price and take or pay. As regards price, the events outlined above, which brought parity with the delivered price of crude oil imported into Japan, gave rise to problems of competitiveness with other fuels, notably coal and nuclear power in the power generation sector, the higher grades of fuel oil in the industrial sector, and kerosene in the residential sector. By 1984, the relativities had become such that electricity generated from LNG was reckoned to be around 25 percent more expensive per unit, than that generated from nuclear power and 20 percent more expensive than coal fired plant.[20]

As far as take or pay is concerned, in the 1970s, many of the Japanese LNG import trades operated for long periods above the design capacity of the facilities country and this was a distinct advantage in an era of excess demand. In a period of excess supply and depressed demand, the position changes and the 100 percent take or pay clauses written into the contracts, have compelled Japanese utilities to take volumes for which they have no immediate use and incur large storage costs. Increasingly the feeling is that contracts must include more flexible take structures which allow for gas not taken to be "rolled over," until the end of the contract if necessary. As in the case of Western Europe, it is necessary to distinguish between two different types of contract: Those which have been running for some years and those which are under discussion, or just commencing. LNG trade with Japan is reaching a mature stage where the first (Alaskan) contract has already been extended for a five-year term and renegotiations on expiring contracts at the beginning of the 1990s are coming into view. At the same time, utilities are being asked to consider a number of large projects where the transportation system will constitute a relatively large proportion of the delivered price of the gas.

As utilities come to renegotiate existing contracts, assuming the reserves exist in the exporting country to carry on the trade, they will be able to rethink questions of price and take or pay. To a modest extent this has already happened in the U.S. contract, where the 1984 revisions have explicitly recognized the situation in which the importers cannot take full delivery due to lack of demand.[21] Similar changes are likely to be implemented in other contracts in the future. The question of price is more difficult since it involves trying to lower the revenues that exporters have been receiving from LNG exports, relative to crude oil prices. The additional issue is whether LNG import prices should continue to bear any relationship to crude oil prices.

Thus, in negotiating new contracts, utilities are faced with the problem of changing a number of important contract conditions which have been in force over a period of years. As mentioned above, projects generally require large capital costs which need to be amortized over a period of years with exporters receiving guaranteed revenues in order to fulfill their financial obligations to creditors; this is the function of the take or pay clause. Where projects require a high production and/or transportation cost, the delivered price must be similarly high if the exporter is to realize a positive value on the gas. To illustrate: Those who are putting forward the notion of exporting large volumes of Alaskan gas from the

Prudhoe Bay field to Japan are facing an enormous commercial problem. The project requires producing the gas under Arctic conditions, transmission through a very long pipeline, construction of a very large LNG plant and a large number of ships. The capital cost of such a system was estimated at more than $14 billion in 1982 dollars, which would be equivalent to more than $30 billion in the early 1990s by which time nearly 2 BCF/D of gas would be flowing.[22] It is immediately evident that to persuade private investors to advance such huge sums, the market prospects must be assured. It is equally evident that such a large quantity of gas will need to be extremely competitive if it is to find a market in Japan. If one makes "back of an envelope calculations" of the simple operating transportation cost of the TAGS system (i.e., leaving out capital cost financing) and then asks what price the gas would need to command in Japan, and the revenue that the producer would receive at the wellhead, the difficulty of financing the project along traditional lines is immediately evident.

The huge project to import LNG from the North Field in Qatar presents the same problems but on a smaller scale. While the production costs of the gas should be low, the transmission distance will be long and the investments needed for liquefaction plant and ships to support a 6 MT per year project will be in the order of $5-$10 billion. The idea of commencing with a relatively small project and scaling up at a later date, is probably not feasible in terms of the economics of the project. There is also the question of whether increasing imports of energy from a turbulent region from which Japan takes two thirds of its LPG supplies, constitutes a wise move in terms of national energy security.

The project to import LNG from Canada has been delayed due to problems from the exporting side relating to both the financial fragility of the original Canadian equity partners and the uncertainty as to whether the netback of exports to Japan would be equivalent to that received from exports to the United States. By 1985, this project was on the brink of being abandoned.[23] Doubts about Canadian organizational capacity and

financial soundness have combined with concern
about the long-term contractual commitment of the
exporter. Nevertheless, the contract may prove to
have been a landmark, even if the project never
goes ahead, as a result of the take or pay clause
which has a form of wording ensuring that even
though the importer may be required to pay before
the gas is taken, there is no way in which gas can
be lost to an importer, even if this means extending the term of the contract.[24]

The initiative to import LNG from Thailand
demonstrates the economic and political desire of
Japanese trading organizations and the Japanese
government to increase their involvement in natural gas trade in Southeast Asia. By 1984, as a
result of a reassessment of Thai gas reserves, it
was evident that reserves were insufficient to
support an export project.[25] With rising domestic
consumption, it is uncertain how much gas would
need to be proved before the Thai government was
prepared to entertain ideas of such a project
again. However it is certain, that if reserves
were to be discovered in sufficient volumes, Japanese importers would give preference to this
source above all others, even those projects where
discussions had taken place over a much longer
period.

The case of the Soviet Sakhalin project is
rather unique for political reasons. In commercial terms the project makes excellent sense: more
than adequate reserves, short transportation distance, small yearly volumes. The one element which
has been overridingly negative over the past ten
years of discussions on the project has been the
political climate between the countries and, less
easy to define but probably even more important,
the psychological attitude of the utilities to
Soviet supplies. The lack of a peace treaty
between the countries following World War II, the
continuing disagreement about Soviet occupation of
the Kurile Islands and the general ambivalence of
the Japanese people toward the U.S.S.R., have been
overlaid by the worsening climate of East-West
relations. Soviet-Japanese relations are at an
all-time post-war low and show little sign of
coming out of their deep frozen state. Moreover,
the attitude of the utilities, mixing distrust

with distaste, militates against natural gas imports in the absence of very strong governmental encouragement. Japanese utilities appear to doubt, despite very strong evidence to the contrary in Western Europe, that the Soviets can be trusted to fulfill contractual relationships over a long period of time.

In summary, international gas trade in Asia is at something of a crossroads. While countries such as Korea and Taiwan will be joining the community of importers in the late 1980s and early 1990s, Japan will remain by far the most important trading force in the region and the principal LNG importer worldwide. Problems of competitiveness have cast doubts on the prospects for future LNG projects beyond the firmly contracted Australian Northwest Shelf venture. All the projects currently under consideration have at least one overriding objection from the political or commercial standpoint. It is almost certain that, following the Australian project, no further projects involving volumes larger than 0.3-0.4 BCF/D, will be arranged in this century. Of the small projects, Thailand would seem the most likely, for political reasons, but politics alone cannot create reserves. The Soviet Sakhalin project requires a good government-to-government relationship, while the main obstacle to Canadian LNG exports is the impression of financial and organizational fragility which has been created from the Canadian side. In any event, new projects will be structured in order to give the importer more flexibility on take and, possibly, to break the direct link with crude oil prices. If exporters resist Japanese demands in these areas, it is entirely possible that no new LNG projects will be concluded for some considerable time. On present demand projections, Japanese LNG importers could make do with extensions to existing projects, plus the Nothwest Shelf, through to the mid-1990s. Their strong bargaining position may make them more assertive in their demands and weaken the position of current and future LNG exporters for the final decade of this century.

NORTH AMERICA

In North America and specifically looking at the United States, one sees the mirror image of the Japanese situation: The biggest gas market in the world; a country which produces 95 percent of its supplies and imports only 5 percent; a country which has the ability to import from two contiguous pipeline sources and need only have limited recourse to LNG imports. The other striking difference between natural gas trade in North America and trade in the rest of the world is the contraction of volumes moving internationally. In 1984, U.S. imports from Canada reach a ten-year low, Mexican imports ceased altogether and LNG import contracts were curtailed to the point where U.S. exports to Japan exceeded the volumes which are being received on the east coast from Algeria (see Table 2.3).

The fundamental reason for this hiatus in North American gas trade is the upheaval which has been taking place in U.S. gas markets in the early 1980s. The process of price decontrol, which commenced in 1978, reached its most important milestone at the beginning of 1985, by which time price controls of around 60 percent of U.S. gas production had been lifted. The effect of these measures on the general level of U.S. gas prices and hence supply and demand remains to be seen, but what is already certain is that the situation for external gas supplies to the U.S. market has been dramatically changed from the situation which existed in the 1970s.

The system of U.S. price controls combined with the regulation of gas transmission which grew up in the 1960s and 1970s, severely limited the incentive both to explore for gas and to sell gas outside states in which it was produced. However, gas imported into the U.S., particularly at a time of overall gas shortage such as occured in the mid- to late-1970s, was able to command a much higher price than domestically produced fuel. Imports were "rolled in" with U.S. domestic supplies in the states in which they were received, and the overall volumes were sufficiently large that the consumer barely registered the fact that bills included an element of Canadian and Mexican gas at a price of

Table 2.3

Natural Gas Trade: North America 1975–84
(billion cubic feet per day)

Year	MEXICO Export	CANADA Export	ALGERIA Export	USA Import
1975	(0.03)	2.68	0.01	2.66
1976	(0.02)	2.70	0.03	2.71
1977	0	2.82	0.03	2.85
1978	(0.01)	2.49	0.24	2.72
1979	(0.01)	2.83	0.71	3.54
1980	0.29	2.26	0.24	2.79
1981	0.30	2.16	0.10	2.56
1982	0.27	2.22	0.16	2.65
1983	0.21	2.02	0.37	2.60
1984	0.15*	2.14	0.10	2.39

*Trade suspended; brackets indicate imports

Sources: U.S. Imports and Exports of Natural Gas 1980, Table 5, p. 7. U.S. Department of Energy EIA DOE/EIA-0188(80) and Fay B. Dillard, "U.S. Imports and Exports of Natural Gas -- 1983," Natural Gas Monthly, May 1984, Tables G5, G6, pp. XXIX-XXX.

$4.94 per MMBTU, rolled in with domestic gas at an average price of $2.50 per MMBTU.

As price controls were lifted, increasing volumes of gas were able to flow across state frontiers to compete in hitherto unprofitable markets. At the same time, natural gas began to lose markets to oil products and this process, combined with falling energy demand in the United States, led not only to shut in domestic production capacity, but severe competition with high price imported supplies which began to find their customers attempting to evade their obligation to take such supplies. The result is that in the mid-1980s, the Lower 48 states is experiencing a glut or "bubble" of gas, only a few years after experiencing a shortage crisis. The basic problem is that almost all import contracts were signed at a time of supply crisis and are not equipped to deal with the diametrically opposite situation. Furthermore, exporting countries became accustomed to thinking that the U.S. would have a permanent and growing need for gas imports and are having to adjust painfully to other realities.

Canada has always been by far the largest external supplier of gas to the United States and has therefore been hit particularly hard by the events of the 1980s. It is important to remember that throughout much of the 1970s, the Canadian government refused to sanction increased exports of gas to the United States, as a result of fears that supplies would be insufficient for future Canadian domestic consumption. In 1977 the Canadian government, with the acquiescence of the authorities in Washington, took over decisions on the pricing of natural gas exports, using a "uniform border price" which was intended to bear a relationship to the price of oil imported into Canada. By the time that the Canadian authorities had agreed to American requests to increase the allowable volume of gas exports and had expressed the price of those exports in terms of a carefully elaborated formula, the U.S. market had changed and importers were no longer interested in such imports, particularly at inflated prices.

These events had extremely serious repercussions in Canada, where the financial distress of producers who had invested in the expectation of export markets were reflected in their urging of the Federal government to allow export prices to fall, if necessary below those of Canadian domestic prices, thus endangering a long standing article of faith in Canadian gas history.[26]   In addition, new projects which had been arranged in order to take advantage of export opportunities have run into grave difficulties, such as the "prebuiilt" sections of the Alaska Natural Gas Transmission Systems (ANGTS), where take or pay volumes have been renegotiated down to less than half the originally agreed volumes.

Mexican gas trade relations with the United States have followed an extremely turbulent path, swinging from expectation of massive volumes to cancellation of contracts.   The rebirth of the Mexican petroleum industry in the late 1970s, with the discovery of very large oil deposits in the south of the country, with quite unusually large volumes of associated gas, led to a decision, taken with undue haste, that these volumes should be exported to the United States.   The subsequent negotiation between the countries which gave rise to a major political crisis in U.S.-Mexican relations can be ascribed to a number of causes, the most important of which were connected with poor American diplomacy and extreme Mexican sensitivity to any hint of high-handed, imperialistic behavior from the U.S. side.   From a purely contractual perspective, the exporter (like everyone else at the time) made the assessment that the U.S. market would be able to take as much gas as could be delivered and assumed that the gas would be able to command a price roughly equivalent to fuel oil parity.   The ensuing argument centered entirely on the price of gas.   With hindsight it is quite clear that the more important question centered on the volume of 2 BCF/D which could not possibly have been absorbed by the market at any price that would have been accepted by the exporter.   However, the Mexican side made the cardinal error of commencing construction of the pipeline before a contract had been signed for the export of the gas.   When negotiations broke down, the government was obliged to reorient what had clearly been designed an export project, to the domestic market, an act which, in the long-term, may be seen to have had far-reaching consequences for both the Mexican energy balance and for exports to the United States.

When the countries finally returned to the negotiating table two years later, the volume of exports on offer had been drastically reduced by the Mexican side and after a hard negotiation on price, a contract was signed which allowed for volumes to rise at some later date. In the event, as a result of U.S. market developments, the opposite occurred, and Mexican deliveries were cut to the contractual minimum by the beginning of 1984. Unlike the Canadian contracts, where U.S. pipeline companies sought unilateral reductions of volume with a great deal of publicity and protest on the part of the exporters, the Mexican contract appeared to be weathering the storm mainly because volumes were not large enough to constitute a significant element for any one pipeline system. It was therefore a considerable surprise when on November 1, 1984, the parties announced that the Mexican contract was being suspended indefinitely.[27] The original problem of the price had inevitably been raised by the importers and the Mexican government, remaining true to its original principles, had preferred to see the trade cease rather than make concessions to U.S. pipeline companies.

Notwithstanding unfortunate episodes in pipeline gas trade in North America, by far the saddest stories are reserved for liquefied natural gas imports. In the 1970s, large numbers of LNG projects were suggested involving imports from Africa, Southeast Asia, South America, the Caribbean, Australia and Siberia.[28] Most of these projects never progressed further than the planning stage, but several involving Algeria were seriously considered and that country appeared destined to become the major factor in U.S. natural gas imports.

That this did not happen was principally the fault of the Algerian government, although the actions of the United States government and the evolution of the U.S. gas market were both very important contributory factors. In late 1978, the U.S. Department of Energy refused permission for two baseload LNG imports from Algeria to go ahead;

another project had already been shelved on account of an accident in the construction of the
U.S. receiving terminal.[28] Although more than 2
BCF/D of Algerian exports were turned down by the
Federal regulatory authorities, three projects
were approved. The peakload Distrigas project has
been running satisfactorily since 1971 even during
the trials and tribulations of other Algerian
projects. The one BCF/D baseload El Paso I project
commenced in 1978 and never reached full capacity,
partly because of technical problems, but mainly
because Algerian demands for price parity with
crude oil led to a suspension of deliveries at the
beginning of 1981.[29] The Trunkline project involving 0.45 BCF/D finally commenced in 1982, two
years behind schedule, after lengthy price disputes, along the same lines as El Paso, and following the commencement of international arbitration
proceedings by the importer. After the importing
company had made efforts to persuade its Algerian
partners to lower the price, it eventually suspended the import, claiming massive financial
hardship (which was linked to its take or pay
obligations in the domestic market) which had led
it to the point of bankruptcy. The Algerian side
promptly instituted its own international arbitration proceedings against the importer.

     The history of U.S. LNG imports is partic-
ularly sad because of the way in which a trade which
commenced with such tremendous prospects has been
reduced to the point where the U.S. LNG exports to
Japan exceed its imports from Algeria. While
Algerian demands were certainly excessive and outside the terms of the original contracts, the U.S.
regulatory process produces nightmares that no
foreigner (and probably very few Americans) can be
expected to understand. Moreover, it is absolutely certain that even had the El Paso contract not
been cancelled in 1981, it would have been a victim
of the market collapse for high price gas supplies
which occurred in the 1980s.

     International gas trade in North America has
to find a new equilibrium which, in commercial
terms, will be dictated by the market established
in the Lower 48. It will then be a question of
whether external suppliers choose to adapt to that
market. Two suppliers, Mexico and Algeria, have

already made it clear that they would rather sac-
rifice exports than adapt to U.S. market conditions. Canada appears to have chosen the opposite
course, partly because of the financial hardship
being suffered by private individuals and companies (by contrast, Mexican and Algerian production
and exports are handled by state energy companies)
and partly because of a hope that this situation
will be of limited duration.

It is the size of the natural gas bubble in the
Lower 48 states that is the critical issue facing
both domestic and external suppliers to that market as they look to the future. Nevertheless, it
would be a mistake to see the situation simply in
terms of market forces, important as these may be
in the short-term. A most important development in
the 1980s has been the abandoning of any kind of
regular trading relationship between U.S. importers and their suppliers. Specifically, participants have shown a willingness to change and, if
necessary, abandon contractual commitments if
these became too onerous, primarily for the importer.

The emphasis of the present policy of promotion of market forces works very well when there is
surplus domestic supply, and consumers have
choices between competing sources of gas, and
between gas and its other energy competitors.
Problems arise first, when the domestic surplus of
gas disappears and consumers start trying to ensure security of their supplies and cannot arrange
firm long-term contracts with pipeline companies
and producers with no certainty that these will be
adhered to. Second, from an international standpoint, the abandoning of long-term contracts is
even more serious for the future. While surplus
capacity remains in the present infrasructure,
there may not be too many problems in gaining
access to increased supplies; although it is by no
means certain that either Mexico or Algeria will be
interested in resuming large scale exports until
the price rises substantially. However, when
current import facilities reach full capacity, new
investments have to be made and it is at that point,
where confidence that contractual terms will be
adhered to over the long-term becomes essential.
This feeling is entirely absent in North American

gas trade where short-term market conditions have determined the course of trading relationships. Thus it is not an environment in which any new large gas projects, such as the Alaska gas pipeline or any other Arctic gas project, large scale LNG trade (involving the construction of new facilities in an exporting country), or indeed any new LNG installation in the United States, can prosper if it is to be funded by private enterprise. This may not be a concern for the U.S. gas market in 1985, but it will be a matter of the utmost seriousness well before the end of the century.

CONCLUSIONS

A major trend which has not been referred to in this paper is the start of natural gas trade in other regions of the world. The concentration on the three major markets, while legitimate in a consideration of developments up to the end of the century, overlooks the fact that there is already a small scale trade between South American countries. Before the end of this decade, other Asian countries will begin to take part in both LNG and pipeline gas trade as Korea and Taiwan join the ranks of LNG importers and Singapore (and perhaps Hong Kong) considers taking pipeline gas from neighboring countries. There are possibilities of trade between Bangladesh, Pakistan, and India. Positive steps have been taken to start a regional gas grid in the countries of the United Arab Emirates, starting with Dubai and Sharjah. There is a real possibility that from these small beginnings a gas grid could spread throughout the Arabian Peninsula.[30] None of this suggests that trade in any of these regional markets will begin to challenge the dominance of the three major markets. However, growth of gas usage in Third World countries by development of domestic reserves and by means of imports from neighbors is a development which should not be ignored.

In terms of numerical predictions, set out in Table 2.4, it seems fair to say that in the West European and Japanese gas trading arenas, the period from the present up to 1995 will be one of considerable expansion, but expansion which can already be foreseen, and for which in the main, contracts have already been signed. No big projects are likely to commence during this period which have not already been largely settled between the parties.[31] In North America, the period up to 1995 appears relatively undramatic, despite a considerable rise in volumes being traded, as the market takes up to slack which it created in the 1970s and early 1980s in anticipation of sharply rising demand.

Table 2.4

World Gas Trade 1984-2005
(Billion cubic feet per day)

Year	U.S.	Japan	Europe		Total
			West	East	
1984	2.4	3.5	11.7	3.3	20.9
1985	5.8	5.6	13.7	5.5	30.6
2005	7.0	6.6	15.5	7.0	36.1

In the following decade 1995-2005, the outlook in all three major markets is for a comparatively slow growth in international gas trade. This is based on present projections of energy demand and prices and the place of natural gas within both of those projections. While I am happy to cast doubt on the validity of forecasts of this sort, I still believe that the period of the mid- to late-1990s will see a stagnation of this trade, with activity not picking up until after the turn of the century at the earliest.

In a discussion of most commodities, the period beyond 2005 would be too speculative even to mention. However, for international gas trade, the first decade of the next century, and particularly the latter part of that decade, is likely to be a most exciting time. Nor is consideration of this time frame of purely academic interest; if the projects which I have in mind are to be realized in this period, they will need to be under serious consideration within five years.

In the context of the three major markets, the regions from which very large quantities of natural gas could potentially be moved into in-

ternational trade are for the North American
market: the Arctic regions, specifically Alaska
and the Canadian Mackenzie Delta and Beaufort
Sea. For Western Europe: the Norwegian Troll
Field and the northern Norwegian waters, and the
Middle East. For Japan: the Middle East and
Eastern Siberia.

In each of these areas a number of specific
projects have already been put forward, but one
region is worthy of further scrutiny. Middle East
gas is probably the last known repository of vast
quantities of low cost conventional energy. In
1984, the region's proven reserves were estimated
to be in excess of 620 trillion cubic feet (TCF).
The aggregate figure is not particularly meaningful; more interesting is the 117 TCF in Qatar's
North Field, 400 TCF in Iran, and 100 TCF of
associated gas reserves in Saudi Arabia, a country where the size of non-associated gas reserves
remains a state secret.[32] Nevertheless, these
reserves remain simply a curiousity until a way is
found to utilize them on a much larger scale than
the present and future requirements of countries
with relatively small populations.

While Middle East gas reserves may have a low
cost of production, their cost of transportation
to any of the three major markets, but realis-
tically Japan and Western Europe, will be extremely high, technically and logistically am-
bitous and politically difficult. The sea voyage
of Middle East LNG to Japan has already been
accomplished, but it is notable that LNG imports
from Abu Dhabi have been among the most expensive
that have been imported into Japan over the past
decade. A number of studies have been conducted
regarding pipeline and LNG transportation from
the Middle East to Western Europe without tangi-
ble result. The impression is that until potential exporters show a willingness to accept the
fact that large scale exports will command a very
low price at the wellhead, both in comparision to
oil exports and in comparison to other gas supplies in world trade, little progress will be
made. Nevertheless, large scale trade in Middle
East natural gas presents one of the greatest
energy challenges of the next century and could

usher in a gas "revolution" in West Europe greater than that started by the Dutch in the 1960s.[33]

Having described the markets, it is striking, and disappointing, how little can be said about them by way of comparison or analystical conclusions. In terms of dependence on international trade, they form a continuum, from the marginal dependence of the U.S., through the significant dependence of Western Europe, to the near total dependence of Japan. The importance attached to the stability of trading relationships is directly correlated with the degree of dependence of the importer. Stability in this context is a synonym for the mutual respect of a long-term contractual and trading relationship between parties. In a world of short time horizons and spot markets, such a statement might seem to hark back to a rather "quaint" business relationship. Nothing could be further from the truth. Although the gas trading relationships of the 1980s and the 1990s will be more flexible than those of the previous two decades, the long-term bond between an exporter and an importer at either end of a transmission system will remain the basic feature of the trade. The strength of that bond will determine whether mutually beneficial trade will be able to continue through a twenty five-year period in spite of constantly changing market conditions which will alternately favor one side and then the other.

One of the challenges is legal: The writing of contracts with sufficiently broad parameters to remain relevant to the range of conditions which will be experienced over a period of two decades. But lawyers are not the salvation of international gas trade. Not every eventuality can be foreseen or catered for. International legal proceedings are almost useless as a means of settling contractual disputes: They require a period of years and, in the final analysis, limited sanction can be applied to a party which does not respect their outcome.

Both West European and Japanese gas trades have broadly shown the resilience over a period of years to suggest that the contractual relationships are solid and stable. While there have been considerable problems between West European countries and Algeria, these have been exceptions in an otherwise satisfactory and, compared with oil, remarkably trouble-free area of commerce. Japanese utilities have generally enjoyed even greater stability in their trading relationships, although it could be argued that their conciliatory attitude toward exporters accounts for this experience. It is in North America that natural gas trade has been at its most turbulent, with suspension and cancellation of trades within a few years of their commencement and the inability of contractual relationships to endure in anything other than the short-term.

Trade in North America, particularly of the past decade, has been mainly a question of setting a price for a commodity, with each side exploiting its short-term position to the maximum possible extent. This is the explanation for the lack of any contractual stability in the North American market, and why trades are suspended when short-term conditions become unfavorable. It is also the reason why it will be very difficult for North American gas trade to grow beyond the confines of the logistics which have already been constructed.

The other area where the three markets have common links is in the role of government intervention. Government intervention in domestic gas industries is not new, whether the industry is private- or state-owned. Government intervention in international gas trade is also not new, but it is becoming more visible and wisespread as natural gas trade has become a more important issue in foreign trade and foreign policy relationships. In many ways this is inevitable given the size of many trades: For most of the exporters to the Japanese market (Australia, Malaysia, Indonesia, Brunei), the LNG projects are the biggest single industrial projects that the country has ever undertaken. In the developing world, the exporter is almost without exception a state energy company with inevitable government involvement. However, even in a country privately owned utilities such as the United States, every important decision in international gas trade over the past two decades has, at a minimum, required regulatory oversight, which amounts to Federal and State approval for virtually every detail of the contract (plus a need to gain permission for any amendment to the contract). Moreover in the case of trades with Canada, Mexico and Algeria (El Paso I), the U.S. regulatory authorities have taken over the actual negotiating process with their opposite numbers. As one writer has wisely observed:

> Once major investments have been made tying buyer and seller inextric-ably together, the condition exists for one side to use its monopoly (monopsony) position against the other. More specifically, the ac-tions of natural gas exporting coun-try governments can leave the U.S. government no choice but to become involved directly.[34]

It is for this reason that the Reagan ad-ministration guidelines on the importation of nat-ural gas are an expression of ideology rather than reality:

> We believe that the buyer and the seller should determine the price based on market realities, with min-imal government involvement in the arrangements which bring gas into the United States.[35]

This is a situation which every actor in the international gas business would like to achieve. The reality is increasingly that natural gas trade is too important to be left to utilities. Despite the industry's complaints about state interfer-ence, governments increasingly believe they have legitimate domestic, foreign policy and strategic interests in this trade which make their oversight necessary. Soviet gas trade has entered into American commercial, political and strategic cal-culations in its relationships with its West Eur-opean Allies.

The problem of state intervention is that natural gas trade is a long-term business, whereas governments -- particularly OECD governments with less than five years tenure -- are concerned almost exclusively with short-term politics and economics. Not only is there no resolution to this situation, but it is likely to get worse in the future and may well prove to be an important limiting factor for the trade worldwide. Indeed, despite the fashionable talk of relying only on "market forces," government intervention may be the most difficult problem facing those involved in this trade in the 1990s.

NOTES

[1] Since this essay is concerned with the major markets, I have not included the South American market which is presently marginal to world gas trade from a numerical point of view, but suggests possibilities for the development of regional markets which may be extremely important in the future, a subject to which I shall return below.

[2] This essay is based heavily on material drawn from my two studies of the subject: International Gas Trade in Europe: The Policies of Exporting and Importing Countries, (Aldershot: Gower Publishing Company, 1984); Natural Gas Trade in North America and Asia, (Aldershot: Gower Publishing Company, 1985).

[3] In the period up to 1980, oil and coal trading relationships were governed by more stable and lasting contractual arrangements than is presently the case, but the length of these contracts did not approach those of the natural gas business.

[4] In some cases, investment in the production system will be made independently for domestic consumption, but in others, such as Norway, it will be solely for the purpose of export since there is no domestic consumption.

[5] Jonathan P. Stern, Gas's Contribution to U.K. Self-Sufficiency, (Aldershot: Gower Publishing Company, 1984).

[6] It is important to acknowledge the viewpoint of Professor Peter Odell who claims that Europe can satisfy its requirements from its own resources without recourse to imports. This involves a view

of European gas reserves which is considerably higher than most conventional views. A number of his arguments are more readily available in World Gas Report, March 19, 1984 and April 2, 1984, pp. 7-9, and pp. 8-10.

[7]Commission of the European Communities, Communication from the Commission to the Council Concerning Natural Gas, COM (84) 583 Final, Brussels, October 26, 1984, p. 6. It should be noted that Norway is not an EC member, so that the Commission counts Norwegian imports with those of Algeria and the U.S.S.R. as non-European.

[8]J.D. Davis, Blue Gold: The Political Economy of Natural Gas, (London: George Allen and Unwin, 1984), pp. 217-218.

[9]Energy Policies and Program of the IEA Countries, 1983 Review, (Paris: OECD 1984) Appendix A, Annex 1, pp. 72-73.

[10]Subsequently there were even claims from the administration that OPEC oil was more secure than Soviet gas, Sumner Benson, "Soviet Gas, Arab Oil and Western Security," The Washington Quarterly, Winter 1984, pp. 129-137.

[11]Walter Ellis, "Gasunie Poised to Step Up Deliveries in Europe," Financial Times, March 31, 1985.

[12]"Gasunie's 1985 Marketing Plan Confirms Conclusion of Talks," Financial Times, International Gas Report, May 10, 1985.

[13]Gasunie Outflanks Soviets in Belgian Spot Deal, Financial Times, International Gas Report, July 6, 1984, pp. 1-2.

[14]Although it is true that the Soviets inserted a "floor price" clause into the contracts which they have evidently had to set aside in this early period.

[15]Dr. Burckhard Bergmann, Natural Gas for Continental European -- Norwegian Gas and Implied Aspects of Energy Politics, a paper presented to the Offshore Northern Seas Conference, Stavanger, August 21, 1984.

[16]Stern, <u>Natural Gas Trade in North America...</u>, Chart 9.2, p. 250.

[17]Gerald B. Greenwald, "Japanese LNG Contracts," <u>Oil and Gas Law and Taxation Review</u>, No. 10, 1983-84, pp. 222-226.

[18]<u>Ibid</u>, Table 7.4, p. 50; J. Estanislao and A. Aquino, "An Economic View of ASEAN," <u>South East Asian Affairs</u>, 1983, Aldershot: Gower Publishing Company, pp. 27-41, Tables 5 and 6.

[19]Shibusawa Masahide, <u>Japan and the Asian Pacific Region: Profile of Change</u>, London: RIIA-/Croom Helm, 1984, p. 150.

[20]Robert Cottrell, "Japanese Finalize Plans for N-Fuel Processing Plant," <u>Financial Times</u>, July 20, 1984.

[21]Greenwald, <u>loc. cit.</u>

[22]General Accounting Office (GAO), Washington, D.C., <u>Issues Facing the Future Use of Alaskan North Slope Natural Gas</u>, GAO/RECD-83-102, May 1983, pp. 99-100. For a list of participants and chronology of the project up to the beginning of 1984, see <u>Yukon Pacific Newsletter</u>, Vol. 1, No. 1, Winter 1984.

[23]In February 1985, Osaka Gas pulled out of the project. Osaka gas was scheduled to take around one sixth of the volumes and the trade could still continue with the remaining partners. Bernard Simon, "Japanese Group Quits Canadian LNG Scheme," <u>Financial Times</u>, February 4, 1985.

[24]Greenwald, <u>loc. cit.</u>

[25]Jonathan Sharp, "Thailand's Bonanza is Still on the Horizon," <u>Financial Times</u>, December 1, 1982; "Le Gaz Naturel en Thailand," <u>Cedigaz</u>, April 1983.

[26]D. Gardner, "Mexico halts natural gas exports to U.S. after price falls," <u>Financial Times</u>, October 25, 1984.

[27]Stern, <u>Natural Gas Tade...</u>, Table 4.1, p. 109.

[28]DOE/ERA Opinion Number Three, Opinion and Order on Importation of Liquefied Natural Gas from Algeria by Tenneco Pipeline Company and Tennessee Gas Pipeline Company, ERA Docket No. 77-010-LNG, December 18, 1978. DOE/ERA Opinion Number Four, Opinion and Order on Application to Import LNG from Algeria by El Paso Eastern Company et al., ERA Docket No. 77-006-LNG, December 21, 1978. The Eascogas project was finally abandoned following an accident during the construction of the terminal on Staten Island.

[29]General Accounting Office, Implications of the U.S.-Algerian Liquefied Natural Gas Price Dispute and LNG Imports, EMD/81-34, December 16, 1980; El Paso abandons LNG deal, Middle East Economic Survey, March 2, 1981, pp. 3-4.

[30]The Gulf Cooperation Council sponsored an initiative to get such a gas grid off the ground. Although the first attempt appears to have been unsuccessful, this idea will certainly surface again.

[31]I do not rule out the possibility that the Troll field will begin production prior to 1995 (although at mid-1985 this prospect appears doubtful), but it is not likely to be producing more than a 0.5 BCF/D, compared with an eventual annual plateau production level which could be ten times that level.

[32]Arab Statistics taken from OAPEC sources. As of January 1984, from: Adnan Abushihada, "Arab Gas and the International Market," a paper presented to the International Gas Prospects and Trends Conference, University of Surrey, April 15-16, 1985, Table 6. Iranian figure is a total as of end 1983, from BP Review of World Gas, August 1984, p. 4.

[33]Many commentators at this point mention the methanol option for Middle East natural gas exporters. I do not give this option much weight because of the loss of 30 percent of the feed gas in the conversion process. If future technological developments should succeed in reducing these losses, then the methanol option could be-

come much more interesting for Middle East gas producers.

[34]Robert S. Price, "U.S. Policy on the Importation of Natural Gas," in Harry M. Trebling (ed.), Challenges for Public Utility Regulation in the 1980s, East Lansing, Michigan: Michigan State University, 1981, pp. 582-594.

[35]U.S. Department of Energy, New Policy Guidelines and Delegation Orders from the Secretary of Energy to ERA and FERC Relating to the Regulation of Imported Natural Gas, Washington, D.C., 1984.

3

International Gas Contracts

Gerald B. Greenwald

COMMENTARY

*The author focuses our attention on the commer-
cialization of gas trades which must remain the only
desirable form in which gas is supplied. What we are given
is unique insight into a process in which great stakes are
involved. If this process were to break down, as occurred
between oil companies and producer governments in the
period 1970-74, then the future of gas would be as
seriously compromised as has been oil. Confidence in the
observance of contracts, with sufficient flexibility to
accommodate market changes, is the priceless ingredient.*

*There is another aspect to gas trades, elaborated upon
in the chapter following on European Natural Gas Industries. In Europe, there is a strong interest in placing
negotiations for gas imports in larger trading contexts
than gas contracts per se can embrace. Pipeline manufac-
turers, compressor pumps, other commodities, concealed
side-offers of trade, and special interest rates for credit
extended have come to be characteristic of increasing
volumes of gas trade. These other ingredients in gas
negotiations totally complicate the definition of gas
"prices." We have made the point that gas must be
competitive with other fuels at the burner-tip. If it is
only competitive because of the presence in gas agreements
of other commercial interests, and highly favored terms, a
distortion comes into the energy market which makes gas'
competitiveness impossible to verify. What Gerald B.
Greenwald informs us is that commercial contracts can be
(and should be) the norm.*

-- Editor --

INTERNATIONAL GAS TRADES

The history of the commercialization of natural gas is instructive. A natural gas reservoir discovered near a town during the late 1800's was brought to an end-use market by means of low pressure distribution pipes. Then gas lighting was threatened when the local reservoir was depleted. Efforts were made to move further afield to discover additional gas reserves and develop technology for long distance transmission. By the 1920's, high pressure long distance transmission pipelines were built. By the 1950's, liquefied natural gas tanker vessels were built. The modern history of natural gas is replete with instances of gas traveling increasingly greater distances, and from more remote locations, in order to replace dwindling closer supplies.

Moreover, there are tendencies which encourage gas to trade at even farther distances than would seem economical in view of more proximate alternatives. Although this phenomenon could produce an economic anomaly, its logic will be rooted in a blend of entrepreneurship, timing and national policies which favor diversificiation of energy supply. Another policy, seemingly becoming more influencial, is the political interest in trade-balancing which can distort gas marketing in order to achieve other economic or political benefits. The most apparent example was French Government intervention in a price negotiation deadlock between Algeria's Sontrach and Gaz de France. The resulting LNG sales price contained a "premium" (for a short time underwritten by the French Government) which was to be compensated by an Algerian/French agreement to increase Algerian imports from France. Consequently, there are a variety of market and non-market forces which have fostered a worldwide effort to develop natural gas resources and markets.

The international gas trade is now about ten percent of the world's oil trade. Gas can be transported over land for long distances through large diameter pipelines at high pressure. Moreover, marine pipeline technology has progressed

quickly and pipelines are used to develop offshore gas for export markets. Existing pipeline
systems link the U.S. with Mexico and with Canada
and link all of Europe in a manner which permits
North Sea gas to enter at the north, Soviet gas
to enter Europe at the east and Algerian gas to
enter at the south, all available for transnational distribution within Europe.

Natural gas is also transported in the
form of liquefied natural gas. Liquefaction reduces 600 units of gas volume to one unit of liquid volume. This change of state and reduction
of volume makes marine transportation of natural
gas viable. LNG first crossed the Atlantic Ocean
in 1958 with 5,000 cubic meters of LNG transported from Lake Charles, Louisiana to Canvey
Island in the U.K. Commercial deliveries from
Algeria to the U.K. under a long-term contract
began in 1964 and from Algeria to France in 1965.
LNG is the means by which an international gas
trade developed in the Pacific. Although each
LNG project is a distinct trade utilizing dedicated land-based facilities and vessels, the number
and location of LNG facilities suggests the possibility of more flexible trade in the future.
At present, nine LNG export terminals are located
in seven countries, and nineteen LNG receiving
terminals are located in seven countries.

Natural gas exports and imports tend to
take place within highly segmented markets. European demand is met by supplies from Norway and
The Netherlands, the Soviet Union and North Africa. Japanese gas demand is mainly met within the
Pacific Basin. After a "false start" development
of base load LNG supplies from Algeria to meet
anticipated natural gas shortages which did not
materialize, U.S. import demand is met mainly by
pipelines carrying natural gas from Canada, and
until recently from Mexico. LNG imports now
serve only the peakshaving natural gas market in
the Northeast United States.

It is possible that in some cases natural
gas of one country can trade into more than one
of these three segmented markets. For example,
Canadian arctic gas reserves are located at an
equal distance from Europe and the U.S. East
Coast. Gas supplies in the far south of Chile

and Argentina have at various times (but without success) sought markets in Europe, North America and Japan. Likewise, Nigeria sought to develop an LNG project which exported gas to both Europe and the U.S. East Coast. The Soviet Union is strategically located to pipeline gas to Europe, but ten years ago considered Siberian based LNG projects to supply in one case the East Coast of the United States and in another case the West Coast of the United States and Japan. As yet, none of these dual-market export trades have thus far been developed.

Canada continues to consider a project which would diversify its substantial natural gas exports to the United States by exporting LNG to Japan. When the Province of Alberta issued a removal permit to permit Alberta gas to leave the province, destined to become LNG bound for Japan, it seemed as though the development of sales to Japan were seen in Alberta as "incremental" to U.S. export sales, for fear that any separate marketing program to Japan might jeopardize delicate pricing relationships with U.S. natural gas.

In sum, for the present at least, international gas trade remains a commerce substantially limited to independent markets of the United States, Japan and Western Europe, each with its unique characteristics of energy supply and demand.

THE UNITED STATES AS AN IMPORT MARKET

The United States is the world's largest gas market. The first long distance transmission of natural gas occurred here in 1925, and since then we have built a nationwide natural gas pipeline grid making natural gas available by 1966 in every one of the lower 48 states, through one million miles of transmission and distribution pipelines. Notwithstanding large investments in domestic production and distribution, the United States is well located to receive significant gas imports on the north from Canada and on the south from Mexico. As yet, natural gas imports have not played a large part in the American natural gas energy balance.

The extensive pipeline transmission system in the United States would permit imported gas to reach distant U.S. regional markets by displacement. A dramatic application of this concept was seen in a study prepared by The El Paso Company which unsuccessfully sought approval in the mid-seventies to pipeline North Slope Alaska natural gas to Southwest Alaska, transform the vapor into LNG, tanker the LNG to a California terminal and distribute gas by displacement to a majority of the lower 48 states.

The United States was an early importer of liquefied natural gas (LNG). Algerian LNG imports first reached the United States in 1968. LNG shipments from Algeria were made to the Boston area starting in 1971 and are continuing today, on a small scale. Thereafter, Algeria and U.S. gas transmission companies developed large-scale projects which constructed LNG import terminals at Cove Point, Maryland, Savannah, Georgia and Lake Charles, Louisiana. Today none of these impressive receiving facilities are in use. LNG import contracts fell victim to excess domestic natural gas supply, falling consumption, and natural gas price decontrol which responded to declining oil prices. In more than ten years of vigorous commercial activities to establish these and other LNG projects, the United States emerged as a leader in cryogenic technology. This technology base, the existence of unused import terminals on the East and Gulf Coasts, and the cyclical nature of energy markets strongly suggests the eventual return to LNG exports to the United States.

Is, then, the United States a major factor in the international trading of natural gas? The pipeline grid which links us with Canada and Mexico is a substantial constraint to any gas trade beyond the continent. Nevertheless, our market is huge, infrastructure is in place for a more distant LNG trade, and there is no reason to believe that we have seen the end of the feast-or-famine cycle in natural gas supply. Import terminals exist to receive Caribbean, Latin American and West African supplies should they materialize as LNG exporters, and even the Norwegian North Sea gas producers would like to have export alternatives to the U.S. East Coast. One can foresee a future LNG import terminal on the West Coast available to receive LNG from Alaska or the South Pacific Basin. Moreover, the eventual exploitation of huge gas reserves on the North Slope of Alaska may include substantial LNG exports, principally to Japan, possibly supplemented by the Republic of Korea and the Republic of China (Taiwan). The U.S. potential for international gas trading exists, but for now Europe and Japan are the dominant international gas markets.

EUROPE AS AN IMPORT MARKET

In 1959, the Dutch discovered the huge gas field at Groningen, which lies within 250-300 miles of West Germany, The Netherlands and Belgium. Dutch gas exports were made to Germany and Belgium starting in 1966, France in 1967, and later to Italy and Switzerland.

These exports necessitated the construction of transmission lines from the Dutch border to the German border and later through West Germany and Switzerland to Northern Italy, the beginning of a transnational European pipeline grid. The Soviet Union contracted to export gas to Austria in 1968, and subsequently exported in the mid-seventies to additional European countries. North Sea gas started flowing in 1977, providing to Norway export opportunities by undersea pipeline from North Sea gas fields to a continental terminal at Emden, Germany and a separate undersea pipeline to the U.K. In 1983 gas began flowing to Italy from Algeria via a TransMediterranean Pipeline System. Natural gas now contributes eighteen percent of the energy consumption of the European Community.

The transportation network for the European gas import market is impressive. Pipelines run from Norway in the north, the Soviet Union in the east, and Algeria in the south. On the south and west coasts of Europe, there are a series of LNG terminals in Italy, Spain, France, Belgium and the U.K. to receive gas from North Africa and perhaps more distant gas supplies from West Africa and the Middle East.

The broad scope of the European gas pipeline grid also presents displacement opportunities. Each national segment of a transnational European system will be operated by domestic companies, but the pipeline itself is likely to be owned in varying percentages by a group of separate national gas companies each making distribution and sales solely within its own national boundaries. Hence, most of the gas in the pipeline grid is the gas purchased by the respective national companies.

This cooperation of shippers extends beyond the interdependent ownership and operation of gas transit pipelines. Trading of imported gas by purchasers within an international context also occurs. The following are some examples of these inter-company transfers.

o   Gasunie of The Netherlands transferred some of its annual imports of Norwegian natural gas to Gaz de France.

o   Pending completion of the MEGAL transport system, Gaz de France transferred Soviet gas to SNAM in Italy in exchange for Dutch gas.

o   Dutch gas destined for Luxembourg is delivered by Gaz de France and the Belgian Distrigaz Company.

o   Belgium Distrigaz made an agreement with Gaz de France to make use of the LNG terminal at Montoir from October 1982. According to this agreement, Distrigaz will cede some Algerian gas to Gaz de France for four years and Distrigaz will take an equivalent quantity of Norweigan gas from the pipeline which crosses Belgium.

The trading of imported gas between purchasers usually indicates logistical adjustments in an otherwise conventional import transaction. However, deliveries of proximate supplies against purchase contracts for distant gas can also be the cornerstone of an international gas project. The most dramatic example was a project known as IGAT II which was signed up in November, 1975 solely as a displacement arrangement. The participants were the state-owned National Iranian Gas Corporation, the Soviet gas export agency, and three European purchasers, Ruhrgas, Gaz de France and Austria's OMV. In December, 1976, Czechoslovakia joined the project. Iranian gas was to be exported to the Soviet Union for its domestic consumption and would have been compensated by Soviet gas exported to Czechoslovakia, and from there to Austria, West Germany and France. Although imaginatively conceived, the project proved to be politically vulnerable, as IGAT II's demise rapidly followed that of the Shah of Iran.

Moreover, the European gas import market is characterized first, by a relatively small number of purchasers, each a state-owned gas transmission company serving as the country's exclusive natural gas importer, or in the case of Germany, a dominant private company which imports 70 percent of German gas trade, and second, by a consortium or cooperative arrangement which unites these transmission companies into a single purchaser group for large gas import transactions from the North Sea and Soviet Union. The results are gas purchase transactions of a magnitude that can foster both economic development of new gas supplies and diversity of gas supply which is broader than any one company (or country) could undertake.

As in the United States, the members of the European Community are endowed with the infrastructure of overland pipelines and LNG import terminals to support a varied and expanded import trade to supplement domestic natural gas supplies.

JAPAN AS AN IMPORT MARKET

A large gas market, and the fastest growing, is in Japan. Japan's importation of gas is in the form of LNG, relying mainly on Pacific Basin supplies under long-term contract from Alaska (starting 1969), Brunei (1972), Indonesia (1977) and Malaysia (1983), and Middle East imports from Abu Dhabi (1977). A contract for LNG supplies from Canada signed in 1982 remains to be implemented on a restructured basis currently under consideration. A contract for import of Australian LNG was signed in 1985 and

is being implemented for deliveries starting in
1989. LNG from the Soviet Union's Sakhalin
Island seems destined for Japan in the early
Nineties. Additional Pacific Basin supplies
could be developed for the Japanese market from
new sources of supply such as Thailand, and from
the Middle East.

In 1982, liquefied natural gas contributed
6.4 percent of Japan's energy consumption. The
Ministry of International Trade and Industry estimates that consumption of LNG in primary energy
will reach 11 percent in 1990. Six electric utilities presently account for 75 percent of all
LNG imports and three gas utilities account for
most of the balance. According to MITI's "Outline of Electric Power Construction Plan," the
breadkown of electric power generation by major
companies in 1983 was oil 36 percent, nuclear 20
percent, LNG 16 percent, hydropower 16 percent
and coal 8 percent. The government favors
cutting down on the use of oil for electricity
generation, leaving LNG to compete with nuclear
power and coal.

In Japan, the buyers of LNG fall into two
categories of public utilities. Public utilities
for the sale of natural gas regasify the LNG and
sell the vapor to their customers for home heating and cooking, commercial heating and industrial fuel. Public utilities for the sale of
electricity regasify the LNG and use the vapor as
boiler fuel for power generation. (There is one
exception: a major industrial company, Nippon
Steel Corporation, is a direct purchaser of a
small portion of the LNG imported from Indonesia.) In Japan purchasers are few, and LNG projects have been based on consortium purchases
involving from two to five buying companies.

In the fifteen years since LNG was introduced in Japan, a series of coastal marine import
terminals have been, and are being, constructed.
Japanese geography and demographics are obstacles
to a far-ranging gas pipeline grid which maxi-
mizes distribution and minimizes supply disruption. But given the high concentration of natural gas use by the electric power industry, LNG
terminal infrastructure provides a degree of
supply/displacement flexibility which can amelio-

rate to some extent the insecurities of potential supply disruption.

This brief survey of natural gas imports into the United States, Europe and Japan describes an existing infrastructure of LNG import terminals and pipeline grids put in place during the past twenty years, and upon which an expanded international trade in natural gas can be built. To some extent, national policies may impede this expansion, but there are also offsetting political considerations which tend to foster international trade in natural gas. Today, it is commercial forces which must provide the impetus to new gas trading. Gas is a complicated commodity to market, and this study now focuses upon contractual arrangements for marketing gas in international trade.

LONG TERM GAS CONTRACTS

Natural gas, alone among hydrocarbons, sells under long-term purchase contracts of fifteen to twenty-five years. A long-term contract offers the promise of stability in commercial relations. The supplier is assured of markets, the purchaser of supply. And the lender is assured of cash flow necessary to debt incurred to construct facilities for production and often for transportation. For oil, these conditions came to an abrupt end in the OPEC era when first, crude purchase contracts became terminable at will upon administered changes in sales price, and second, contract quantities became renegotiable at frequent intervals in order to reflect falling worldwide demand for crude oil.

For natural gas, the long-term purchase contract persisted, primarily because of the need for intensive capital investment to develop the infrastructure of the gas trade, namely gas fields, pipelines, gas processing plants, and in the case of LNG projects, also liquefaction plants, LNG storage tanks, marine terminals and LNG vessels. Yet, it was impossible for gas contracts to avoid the forces that propelled the crude oil trade into a increasingly "spot sale" business whether on the spot market or under so-called term contracts. The adaptation of gas

purchase contracts   has been slow,
revolving around terms for quantity and price,
and take-or-pay clauses which obligate the
purchaser to pay at or near the contract price
for gas which the purchaser fails to take in each
year of the contract.

THE STRUCTURE OF GAS CONTRACTS

The natural gas sales and purchase
contract has unique features. Although legally
a contract for the sale of goods, the commercial
sale is measured and priced in terms of the
heating value or volume of the goods. The
contract must also be concerned with measurement
of qualities. Natural gas is both a mixture of
various hydrocarbons in a gaseous state and a
mixture of hydrocarbons and other constituents,
such as hydrogen, carbon dioxide or sulphur and
can contain damaging impurities. In the end,
heating value is determined in relation to
volume, temperature, pressure, density and
molecular constituents. These physical aspects
of the commodity require sampling procedures,
measurement standards and practices, and related
test equipment, which reveal the quantity and
quality in a commercial sale. Project facilities
and scheduling of deliveries are also central to
effecting gas sales.
In the natural gas pipeline trades, the
estimated quantity of deliverable reserves from a
single field can often set project parameters for
field development, pipeline capacity, storage
capacity, and delivery quantities on a daily,
weekly, monthly and annual basis.
Similarly, the LNG trade requires matching
specialized facilities, such as a liquefaction
plant, tank storage, port and marine loading
facilities at the loading port, LNG tankers to
provide transportation, and port and marine sun-
loading facilities, tank storage, and a regasification plant at the discharge port. Moreover,
the marine interface at each end of the trade
gives rise to specialized contract clauses
designed to accomodate both the physical proper-
ties of LNG and commercial practices of ocean
transport.

Another layer of contract terms are those customary to international sales contracts generally, such as transfer of title and risk of loss, currency adjustment, invoices, payment, duties and taxes, force majeure, arbitration and applicable law.

QUANTITY

A seller's view of gas quantity is straightforward. Quantity should match as closely as prudent to the productive capacity of natural gas field facilities, and in the case of LNG, the LNG liquefaction plant. Optimally, the field and plant operate on a daily basis except during scheduled maintenance periods. Storage capacity is limited and expensive. Transportation capacity, whether by pipeline or ship, is limited and expensive. Thus, the "system" requires that deliveries occur with the same constant periodicity that matches optimization of production, transportation, processing and storage. This is indeed a rigid view of product deliveries which must survive intact for two decades.

Generally speaking, the buyer's view of gas quantity in an LNG project is almost as rigid. Like the seller, the buyer has invested in physical facilities which it wishes to optimize by receiving deliveries at the same relatively constant intervals. Moreover, the end-use of gas is usually as a base load fuel either for electric power generation or natural gas distribution. Either use supports a constancy of service which, while subject to peaks and valleys, must rely upon a constancy of supply. As would be expected from this description, the sales contract terms for the long-term sale of a quantity of natural gas will exhibit considerable rigidity.

PRICE

Contract terms for quantity are "rigid," but contract terms for price have come to be exceedingly "flexible." This flexibility is achieved by a variety of price-adjustment methods which may operate independelty. One can expect to find in gas contracts some or all of the following:

o   Base Price;

o   Commodity escalation of the Base Price, tied to crude oils or oil products. Crude oil prices may be determined F.O.B. or C.I.F. designated markets and usually blend a variety of crudes. Specific products selected to approximate competitive alternative fuels are priced in the purchaser's market.

o   Floor price, sometimes related to capital and operating costs of the project or initial sales price.

o   Currency adjustment, often relating the currency of the contract price to a basket of internationally convertible currencies.

o   Periodic price reconsideration, often provided for at intervals of three or four years, which permit renegotiation of the base price or escalation formula on the basis of significant interim changes in the energy market which are perceived as disadvantageous to one party or the other.

Although prices change periodically by virtue of the application of these various price determinants, there may be no assurance that the gas price at any particular time will be competitive in the end-use market with the price of alternative fuels available to an end-user which can switch away from gas or otherwise reduce gas consumption.

TAKE-OR-PAY

Cash flow from gas sales is assured by several further concepts, namely, "take-or-pay" payment when quantities are not taken, and "carry-over" to a later period of quantities which could not be delivered or not be taken due to events of force majeure.

Take-or-pay plays an essential role in gas project development and financing. First, it provides a potential cash flow which has been sufficient to stimulate investment and to attract financing, both essential for the development of vastly expensive facilities customarily dedicated

to a single trade. Take-or-pay terms also substitute liquidated sum (take-or-pay, price multi-
plied by take-or-pay quantity) for an uncertain
sum difficult to calculate and possibly subject
to set-off or defense, which represents the
Seller's monetary damages arising from the Purchaser's failure to purchase contract quantities.
Take-or-pay terms, however, operate in a contractual setting of rigid quantity requirements and
changing prices.

The purchaser has only limited contractual
assurance that natural gas paid for but not
taken, can be taken at a later date at a price
which reflects a credit for the amount of the
earlier payment. This assurance is "limited"
both by physical and commercial constraints.
Since projects are sized to operate on an optimal
basis and excess storage capacity is usually
severely limited, the capacity to deliver quantities, and often to receive quantities, in excess
of these optimal quantities is often constrained.
Nevertheless, the purchaser's right of "make-up"
must be recognized, and the parameters for the
exercise of this right must be negotiated.

Another set of quantity terms may concern
so-called "carry-forward" of quantities taken by
the purchaser in any year which are in excess of
its annual contract obligation. Carry-forward
permits these excess quantities to be credited
against the quantity obligation of a subsequent
year. Normally there will be a time limitation
of several years on the purchaser's exercise of
carry-forward rights. Another clause may require
adjustment of the price of the excess natural gas
in order to reflect the price in the year when
the quantity obligation is avoided, rather than
the price in the year when the excess gas was
taken and paid for.

Project cash flow can also be made more
secure by protecting the aggregate contract quantity against reduction caused by force majeure
events which interfere with either party's performance during the short run. Quantities missed
during the year due to force majeure can be added
to the quantities for the remaining contract
term, or, less frequently, can stretch out the
contract beyond its original term until all of

the aggregate contract quantities are delivered. In some cases, the purchaser's obligation to purchase missed force majeure quantities can block the exercise of the purchaser's right to "makeup" quantities previously paid for but not taken.

The point to be made is that it is the interplay of contract terms with respect to quantity, price and take-or-pay which are at the heart of the commercial negotiation. And it is the contractual means of relating these concepts that will determine the resiliency of the commercial transaction to respond and adjust to the cyclical nature of energy markets which characterized the past decade and is likely to continue over the next decade or more.

THE IMPACT OF VOLATILE ENERGY MARKETS

The rise in gas export trading coincided with the period of rapid escalating oil prices which also drove up prices of all alternative energies. In recent years, "oil gluts" and "gas bubbles" characterized oversupply which generated declining prices for all hydrocarbons. Volatile prices are a problem for marketing of any commodity. But the problem is intensified in the natural gas trade because long-term gas purchasers are invariably short-term resellers of energy. Contract terms for periodic price adjustment often lag both the fall of prices of competitive fuels, and contract terms for inflexible deliveries of fixed quantities cannot respond to periods of falling demand. When gas is used as boiler fuel, the resulting electricity must be sold to end-users who have a range of options, including reduced demand in periods of recession and conservation ini periods of rising prices. Natural gas purchased by natural gas transmission companies is resold to gas distribution companies and ultimately to gas consumers who often can make alternative choices among LPG, heating oil or coal. During the recent period of worldwide recession contracted quantities have frequently exceeded demand in the local gas or electricity markets. As a result, the recent experience with the sanctity of long-term natural gas contracts has not been all that good.

TERMINATION OF CONTRACTS

In the extreme case, gas supply contracts broke down, notably in the case of Algerian LNG export sales to the United States. In 1969 El Paso contracted with Sonatrach for a twenty-five year supply of LNG, and the following year this supply was resold to three U.S. pipeline companies. Sonatrach encountered start-up delays and construction cost overruns, and the deliveries did not begin until 1978. By then the project was confronted by both the full impact of OPEC upon oil prices and the political shift in Algeria to a new regime not wedded to the gas pricing terms accepted by its predecessor. Contract renegotiation resulted in a signed amendment to the pricing terms, but Sonatrach later advised El Paso that the amendment was not acceptable to the Algerian government. In the spring of 1980, deliveries ceased. When El Paso and Sonatrach could not reach a new agreement, the U.S. Department of Energy, with the assistance of the State Department, began negotiating with Algerian officials. The United States would not accept the Algerian principle of BTU price parity between natural gas and crude oil at the point of export. Rather, the U.S. insisted upon a delivered price no higher than the cost of alternate fuels in the consuming area, which they determined to be about comparable to the $4.47 MMBTU price of Canadian and Mexican pipeline gas imports. These alternate fuels were about $3.50 lower than the Algerian price request, once shipping and regasification costs are added. Government to Government negotiations ended. Negotiations to restart the project continued between Sonatrach and some of the U.S. pipeline company purchasers from El Paso, but no settlement has been reached.

In December 1983, a purchase contract for Algerian LNG was suspended by Panhandle Eastern Corp. Panhandle halted deliveries under its long-term LNG purchase contract with Sonatrach signed in 1975, and under which deliveries of Algerian LNG to Lake Charles, Louisiana began in 1982. Panhandle was reported to have advised Sonatrach that the contract is "temporarily suspended . . . for an indefinite period." Panhandle cited the extreme financial pressures generated by its purchase contract under which LNG cost Panhandle more than twice as much as Panhandle paid for its domestic natural gas in the United States. Continued performance of the Sontrach contract was said to jeopardize Panhandle's solvency. Thus, in 1983 Panhandle announced its decision as a choice based on economic self-preservation. Notwithstanding Sonatrach's invocation of the arbitration clause of the contract, it is reported that Sonatrach and Panhandle continue to meet and work toward a solution.

Since late 1973 it has been accepted practice in the gas trade that gas prices under long-term contracts will fluctuate in accordance with an adjustment formula based on price changes in other forms of energy, usually designated crude oils or refined oil products which respond to short-term price changes. Notwithstanding this price responsiveness, there can be mistrust of the long-term operation of the formula used in the price adjustment clause.

PERIODIC PRICE REVISION

There are basically three strategies for achieving greater flexibility under gas supply contracts. The first is to abandon reliance upon long-term mechanisms and explicitly provide for reopening of negotiations of price/quantity and other commercial terms during the twenty-year contract period at frequent intervals, perhaps three to five years. This approach was promoted by Algeria in its LNG sales contracts during the halcyon days for energy sellers, and the implementation of these clauses is now eagerly awaited by European purchasers of Algerian LNG. Similarly, the latest contracts for pipeline export of Canadian natural to the United States provide for renegotiation of at least the price terms, and usually the quantity, annually.

Periodic price reopening has also become a feature of Soviet and North Sea gas exports to Europe, and more recently in Gasunie's export sales on the Continent. In the case of Soviet and North Sea gas sales contracts, "floor prices"

provisions may operate as a limitation on the negotiation of lower pricing terms. Both Soviet
and North Sea sales were based upon development
of new gas resources and infrastructure. Dutch
and Canadian contracts which will utilize existing deliverable gas resources and transportation
systems do not have similar "downside" protection.

In a sense, periodic price revision
clauses avoid the question of long-term stability
in contractual relations because these long-term
contracts include short-term contracts with respect to one or more vital commercial term of the
sale.

HARDSHIP CLAUSES

A second approach is the so-called "hardship clause" which permits either party to reopen the economic terms if the operation of the
contract's long-term provisions cause a substantial adverse economic effect upon one of the parties. For example, in the 1973 Ekofisk Natural
Gas Sales Agreement between Phillips Petroleum Co
Norway Group and the Gaz de France Group, the
concept of "substantial hardship" is defined as
follows:

> ". . . if . . . during the term of this
> Agreement, without default of the party
> concerned there is the occurrence of an
> intervening event or change of circum-
> stances beyond the said party's control
> when acting as a reasonable and prudent
> operator such that the consequences and
> effects of which are fundamentally differ-
> ent from what was contemplated by the par-
> ties at the time of entering into this
> Agreement . . . which consequences and
> effects place said party in the situation
> that then and for the foreseeable future
> all annual cost . . . associated with or
> related to the processed gas which is the
> subject of this Agreement exceed the
> annual proceeds derived from the sale of
> said gas."

A clause as limited as this operates to provide cost protection or cash-flow protection on the "down-side," but should also include limitation of benefits derived from unanticipated increases in prices of other forms of energy in order to provide benefit to both parties.

Even in the absence of a hardship clauses, fundamental change in energy markets such as that which took place in late 1973, tended to result in increased energy prices under existing gas sales contracts in order to give recognition to the substantial increase in the market price of energy. These increases occurred by government fiat, as in the case of Canadian gas exports, or by contract renegotiation.

The 1967 contract for the export of Alaska LNG to Japan is a classic example of such renegotiation. Title and risk of loss of goods passed at the flange connecting the unloading piping of the LNG tanker with the piping of Tokyo Gas at Negishi in Yokohama Bay. The price was 52 cents per million BTU's delivered, about one-ninth of the current price. In the tumultuous energy market of the 1970's, there were 13 amendments to the pricing provisions of the Agreement in the period up to May 1982.

These amendments fixed the base contract price at levels consistent with prices of Japan's other LNG imports as adjusted monthly by a formula indexing the base price to the weighted average of the Government Selling Prices of the 20 leading crude oils imported into Japan. Notwithstanding the price indexing to imported crudes, the contract provided that, "Sellers and Buyers shall be free to request a renegotiation of the prices if there are significant changes in circumstances."

RENEGOTIATION

The third strategy for achieving greater flexibility in natural gas terms is to tinker with terms for price, quantity and take-or-pay in order to provide a degree of contractual resiliency which can react to changing market conditions in the Purchaser's resale market. This objective has been pursued in a large number of renegotiations of long-term international gas contracts. However, in most cases the modification has been made effective for only a short period of one, two or three years. This caution itself reflects the parties own uncertainties about designing "flexibility" into long-term contracts. Nevertheless, these changes illustrate a range of choices available to meet cyclical market conditions.

In recent years, Sonatrach's LNG export contracts to Europe bent somewhat, but did not break. By and large, Sonatrach obtained premium prices for its LNG from European purchasers and was consistently unwilling to lower those prices. In turn, European purchasers refused to accept delivery of full annual contract quantities. Agreements were ultimately reached which reduced contract quantities on a temporary basis of perhaps several years but added the reductions back into the contract quantities for later years of the contract. Also, take-or-pay liabilities of purchasers, which could have been substantial, were compromised at a subtantially lower amount or in some cases may have been forgiven altogether.

During this period, Japanese LNG contracts were relatively unchanged, probably because over 75 percent of gas imports were used to fuel boilers for electric power generation. Electric companies rely on a wide variety of fuels. During the period of declining demand, they were apparently able to reduce spot purchases of oil and LPG in order to utilize a larger proportion of gas in their energy balance. Nevertheless, the effect of foregoing oil and product purchases during the falling spot market must have increased average fuel costs of the electric utilities. As a result, Japan likewise became insistent upon greater flexibility as the quid pro quo for new LNG purchase contracts to serve its expanding gas imports.

In the U.S. market, Canadian export contracts were systematically renegotiated to reduce quantity (and later price), to increase flexibility of take, and reduce the impact of take-or-pay.

Canada is a major exporter of natural gas to the United States. The U.S. gas market is huge, and Canadian gas increasingly filled the supply gap created by diminishing U.S. gas production in the seventies. But in recent years U.S. domestic gas production increased and domestic gas consumption fell sharply. Canadian sellers and U.S. buyers were forced back to the bargaining table.

The original gas purchase contracts between Great Lakes and TransCanada Pipelines, Ltd. reflected the following take-or-pay arrangements:

1. The take-or-pay level was 75%, determined and payable on a monthly basis.
2. The take-or-pay price was the full import price.
3. There were no make-up rights.

By early 1984 these provisions were renegotiated to effect the following changes:

1. The take-or-pay price was changed to a price which has been approximately 60% of the full import price.
2. The take-or-pay payments are due on an annual basis rather than a monthly basis; similarly, the take-or-pay volumes were based on 75% of the annual contract quantity.
3. Provision was made for make-up of LNG paid for but not taken. Not only do the make-up rights extend to the full term of the contract, plus one year, if necessary, but the make-up volumes occur at any time a quantity in excess of 75% of annual contract quantity is purchased in any contract year. Thus, take-or-pay make-up can occur within the annual contract entitlements as opposed to a requirement that volumes in excess of the annual contract entitlements must be purchased in order to obtain make-up credit for past payments.

More recently, another round of renegotiation resulted in further modifications as follows:

1. For the contract year ended October 31, 1983, the take-or-pay volumes were reduced from the level of 75% to 50%. During the contract year commencing November 1, 1983 and ending October 31, 1985, take-or-pay obligations are 50% of Annual Contract Quantity and past deficiencies can be made up by purchase of volumes above 50% of Annual Contract Quantity.

2. Any take-or-pay amounts incurred will be deferred automatically for a period of four (4) years. During such four years the only obligation will be to pay interest on the take-or-pay amount.

3. The 75% take-or-pay level is reinstated on and after November 1, 1985.

4. All of the take-or-pay gas is subject to make-up rights which extend to the full contract term, plus one year, if required.

Natural gas sales contract amendments negotiated between Canadian exporters and U.S. importers during the past several years provide the following catalog of techniques for increasing the flexibility of the Buyer's take-or-pay obligations.

o Take-or-pay percentage of annual contract quantity was reduced.

o Price for natural gas which is paid for but not taken was reduced.

o Base time period for calculation was increased, e.g., from quarterly or monthly take-or-pay calculation to annual take-or-pay calculation, and take-or-pay obligations based on different time periods were scaled down, e.g., a lower take-or-pay percentage per quarter than per annum.

The recent amendments of these various Canadian contracts also contain a variety of related marke-up provisions which likewise reduce the adverse impact on the Buyer of its take-or-pay payments. These are examples:

o   Volumes paid for but not taken may be
     made up during the remaining years of
     the contract.
o   Volumes paid for but not taken may be
     made up during a one-year extension
     period of the contract.
o   All volumes in excess of the take-or-
     pay percentage shall be treated as
     make-up quantities.
o   Payments made for natural gas which
     has not been made up by the end of the
     contract term will be refunded.

Long-term contracts could not protect the
Canadian sellers from returning to the bargaining
table to reduce the effects of a depressed gas
market upon their purchasers. Given these
events, one wonders whether it is possible to
build into long-term gas contracts concepts which
are more attuned to short-term changes in the
purchaser's resale market. Some of these concepts are beginning to be seen in international
gas sales contracts.

NEW DIRECTIONS IN NATURAL GAS TRADE

It is safe to predict that in the future
gas will be traded across national borders in
greater quantity than at present. It is considerably more difficult to predict the changes
in commercial arrangements which will accompany
this expanded trade. On the assumption that the
seeds of future contracts have been sown in the
recent spate of changed contracts and evolving
deregulation of natural gas markets, it seems
worthwhile to note certain developments which
seem likely to be accelerated. These developments are incentive pricing, take-or-pay caps,
spot sales and contract quantities based on the
"requirements" of the purchaser or its "best
efforts" to exceed a minimum quantity obligation.
Also, we can speculate on whether natural gas
contracts may in some cases evolve away from a
"sale of goods" which compels sellers and buyers
to be commercial adversaries. Joint ventures and
cooperative marketing arrangements are not
uncommon formats for international commerce in
manufactured goods. Perhaps these concepts can

be adapted to foster a more cooperative mode of international gas marketing.

INCENTIVE PRICING

During 1980-83, Canada imposed a single U.S. border reference price for all export sales of Canadian natural gas to the United States. As U.S. natural gas demand declined in 1982, U.S. companies took delivery of only fifty percent of the 1.5 TCF authorized for export by the Canadian Government. In 1983, Canada's National Energy Board estimated a decline to forty-four percent. In April 1983, the minimum price at the Canada/U.S. border of $4.84/MMBTU was cut to $4.40/MMBTU by the Canadian Government. Three months later Canada established an interim Volume Related Incentive Pricing (VRIP) system to last sixteen months. U.S. gas purchasers paid $4.40/MCF for the first fifty percent of the gas volumes contracted for and $3.40/MCF for quantities in excess. The $3.40/MCF price also applied more generally to any shipment above the amount exported in 1982.

Thereafter, Canada moved to align itself with U.S. policies favoring market oriented gas pricing. Recent Canadian natural gas sales to the United States relate unit price to load factor, i.e., the percentage of daily maximum contract quantities delivered to the purchaser. Price per unit declines as load factor increases. Most of these Canadian export contracts state the highest price for quantities at one-third or one-half load factor, with price moving downward in two or three increments until take reaches 100%. The same result, namely, reduced incremental pricing for increased purchases can also be achieved by means of restructuring natural gas pipeline tariffs of the commodity seller. The press recently reported that Pan Alberta's export contracts with Northern Natural and Panhandle Eastern employ a heavy demand charge and a low commodity charge that makes Canada gas "very attractive on an incremental basis after the demand charge has been paid."

In Europe, a British gas industry official reportedly suggested that Norway's high cost gas supplies be marketed with a different gas price and/or price escalation for each tranche contained in the contract quantity. The first tranche could function to assure minimum project revenue necessary in order to support financing; subsequent tranches to permit adaptation to changing market conditions.

The existence of two or more prices, based on quantity levels, does not of itself provide a means to reflect changing conditions in the seller's market or the purchaser's market. Rather, incentive prices produce a contract climate more conducive to aggressive marketing by the gas purchaser to its own customers by its own system of either incremental or rolled-in pricing. In principle, use of quantity discounts seems fully consistent with a realistic gas marketing strategy in which initial quantities supply the highest price market of domestic customers (or other price inelastic end-users), but in which aggressive pricing is needed to expand the market to industrial customers (or other elastic end-users).

TAKE-OR-PAY CEILINGS

In the Northwest Alaskan Pipeline case, the Federal Energy Regulatory Commission (FERC) considered the sale of Canadian natural gas transported to the United States by the so-called "Pre-build" section of the Alaska Natural Gas Transportation System. In approving the sale, on June 20, 1980, FERC limited the purchaser's take-or-pay obligation to a "revenue cap" calculated by multiplying the fixed annual take-or-pay quantity by the original contract price as escalated by a general index of inflation. The pricing terms of the sales contract provided for more generous price escalation, and FERC did not modify any of the pricing terms. As the price escalated under the natural gas sales contract at a rate faster than the rate of inflation, the effect of the FERC cap was to reduce the amount of the fixed quantity which gave rise to the purchaser's take-or-pay obligation.

FERC thereby expressed take-or-pay as a monetary obligation, rather than a quantity obligation. FERC's theory was that take-or-pay should be based on project economics underlying the original contract price. Capital costs and debt service being relatively fixed at inception of the project, it was assumed that the "first contract year" level of revenue would be sufficient to keep the project economically viable. The use of a general inflation index as the take-or-pay escalator was seen as a means of covering escalation in project operating costs.

Perhaps this concept of take-or-pay revenue caps has its counterpart in gas sale contracts which, in addition to a contract price and a price escalation formula, contained a floor price, that is, a price below which the contract price could not be reduced by operation of the escalation, or rather deescalation, formulas. In that context, the producer was able to obtain assurance of a minimum revenue sufficient to service debt, operating costs and possibly, a projected rate of return on investment. The corresponding concept of a "maximum price" which would limit the operation of price escalation formulas never developed because gas sellers have been intent upon obtaining the full commodity value of gas in the energy market. The FERC decision struck a balance, permitting the gas seller to obtain the full benefit of contract price escalation, but imposing a reduction on the purchaser's contract quantity obligation to the extent price escalation exceeded inflation. There may be long-term benefit in capping quantity rather than price. A take-or-pay revenue cap can provide minimum revenue assurance during recessionary periods, but in this instance the purchaser is accommodated by a ceiling on quantity required to be taken in a period of rapidly escalating energy prices.

SPOT SALES

During 1983 and 1984, FERC approved proposals of natural gas transmission companies in the United States for special marketing programs to develop a spot market for domestic

U.S. natural gas which would otherwise be lost to residual fuel oil. Prices to end-users of natural gas, in one plan called "PanMark," were determined by the average of competitive prices of residual fuel oil in the regional market of the end-user. The price paid by PanMark to gas producers who choose to participate in the program was a net back price determined by the end-user's price, less costs of pipeline transportation and distribution. These net back prices were adjusted monthly to reflect any differences in competitive prices of residual fuel oil.

Such programs were approved for a relatively short term (less than one year), and subject to monthly reporting to FERC as to the program's operation. The experiment tests the viability of utilizing the interstate pipeline company as a transmitter of short-term market signals between gas producers and end-users. This experiment took place within the peculiar environment of the U.S. natural gas market, a large and complicated domestic commerce which is in the process of adjusting to regulatory change and cyclical demand.

At the end of February 1985, the Economic Regulatory Administration of the Department of Energy which must approve gas imports and exports extended the spot market concept to include natural gas imports overland from Canada and as LNG from Algeria, observing that "both short-term and long-term imports have roles to play in the marketplace."

Northwest Alaskan Pipeline Co. was permitted to divert to the spot market a portion of Canadian gas it is already authorized to import, but cannot sell to its long-term U.S. customers. Cabot Energy Supply Corp. of Boston will look for spot customers of LNG and then seek the supply from Sonatrach of Algeria, which sells LNG under long-term contract to Cabot's affiliate, Distrigas Corp. In both cases, the international spot sale concept developed within the context of existing long-term supply arrangements and the existing infrastructure and facilities which serve the long-term arrangements.

This same pattern has also emerged in the European market, where the Soviet Union offered spot sales to Distrigaz of Belgium, and in the Japanese market, where Pertamina has sold a few extra cargoes of LNG on a spot basis to its long-term public utility customers.

The international gas trade is now sufficiently widespread that one can easily foresee increasing throughput of spot sale quantities in existing infrastructure and hitherto dedicated solely to servicing long-term gas sales contracts. With low marginal costs, it is relatively easy for spot sales to be made at prices different from those provided in long-term contracts, permitting both lower prices in weak markets, and higher prices in strong markets. If spot sales to existing long-term customers become more common, it is possible that sellers will come to view their market as a combination of baseload quantities and supplemental spot sales, which will permit a greater flexibility in overall quantity obligations of gas purchasers.

REQUIREMENTS CONTRACTS

The tension in gas contracts lies in the interplay of obligations regarding quantity and price. The lightning rod for this tension is the purchaser's promise "to take or pay if not taken." Historically, this triad of quantity, price and take-or-pay convenants worked relatively well during periods of stability in energy prices. But in the last decade they have played havoc with gas contracts and gas contract negotiations. In theory, a long-term contract which adjusted prices very frequently in order to meet market competition could always market a fixed quantity, but, in fact, gas contract price clauses have not been that sensitive, and factors other than price, such as conservation and government policy, influence consumption patterns. Also, in cases of both rising and falling prices, interfuel competition and competition and attendant fuel switching by consumers exacerbate the burden of long-term quantity obligations.

Ideally, increasing flexibility in quantity obligations of gas purchasers should provide some corresponding benefits to gas sellers. A move in this direction was made in late 1984 when Pacific Northwest Pipeline in the U.S. agreed to purchase 42.5% of its total aggregate gas requirements from Canada's Westcoast Transmissions, Ltd., and to take additional quantities equal to 75% of Northwest's market growth until Westcoast's total sales reached 50% of Northwest's total requirements.

Requirements contracts impose quantity risks upon the supplier caused by reduced demand of the purchaser's customers, but confer benefits of increased sales to meet the resale customers' increased demand. Thus, the gas supplier is more closely linked to the end-use market throughout the changing supply/demand cycle.

A related concept imposes upon the gas buyer an obligation to take, or pay for, a fixed quantity, but also to use its "best efforts" to purchase additional supplies up to a maximum quantity in order to meet any increase in its requirements. In return for setting take-or-pay levels at a lower level, the seller gains priority against other gas sellers and/or against competing fuels in meeting the purchaser's additional demand.

It was recently reported that Alberta and Southern Gas Co., Ltd. of Calgary sought to renegotiate its producer contracts in order to become more competitive in serving the U.S. export market. One proposed change was the abolition of minimum quantity obligations in favor of "equitable purchasing." We assume that doing equity in this context requires non-discriminatory treatment of producers who will share ratably in supplying the export quantities which can be marketed by Alberta and Southern.

A single importer can agree not to discriminate among multiple gas suppliers, or even among competing fuels, when faced with reduced demand, but to spread its reduced purchases ratably among all suppliers. When Sellers obtain their supplies from various gas producers, Sellers can make the same undertaking to producers. Similarly, all can share ratably in supplying the renewed demand. Concepts of "requirements," "best efforts" and "equitable purchasing" are all designed to accommodate long-term purchase and sale obligations to the vagaries of cyclical energy markets. One can expect these concepts to become more highly developed in the next generation of international gas sales contracts.

JOINT VENTURES

Long-term gas supply contracts have consistently followed traditional legal principles for the sales of the access is goods. The commercial contract apportions risks between the seller and purchaser and the commercial law enforces those risks against the defaulting party. Under the contractual terms, a seller must sell and a purchaser must buy an agreed quantity at an agreed price. The failure to do so causes the contract to be breached. Damages are then due in order to compensate for injury caused by the breach. As we have seen, the longer the term of the contract the greater likelihood of conflict between the parties during rapid short-term swings in their respective markets. To reconcile the unique requirements of gas sellers with those of gas purchasers, one can consider whether there is a place in the gas trade for revising the structure of the transaction so that it resembles some other form of commercial arrangement, such as a joint venture.

A joint venture creates a legal relation akin to partnership. It is premised upon a common benefit to be apportioned among the participants and their sharing of risks in order to achieve that benefit. The benefit in this case is the ability to exploit the demand of end-users for natural gas. The seller has access to a potential gas supply which can be made available to the market only through capital investment and technical development. The purchaser has access to an end-use market (or a chain of markets which link transmission, distribution, retail sales and end-use), but that access is usually subject to competitive conditions which influence price and/or quantity. In pre-OPEC days, the rewards of this commerce in oil fell to the marketer; in the OPEC era the rewards of oil commerce enriched the resource producer. But the long-term gas market has been subjected to considerable strain during this process. Perhaps one lesson to be learned is that gas marketing will be stabilized if the risks and rewards of gas commerce can be shared among the major participants.

A case can be made that gas demand at the margin competes against all other fuels in two ways. First, the premium residential market is expanded by conversions to gas from coal, briquets, fuel oil, kerosene or electricity as consumers predict a competitive price advantage for natural gas. Second, the lower price industrial fuel market is readily expandible to the extent that gas can be priced competitively with coal and residual oil and other boiler fuels. In both cases, market penetration is aided by a long-term strategy, and among all competing hydrocarbons only natural gas is marketed under long-term arrangements which can accommodate long-term marketing strategies. The obvious point is that if both suppliers and marketers share the marketing strategy, then they both are more likely to derive the maximum benefit from their long-term supply arrangement. This is easier said than done.

To a large extent, gas purchasers currently seek to limit risk in view of limitations on reward imposed either by public utility regulation or by interfuel competition for end-users. Sellers currently seek protection of their investment, transporters seek cost of service (including return on equity) and lenders to all participants in the gas trade demand assurance of repayment. The current period of difficulties in international gas contracting has fostered a greater understanding of dynamic supply and demand factors. This greater understanding may be the first step on a journey to find new contractual means for conducting old business.

4

Europe's Natural Gas Industries

Simon A. Blakey

COMMENTARY

    The following detailed discussion of European gas in terms of its industries, the role of governments, prospects, and security issues arising out of imports reveals the "inner workings" of a gas market very different from that of the United States (as described in the contribution by Daniel E. Gibson and Mason Willrich from the perspective of a giant utility), or of Japan (in the chapter by Toyoaki Ikuta and Norio Tanaka).

    Simon A. Blakey makes clear the intricate relationship between gas companies and governments. In doing so, he draws our attention to the many economic factors implicit in Europe's gas trades and then weaves about them the security concerns which form part of Europe's gas prospects -- issues unlikely to disappear.

    The author makes entirely clear why the Editor's vision of a far greater opportunity for gas is at variance with present and foreseen circumstances, at least in Europe.

    However, when the gas potential for Europe was first discussed after World War II, the Groningen field of the Netherlands had not been discovered. When it was, and Shell and Esso proceeded to exploit the asset in a very major effort, they transformed the energy scene in that region. What Groningen did then, the vastly greater reserves of the Soviet Union, North Africa, and the Middle East could accomplish in the decades ahead. Until those supplies are incorporated into gas planning, the limits to gas growth will remain more evident and persuasive -- or so is still the belief of the

                                      -- Editor --

INTRODUCTION: BACKGROUND AND STRUCTURE

In many respects the industries which supply natural gas to homes and businesses in Western Europe[1] today are a mirror of the political and commercial life of the continent. There are several national industries, not one European industry, with distinct forms of organization and culture. These profoundly affect their behavior, from customer relations to gas purchasing strategies through many other aspects of their operations. Through their relationships to their own national governments, as well as in their direct commercial relationships, each national industry adopts certain attitudes toward gas supplying companies and countries both inside and outside Western Europe. Most of them hold a few things strongly in common, notably a heavy technical orientation and a conservative corporate outlook. There are also formal layers of integration between the various national industries through common ownership of transnational pipelines and, in some cases, common shareholders. These formal aspects of integration are reinforced by the presence of a generation of senior corporate executives in each country who have a shared experience of an industry which has passed through major technical, commercial, and political challenges in its twenty five years of existence.

It is important to appreciate both the extent of national separateness and the degree of international integration in order to understand the present situation of the natural gas industries and the future challenges which these industries will face. To attain this appreciation, we must know how they have evolved. Their evolution has been very different from the evolution of the natural gas business in the United States.

In the first place, the big gas industries of Great Britain and Germany have their origin in the days when gas was a co-product of coke manufacture. Massive regional concentrations of coal and steel production provided the basis for an urban gas supply from the first half of the nineteenth century. In over a hundred years of evolution, these industries have changed the principal end-use of their product as technology has changed -- from public gas lighting to domestic cooking in the early twentieth century, to industrial steam-raising and domestic and commercial space-heating in the late twentieth century. They have changed the source of their product as well, with coke-derived gases being supplemented with naphtha-derived gas in the era of cheap oil in the 1950s through to the 1970s, and now both types of manu-factured gas being replaced with natural gas. The coke- and steel-based regional companies were transformed by government initiative in both Ger-many and Great Britain into more suitable vehicles for supplying gas on a national level. In Great Britain, the post-World War II Labor government performed a conventional nationalization on local and regional companies to create the British Gas Council (1949). In Germany, a kind of private-sector nationalization was implemented before World War II by the establishment of the so-called "Demarkationsvertrag" which defined relations be-tween the various regional gas companies in order to achieve an efficient overall structure. This agreement is still in force today.

The changes of use and change of supply source have permitted a seven-fold increase in the useful energy supplied by gas in Great Britain between 1960 and 1985, and a twenty-fold increase in the Federal Republic of Germany. Massive technical and commercial changes have been involved, and yet the legal and organizational structure in both countries, although very different from each oth-er, has remained virtually unchanged throughout the period of introducing natural gas. In the ownership and corporate structure of Ruhrgas, the largest German gas company, there are still strong residual elements from the days of manufactured gas.

Secondly, today's gas industries in Italy and France have been created much more with the support and sponsorship of central government, although the corporations which distribute gas and dominate the business are independently motivated. Italy's SNAM is a part of the ENI group which acts as Italy's national oil company. As well as oil and natural gas, ENI has engineering, chemical, and financial interests. SNAM has been responsible for the distribution and sale of natural gas since 1953, when the ENI group was formed; the first gas fields in the Caviaga region in northern Italy were put into production as early as 1944. The Italian gas industry therefore has the longest history of natural gas operations in all of Western Europe. SNAM's joint expertise with the production (AGIP) and the engineering (Snamprogetti) arms of ENI has given it an important advantage in the operation of depleted gas fields for storage purposes, which has in the 1980s come to have an important commercial and political as well as technical dimension.

Gaz de France, the French state-owned gas distribution company was also initially established to handle French-produced natural gas, produced by Elf, from fields near Lacq in the province of Aquitaine. Distribution of gas in and around the region of Aquitaine is handled by the Societe Nationale de Gaz du Sud-Ouest (SNGSO) which is a joint venture owned 70 percent by Elf and 30 percent by Gaz de France. The integration of the gas industry with national oil company operations and with petroleum and chemical engineering (where the principal French company is Technip, itself a part-subsidiary of Elf, Gaz de France, the Compagnie Francaise de Petrole and the Institut Francais de Petrole) is not as formal as it is in Italy through the ENI group. Nevertheless, integration is strong, and senior appointments are made interchangeably with the civil service and government administration. Gaz de France and SNAM inherited and absorbed the town gas industries of France and Italy, which, while not insignificant, had been smaller than their counterparts in Great Britain and Germany.

Thirdly, in the Netherlands and Belgium, the transmission, wholesale distribution, and export of natural gas is in the hands of Gasunie and Distrigaz respectively, single companies each with a national monopoly. Each of these companies is owned partly by the state and partly by private sector interests. In the case of Gasunie, the state owns 50 percent directly or indirectly, and the other 50 percent is owned by the Nederlandse Aardolje Maatschappij (NAM), an oil and gas producing company which is a 50-50 subsidiary of Royal Dutch/Shell and Esso Europe. In operational and

staffing terms, Shell tends to be the dominant
partner. Distrigaz of Belgium is owned 16.7 percent by Shell, 37.2 percent by the Belgian government and various state-owned companies, and the
remainder by large electrical producers and engineering concerns. Distrigaz of Belgium also supplies customers in Luxembourg. The joint public/-
private sector ownership is of most interest and
significance in the Netherlands because of the
importance of Dutch gas exports, both in volume and
technically as a "load-balancing" supply, to other
European nations (Belgium, France, Germany, Italy,
and Switzerland). Indeed, the natural gas industry was built to today's scale in these countries
largely on the back of these exports. It is worth
remarking, therefore, that this has been done,
along with the development of the Netherlands' own
domestic natural gas system, entirely without national legislation in the Netherlands to define
the rights and obligations of Gasunie. Gasunie
operates on the basis of its private law incorpor-
ation as a joint-venture between the oil companies
and the State. Its policy direction depends on a
series of formal or informal understandings between the partners, which have developed in a
pragmatic way according to changing circumstances.

A physical description of the European gas
scene can focus on these six countries -- Great
Britain, West Germany, Italy, France, Belgium
(with Luxembourg) and the Netherlands -- which
account for 95 percent of all gas consumed in
Western Europe. The other major actor on the scene
inside Western Europe is Norway, which produces
large quantities of gas (over 2.6 BCF/D in 1985)
but exports it all and does not consume any. All
six major consumer nations are members of the
European Economic Community. All except Belgium
produce significant volumes of natural gas within
their own national territory as well as importing
from elsewhere. Companies in Germany and Belgium
are involved in the transit trade of large volumes
of gas from the Netherlands to Italy and France.
Germany is also involved in the last stage of
transit of gas from Soviet Asia to France.

There are seven smaller national natural gas
industries in Europe. Finland uses only imported
Soviet gas. Austria, Switzerland and Denmark are

all connected to the German grid. All have at times received natural gas from German companies, although Austria's principal supplies have always come from its own fields and from the Soviet Union, and Denmark is more than self-sufficient with its own North Sea gas. Denmark now exports small quantities to Germany and to the brand new (1985) gas importer in Sweden. Switzerland's principal supplies have been Netherlands' gas, repurchased from SNAM of Italy, whose Dutch purchases pass through Swiss territory. Spain and the Republic of Ireland both use natural gas as well as naphtha-based manufactured gas; each country is supplied from its own offshore fields, and Spain receives liquefied natural gas imports from Algeria and Libya. There is no connection between the distribution grids of Spain, Ireland, and Finland, and the main continental Europe or British transmission networks. Northern Ireland is connected neither to the Irish nor to the British grids, because it has hitherto proved too costly to make either connection. The major cities of Northern Ireland as those of Norway, Portugal, Greece and Turkey, and large parts of Spain, Sweden and Italy remain for the time being dependent on various forms of manufactured gas and are still waiting for pipeline connections to make natural gas available. Connection of several of these cities is likely to be one source of increasing demand for natural gas in the next few years, at the expense of further diminution in oil demand.

Of the natural gas industries in the major European countries it may truly be said that they are _derivative_ industries. They derive either from the coal- or steel-based industries of their nations' own industrial heartland, or from the ancillary natural gas and engineering operations of major multinational or national oil companies. In their present form they mostly reflect a combination of the two. Nowhere is this more clearly visible than in Germany, where oil companies wholly-own the second and third ranking regional gas companies (Thyssengas and BEB) and where Ruhrgas, the pivotal front-ranking company, has oil company representation among its shareholders, but is essentially dominated by coal and heavy industrial interests from the Ruhr region (see Chart 4.1).

Chart 4.1

The Ownership Structure of Ruhrgas

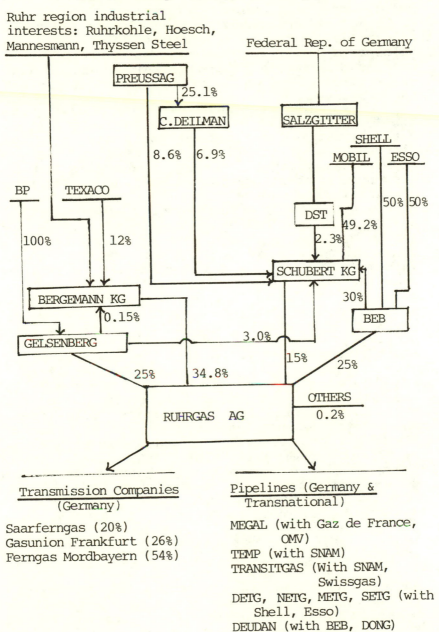

Transmission Companies
(Germany)

Saarferngas (20%)
Gasunion Frankfurt (26%)
Ferngas Mordbayern (54%)

Pipelines (Germany &
Transnational)

MEGAL (with Gaz de France,
OMV)
TEMP (with SNAM)
TRANSITGAS (With SNAM,
Swissgas)
DETG, NETG, METG, SETG (with
Shell, Esso)
DEUDAN (with BEB, DONG)

The government of the Federal Republic of Germany, which is normally vigilant through its Cartel Office against concentration and abuse of oligopoly power in industry, is content to let the gas industry in Germany remain independent of the authorities' supervision, because it believes the balance of power between coal and oil interests creates a suitable equipoise which ensures adequate competition in the energy market to protect the consumer.

This derivative nature of Europe's gas industries -- its arising from already established large industrial interests -- explains many of the differences between Europe's industries and that of the United States. In the United States natural gas supplied energy needs on a local basis for many decades following the first developments in the nineteenth century. The industry operated side-by-side with a manufactured gas industry, depending on locality, for many decades. Only in parts of northern Italy has anything comparable occurred in Europe. The need for public authorities to exercise legal supervision in the interests of consumer protection arose early in the United States as fly-by-night operators in the early years of this century had to be prevented from supplying a community for a quick profit for a short time and then abandoning the responsibility once easy-to-exploit gas reserves were depleted.[2] From those days onward, the natural gas industry in the United States has had a relatively high public and political profile. Legislation, regulation, and court judgments have been an integral part of the industry's operation through a whole series of major rulings of nationwide impact (such as the 1954 Phillips decision by the Supreme Court) to rulings with strictly local impact on the behavior of gas distribution companies. Nothing comparable has existed anywhere in Europe since the development of natural gas supply on a major scale in the 1960s. It is fair to say that the industry has a very low public and political profile except as regards consumer prices to households. Outside the realm of commercial and industrial law there is virtually no involvement at all by the courts on behalf of citizens or communities. The business of supplying and transmitting gas and running the gas

industry is left, at a national level, to the
management of the large companies already mentioned.   At a local level, it is left to the
transmission companies themselves, in the case of
the British Gas Corporation and Gaz de France, or
to municipal authorities, in the case of Germany,
Italy, Belgium and the Netherlands.   Government
involvement is through ownership, with administration and civil service departments the means of
exercising public policy, which contrasts strongly
with the United States where the government is
involved through legislation, with regulators and
courts the means of exercising public policy.

The importance of these structures is coming
to be recognized more and more, particularly as the
natural gas industry in Europe has moved into the
political limelight. The ideas and commitments of
relatively few people take on great importance in
the strategic decisions of the various national
industries. Personal bridge-building between, for
example, German industry representatives and their
Soviet counterparts, or between Dutch and Belgian
company and government officials, has helped to
smooth over difficulties of a political and commercial nature at particularly sensitive times.
Where personal relationships have not developed
well, this has contributed in large part to difficulties with the implementation of actual contracts, or cancellation of otherwise acceptable
proposed deals.   Negotiations between a German
buyers' consortium and Algeria's national oil company Sonatrach in the late 1970s and early 1980s
are a case in point.   Similar factors may have
contributed to the collapse in 1985 of the agreement by which Britain would have imported gas from
Norway's Sleipner field.

In a continental-scale industry which must
nevertheless operate across national boundaries,
and in the context of different national tradi-
tions, such personal links are essential. It is a
commonplace of the natural gas business, whether
in Asia, America, or Europe, that success depends
on long-term relationships, on confidence, on mutual interdependence between buyer and seller. In
its extreme form this has been expressed in an
unwritten rule that "no party to an agreement
should be making profits while the other is making

losses." [This commonplace has recently been questioned in the United States in the context of a surplus of deliverability and the emergence of new market structures around the edges of the long-term contracts which are the basis for producer, pipeline, and distribution company operations. No such questioning has happened or is likely in Europe, where unilateral abrogation of contracts (as has been seen in the United States) will frequently have major political ramifications.] In order to build and sustain this confidence the personal links must be strong, and the sense of a shared industry culture must transcend different national cultures.

Seen in this light it becomes easier to understand the strength of the European industries' reaction to the U.S. government's attempts to influence decisions on the supply of gas from the Soviet Union to some European buyers. The same forces, however, have been repeatedly at work in less-publicized events. One example would be the pressure from fellow-buyers on a financially-exposed member of the consortium buying gas from Norway who wished to claim force majeure on account of the price terms of the contract. The fellow-buyers prevailed in the expectation of negotiating an improvement in the name of the long-term relationships. Such illustrations of the strength of the corporate culture and the depth of the commitment to long-term understanding are fairly commonplace. The future direction of Europe's gas industries will in all probability continue to be molded by this transnational industry culture, as well as by the national political and market conditions.

Speculation on future trends frequently includes such questions as the emergence of "spot" gas trading, or whether or not the European industries will become "more like" the U.S. industry, or whether there are circumstances under which gas could increase its share of the European energy market from today's 16 percent or 17 percent to U.S. levels of 25 percent or more. Such speculation can be reviewed and assessed in a more balanced way if the features of the European gas industries described above, especially the industry culture and the strong ethos of cooperation, together with their likely future impact, are taken fully into account.

DEMAND FOR GAS -- FUEL OF THE FUTURE?

In 1984, the fourteen gas-consuming countries of Europe consumed just over 19.3 BCF/D of natural gas. Recovery from the economic recession of 1981-83 was very slow, and energy demand was stagnant, yet consumption of natural gas grew by 6 to 7 percent over the previous year's level and exceeded its previous peak in 1979. Gas was therefore increasing its share of the energy market which stood at 16 percent in 1984: three factors account for this, each of which illustrates something fundamental about the European gas market, and contribute to understanding possible future trends.

The _first_ factor is the steady growth of natural gas' share of the heating market in the residential and commercial sector. Some 9.6 BCF/D of natural gas was used in this sector in 1984, slightly less than half the total. This compares with only 6 BCF/D out of a total of 16.4 BCF/D in 1975. Growth in absolute and relative importance of sales to this sector has taken place in nearly every gas-using country in Western Europe. The only exceptions have been the Netherlands, where the residential market is already saturated both in terms of the number of households connected to the distribution grid and in terms of heating standards and comfort levels, and Belgium, where residential gas prices have recently been higher relative to heating oil prices.[3] Elsewhere, there has been a continuing trend to install gas-fired central heating (as in Great Britain and parts of Germany) among single-family households which already have gas supplies for lower volume uses such as cooking and water heating. In Austria, Italy, and Germany the gas distribution grids continue to be expanded and new connections made. Some of this expansion is taking place in well populated and relatively prosperous areas, such as Bavaria and parts of northern Italy, which have not received gas in any form before. In the smaller markets of Denmark, Ireland, Finland, Spain, and Sweden residential markets for natural gas are only now beginning to be developed.

The scope exists for these trends to continue. The 9.6 BCF/D of natural gas which is consumed annually in this sector is the equivalent in energy terms of about 1.8 MMB/D. Consumption of oil products in this sector, mostly for heating purposes, runs at around 2.5 MMB/D. Gas will not be able to compete with all of this, because of transport limitations. However, the potential exists for gas to capture at least some of this sizeable market, if there is sufficient incentive for gas distribution companies to wish to do so. There is every indication that this is the case. Residential and commercial sector sales offer secure long-term sales outlets, compared with the vulnerability of industrial markets to economic change. The unit costs of delivering gas to these markets, but also the sales prices, can be higher than costs and prices to industrial markets. The key factor in determining whether incremental sales to residential markets can profitably be made is whether the supply system is able to meet the seasonal and daily variations in supply which these markets require. All European gas utilities at present expect to be able to expand their sales in this sector, and appear willing to invest in additional storage facilities if this is needed to meet the resulting changes in the pattern of demand.

Recent estimates of potential demand for gas in this sector vary in a range from 11.7 BCF/D to 15 BCF/D per annum by the early years of the next century. Estimates from Shell[4] and the EC[5] would tend to be at the lower end of the range; those from the International Energy Agency[6] and from the International Gas Union[7] toward the higher end. Precise forecasts vary according to differing assumptions used for price relationships between different fuels, economic activity, comfort levels, energy conservation and the rate of change in the average efficiency of gas-using equipment. The extent to which conservation may reduce or limit growth in demand for all energy in this sector is the main uncertainty which leads to variations in the estimates of future potential demand for natural gas.

The second factor in the strength of natural gas demand in Europe in 1984 was the increase in gas burned in power stations to generate electricity. This was contrary to a trend established since 1979, when policy decisions in Germany and the Netherlands led to a gradual withdrawal of gas from this sector. In 1984 Italy began to switch significant volumes of gas (0.6 BCF/D) into power stations to displace fuel oil. This resulted from an inability to find other markets for the build-up of supplies from Algeria through the trans-Mediterranean pipeline, and may therefore be interpretated as essentially a supply-driven phenomenon. At the same time, more gas continued to be used in power stations in the Netherlands under special contracts made in 1983 to help with electricity generating costs and to protect the balance of payments (because the alternative has been to use imported fuel oil). In Germany, the decline in gas use in power stations was halted, partly for environmental reasons, and partly because certain domestic gas fields which have well-head sulphur-strippers because of the gas' high sulphur content can only be operated ecnomically if there is a steady base-load offtake provided by local power stations. In Belgium, in early 1984, an over-commitment to take Algerian gas was also relieved by special sales to power stations.

It is widely expected that in future less gas will be used to generate electricity than has been normal in the past. Power generation does not represent a major market in Europe (around 2.4 BCF/D per year is consumed) and in recent years there has been a political prejudice against using what came to be regarded as a "premium" fuel in the raising of steam to drive electric turbines. Forecasts for end-of-the-century annual gas burn in this sector are usually in the range of 1.9 BCF/D to 2.4 BCF/D, not significantly different from today. Most of this is expected to be the use of domestic gas in the Netherlands and Germany. Nowhere in Europe are there large low-cost supplies of natural gas fed directly into power stations on the scale of the electricity generation in Texas or Louisiana, which accounts for the major part of this use for gas in the United States. Absent the discovery of such supplies in onshore areas it is very unlikely that such a market could develop.

However, one or two words of caution are due about forecasts for this sector. One lesson at least can be drawn from the events of 1984 and the recovery in gas consumption. This is that factors external to the simple economics of relative fuel prices and demand can have an important bearing on the use of gas in power generation from time to time. There is always a risk that committed supply will not match aggregate demand for gas in an industry where so much depends on long-term factors; electricity generation, which itself is an industry very much under direct government control or influence in most European countries, offers the possibility of taking large tranches of gas supply to restore contractual equilibrium. "Supply-driven" demand may be a feature of this sector's use of gas into the medium-term, and may recur over the longer-term as and when large discrete new tranches of supply appear on the market. There is no reason to suppose, either, that balance of payments questions will cease forever to trouble the Netherlands; so that use of more domestic natural gas in power stations may remain an attractive option in that country. In the longer-term, there may be new markets for natural gas as a fuel for power generation in Scandinavia; Norway is currently examining this as an option for the day when environmental limits prevent further exploitation of hydroelectric power, and Sweden may have to consider gas among other fossil fuels if the decision made by referendum in 1980 to phase out nuclear power after the turn of the century is maintained.

It is in the field of power generation as well that the greatest area of uncertainty lies regarding the possibility of technical change -- which can always throw out the calculations of the best energy forecasters. Combined cycle power generation -- in which a steam turbine is combined with a gas turbine driven by the combustion gases -- offers significant efficiency gains and certain technical advantages in the generation of electricity, and may prove economically attractive to quite a wide range of users. It is difficult to judge how widely this technology will spread, or to what extent it will cause gas to displace other fuels in power generation. However, it is now widely perceived that this may add a significant new area of demand over and above existing gas use in the next twenty to twenty five years. A doubling of gas demand for power generation (to 4.8 BCF/D) as a result of major inroads by combined cycle technology would represent a displacement of only 8 percent of Europe's existing fuel inputs in this sector. A major obstacle to development of this technology on wide commercial scale could, however, be the desire of electric utilities to maintain highly centralized large-scale generation of electric power. The possible contribution of combined cycle equipment to gas demand remains a large unknown element in the picture.

The third factor in the resilient demand for natural gas in 1984 was the large volume required for the chemical industry's operations. The manufacture of methanol and ammonia and therefore of most fertilizer products, is essentially methane-dependent; olefins, aromatics and ethylene-based petrochemicals are not however major consumers of natural gas in Europe -- naphtha and, increasingly, natural gas liquids are the principal feedstocks. The chemical industry's demand accounts for about 40 percent of total industrial gas demand in Western Europe. Ammonia manufacture is subject to wide annual variations, partly in response to the exaggerated stock cycle of any intermediate industrial product, and partly in response to the large season-by-season swings in demand for fertilizer (which depend on farm incomes in the previous year and climatic and soil conditions in the year in question). 1984 was a boom year in the industry of all counts, and industrial sector demand for gas was correspondingly buoyant in all the major ammonia-manufacturing countries. In this respect, when examining the outlook for gas demand in Europe, cyclical effects in 1984 should be discounted.

Industrial gas demand of just over 7.2 BCF/D may grow, rather more slowly then residential and commercial demand, and most analysis puts it in the range of 8.4 BCF/D to 9.4 BCF/D by the turn of the century. Gas distributors in Germany, France,

Belgium, and the Netherlands responded to restore the price-competitiveness of gas to industrial users after losing markets to fuel oil in 1982. Their suppliers appear likely to want to maintain this flexibility in future in order to achieve demand growth in this sector. Both these factors suggest that serious efforts will continue to be made to preserve competitiveness and to push out oil, or coal if need be, in industrial uses. Given the importance of sales to the chemicals sector, however, a severe erosion of the competitiveness of European fertilizer industries could cut back this growth considerably. The lowest forecasts recently made available (Shell) suggest that by 2010 a reasonable low end of the range for industrial gas demand might be as low as 7.7 BCF/D.

Adding up these sectoral estimates, the range of demand for natural gas in Europe by the year 2000 is therefore expected by most forecasters to be between 23 BCF/D and 28 BCF/D per year (between 235 and 285 billion cubic meters). As an upper limit, assuming limited conservation in the residential sector, rapid spread of combined cycle power generation and maintenance of a substantial fertilizer industry, 29 BCF/D of gas might be required. Compare this relatively narrow range of uncertainty in Europe with the range of about 34 BCF/D to 68 BCF/D which a collection of forecasts by oil companies and others would propose for the United States by the year 2000.

Surplus supply conditions exist in all energy industries in Europe, as elsewhere in the world, in the mid-1980s. Natural gas supplies, discussed in sections below, appear to be plentiful both in terms of immediate commitments of contracted gas and in terms of the ultimate reserves of major supplying countries. Against this background the question has been asked "What if gas were priced low enough to drive out other fuels in all competing sectors?" In the 1950s and 1960s oil drove out coal as the major primary energy source in Europe. Could gas repeat the experience and drive out oil in the 1990s? As recently as 1960, coal and other solid fuels accounted for some 60 percent of European primary energy; by 1973 oil demand had increased so fast that oil accounted for 60 percent of energy. Since 1973 the share of oil has been declining -- to 46 percent in 1984 -- as steady growth in the share of natural gas and primary electricity (nuclear and hydro) has gradually displaced oil. In future, could enough gas be made available to meet demand at prices low enough to lead to equally rapid displacement of other fuels in all sectors of consumption? No doubt the possibility exists, and it may be beguiling to think in these terms, but close examination of the underlying factors at work suggest it is unlikely to happen over the next fifteen to twenty years.

In the first place, gas is not technically as versatile as oil. It does not compete as a fuel for mass transportation. It is likely only to make inroads into some dedicated fleet markets as compressed natural gas (CNG) where there is differential tax treatment on gas and diesel fuels as well as a differential in the base price. The transport sector accounts for 25 percent of final consumption and 18 percent of primary energy in OECD Europe. This market is effectively closed to gas. Natural gas is also effectively kept out of that large part of the petrochemicals market whose products are ethylene, olefin and aromatics-related. The stability of the methane molecule means it is unsuitable for cracking into chemical derivatives, as compared either with ethane and other natural gas liquids (NGLs) or with naphtha and other oil-derived products. There is a trend toward increasing price-based substitution of natural gas liquids for oil products in these petrochemical industries in Europe, but this will not impact directly on natural gas consumption. On purely technochemical grounds, this closes a further 3 to 4 percent of the European energy market to gas.

We are left with little over three quarters of the energy market which is made up of heating, process and power generation uses of energy in the residential, commercial, industrial, and electricity sectors. A second major technical constraint on gas, compared with oil and other primary fuels in all these sectors, is that gas is a "grid-dependent" energy carrier. Its economic competitiveness will thus depend on the economics of grid construction, including the associated risks of such an inflexible means of delivery -- risks of underusing installed capacity which cannot be re-directed to another location at some future date. In practice, of course, this "grid-dependency" rules out the supply of gas to consumers in remote areas. Work undertaken by the International In-stitute of Applied System Analysis in Vienna on natural gas demand has defined "energy density consumption areas" as a basis for quantifying the possible economic and competitive effects of "grid dependence."[8] As a rough estimate, based on this work, up to four fifths of the 2.5 MMB/D of heating oil currently used in residential and commercial sectors in Europe may be inaccessible to gas be-cause of this factor. Allowing a wide margin for the uncertainty of this type of calculation, about another 5 to 8 percent of the primary energy market can thus be counted as closed to gas.

So far we have only considered technical as-pects. There are also institutional, historical, and economic factors to be taken into account. There are today in Europe, as there never were before the 1970s, major government-backed moves toward balance and flexibility in fuel supply. There is also massive institutional support in many countries for electricity industries based on nuclear power and domestic coal. These, together with the substantial hydropower resources of Scan-dinavia and the Alpine regions, will continue to provide the baseload of electricity supply at least for the economic lives of existing power stations, irrespective of the cost of gas. Power generation represents about one third of all pri-mary energy input in Western Europe. Much cheaper gas would be a necessary but even then not a sufficient condition for there to be any chance of penetration of this baseload market. There would have to be as well a complete reversal in long standing government and utility support for domes-tic coal and nuclear power. This is very unlikely in the next fifteen to twenty years, barring a major accident involving nuclear power resulting in nuclear becoming completely unacceptable to a wide public.

Something rather less than half of the primary energy market remains as the bounded area in which natural gas must compete against other fuels for market share. There is thus no possibility that gas could repeat the explosive growth of oil in the 1950s and 1960s to the point at which it had a 60 percent market share. Such explosive growth in the share of one fuel is of course easier to achieve at a time of rapid growth in the total use of the energy; in the 1970s oil consumption grew relative to other fuels more because it supplied almost 100 percent of the incremental growth in energy demand than because it substituted for other fuels in established uses (although it did that as well). In a period of much slower growth in total energy demand, rapid growth in the market share of another fuel, such as gas, would require replacement and substitutionary investment on a much more massive scale. Very much lower gas prices, even if associated with lower prices for oil and other fuels, do not seem likely to stimulate renewed and sustained rapid growth in energy demand in Europe, given (1) the much higher basic levels of comfort in heating today compared with twenty five years ago, and (2) the lower energy intensity of prospective growth industries compared with that of the growth industries of the 1950s and 1960s. All these structural factors combine to give much more limited prospects for gas in the 1990s, whatever the supply picture, than oil had in the 1960s.

Finally there are major differences in attitude and commercial interest between the oil supplying companies of the post-World War II world and the gas-supplying companies of today. The oil majors, the "Seven Sisters," and their smaller brethren, were able to aim for volume sales growth at low prices over a period of years in order to maximize their upstream revenues and thus to stimulate the growth of oil's market share. At no stage in the era of oil's dynamic growth was there a strategy of pricing oil up to a "coal-equivalent substitution price" in order to maximize revenues. However, among gas companies, many of whom are part-owned by oil interests, there is today a widespread consensus that pricing strategy should be geared to an oil-substitution price. Evidence of this approach among Europe's gas suppliers can be found not only by looking at the policies of the reputedly "high-price" sellers, such as Algeria and Norway, but also at the Netherlands, with abundant reserves and relatively low delivery costs to major markets. It was Dutch government policy which, through the Spirenberg negotiations in 1980 and 1981, forced the transition of pricing principles for gas supply from a simple general inflation-linking to an alternative fuel basis. Even more surprising is the general acceptance of this principle further downstream, among continental European gas utilities. The tariff structure of companies like Enagas in Spain, Distrigaz in Belgium and many German gas distributors is calculated according to the principle that the end consumers should pay for gas at the avoided cost of his alternative fuel. In some cases this produced highly sophisticated tariffs and multiple metering of gas supplies -- as for example in the ceramics industry in Spain, where a customer will pay a lower rate for gas used to fire the basic "bizcocha" for tile manufacture, and a higher rate for gas used in glazing the surface. In the case of the "bizcocha," the alternative fuel would have been heating oil or even coal, whereas for the glaze the alternative fuel would be LPG or electricity. Or again, the principal German importing company Ruhrgas has repeatedly stated that it is willing to give priority to Norwegian over Soviet or any other supplier for its next major gas import contract as long as Norway's gas can be delivered to the end consumer at a price which is competitive with the appropriate alternative fuels. Existing strategies do not tend to promote gas versus gas competition; as long as suppliers and transmission companies maintain this position it will further diminish the possibility for gas to imitate the dynamic growth of oil.

Against this background, technical, historical, and institutional, there is a general expectation, arising from analytical work on the dynamics of the gas market, that natural gas demand in Europe is more price elastic with respect to rising prices than to falling prices. For example, a 1982 study by consulting engineers Purvin and Gertz, concluded that a 20 percent decrease in the relative price of gas to heavy fuel oil would be required to increase the volume of demand by about the same amount as that which would be lost by a mere 10 percent increase in the relative gas price.[9] Subsequent work by the same consultant and by others has not cast any serious doubt on this indicative conclusion, and there is a kind of consensus in the industry that a unit increase in price would threaten more loss of gas market share than a unit decrease in price would offer gain. Some new or immature markets may provide exceptions to this rule, but as a description of the core European gas market it probably remains valid.

In summary, there is a conventional wisdom view of the future of European natural gas demand, which holds that there is room, although limited room, for expansion of the market to residential, commercial and industrial space-heating, and process users of energy. The degree to which this is exploited will depend on factors outside the gas industry's control -- environmental standards, economic activity, conservation, the general level of energy and especially oil prices, as well as on the ability and willingness of governments, suppliers and distributors of gas to bring gas cost-effectively to market. But however price attractive gas is made to appear as a result of the interplay of all these factors, there are technical and institutional limits to the size of the energy market in Europe in which gas ultimately competes and these limits are unlikely to be breached. It is therefore difficult to question seriously the general lines of evolution of gas demand in the overall energy picture which that conventional wisdom portrays.

THE PRICE OF GAS -- PRINCIPLES AND PRACTICES

PRICING PRINCIPLES

If gas is to achieve its potential in its contribution to overall energy supply in Europe, the question of appropriate prices at which it can do this will have to be resolved. According to an apparently impeccable logic, the transmission companies who purchase gas maintain the argument that their suppliers must make gas available at prices which can compete with alternative fuels (mainly oil products but possibly also coal and electricity in some uses) if gas is to increase sales and/or its market share. There are, however, major problems in setting appropriate pricing principles and crystallizing them into contract terms. Probably as much effort is put into, and as much fun had out of, negotiating over the principles as over the prices. Some contractual agreements for supplies in the far distant future (as with the 1985 agreements to extend Dutch gas exports into the first decade of the next century) in fact include only negotiated agreement on principles; actual prices must be resolved nearer the delivery date.

The main competing fuels are of course gas oil (N° 2 fuel oil) and low sulphur fuel oil (N° 6 fuel oil). Indexation terms therefore usually contain some reference to the prices of these two fuels. But indexation terms which take gas oil as an indicator make gas prices respond to movements in the price of a fuel which is itself influenced by, for example, the demand for diesel fuel in the transport sector. More generally, the relative price of gas oil and heavy fuel oils will be influenced by a complex configuration of different events and different markets. These will include: imbalances between refinery upgrading capacity and light and heavy oil product demand, the yield of products from a changing slate of crude oils, and the shape of the barrel of imported oil products from outside the main European refining centers. All these variables are subject to analysis, but scarcely to prediction, and they complicate the calculation of the effects of any particular set of indexation terms. Buyers and sellers adopt preferred positions on indexation terms, and the final settlement on which terms to use is the subject of intense negotiations. The results however can often be paradoxical and even perverse.

For many years, for example, Dutch gas export prices have been indexed only to the price of low sulphur fuel oil, with no reference to light heating oil (gas oil). From the beginning of 1985 an element of gas oil-related pricing was proposed by the exporting company Gasunie, and accepted in varying proportions by different customers. Gasunie have stated that they expect the change to be "broadly neutral" in its effect on the price in the medium-term but that the change will more closely reflect changes in the value of gas to end users, whose alternative fuels include light heating oil as well as fuel oil. A reduction in the base price was negotiated at the same time, in the context of a weak outlook for energy prices generally, growing interfuel competition, and a strong buyers' market. Within three months of the new terms being agreed, there was a 25 percent collapse in heavy fuel oil prices, as a result of energy market developments completely unrelated to gas, whereas light heating oil prices remained stable. The new terms acted as a significant support to the price of Dutch export gas, in direct contradiction of the expectation that the effect of the change would tend to be neutral compared with the oil formula. It may be of course that in the longer-term the effect will indeed be broadly neutral.

A similar illustration of the possible perversity of negotiated pricing principles is given by the Algerian experience as a seller of gas to Europe. High base prices were agreed in 1980 and 1981 in a sellers' market, after political intervention in most cases. The index against which prices were to move was crude oil, reflecting Algerian fears that consumer country taxation policies could influence the price of oil products. But the mechanism by which gas prices were to move was also negotiated in a way expected to be favorable to the seller -- namely that increases or decreases in the price of gas would not merely be proportional to the percentage change in the price of crude oil, but would reflect the full change in the value of a BTU of crude oil. For increasing crude oil prices (which was how both sides of the negotiating table envisaged the future at the time) this would have meant a more than proportional increase in gas prices. In fact, of course, since the prices were agreed in the early 1980s, crude oil prices have fallen, and the decline (albeit from a high base level) in Algeria's gas prices has been more than proportionate to the decline in crude prices (see Table 4.1) as a result

of the distinctive indexation mechanism. It has
been calculated that Algerian gas would become
cheaper than alternative pipeline supplies in
France and Belgium if crude oil prices were to fall
to the $24-$25 per barrel range.

Table 4.1

Illustrative Example of Algerian Gas
Price Indexation Mechanism

Crude Oil Price

	$/Barrel	$/MMBTU
1982	34.0	5.85
1985	27.0	4.65

Change from
1982 to 1985

	a) Proportional change: -20.5%	b) Full BTU value change: -1.20

Illustrative Gas Price Response
$/MMBTU

1982 Base Price	5.12
1985 a) Adjusted by proportionate change	5.12 - 20.5% = $4.07/MMBTU
b) Adjusted by full BTU value change	5.12 - 1.20 = $3.92/MMBTU

Norway too has had difficulty in finding
appropriate price indexation terms to ensure that
sufficient comfort is given to providers of finance to capital-intensive gas projects while
maintaining the competitiveness of Norwegian gas
in the final market place. Some kind of redefin-
ition of the 1981 contract terms for gas to be
delivered through the Statpipe pipeline system
appear likely to be made when the gas actually
starts to flow for the winter of 1985-86.

In general, there is perhaps a trend toward recognizing that the difficulties of "getting it right" in terms of gas pricing can best be dealt with by a willingness to agree only on general principles at the early stages of committing to a project, and to postpone settling precise terms until the energy environment at the time of delivery is known. In the Soviet Union, such a pragmatic approach has a fairly long history. It has often been interpreted by observers as a standing willingness on the Soviet side to supply gas in a way which always undercuts competition "at the going rate." The pragmatism arises perhaps because there is rather less respect for the letter of a contract and more respect for its spirit, in a business culture less dominated by what in Marxist terms is said to be the "bourgeois" concept of law. Respect for the spirit rather than the letter of a contract is something which tunes in well with the practical needs of the gas industry, with its long-term commitments of producer to pipelines and distributor. It is something also which gas industry leaders from many different European countries have been at pains to emphasize over the years, and which will remain a vital element in the equation if gas is to fulfil its potential in Europe's future energy supply.

THE LEVEL OF PRICES

Table 4.2 gives the author's estimates of some recent prices for gas at the inlet of importers' transmission systems. In part they are based on diverse sources such as the trade press, in part they are based on back calculations from customs' reports of volumes and values of gas traded between countries, and on the estimated effects of indexation provisions in gas contracts. They cannot be considered wholly reliable, but they are probably as good as can be obtained without being privy to details of all individual contracts.

A more important caveat about the accuracy and meaning of gas prices is that a price never stands alone in a gas contract. Price for a unit of energy is always associated with a greater or lesser degree of flexibility in supply and offtake -- a flexibility which has a cost to the seller and

Table 4.2

European Gas Prices at Inlet of Distributors'
Transmission Systems

$/MMBTU[a]

	Second Quarter 1984	Second Quarter 1985
NETHERLANDS TO:		
Germany	3.75	3.40
Belgium	3.75	3.35
France	3.90	3.50
Italy	3.90	3.50
SOVIET UNION TO:		
Germany	3.70-4.05	3.35
France	3.50-3.95	3.50
Italy	3.68	3.50
Austria	3.58	3.40
NORWAY TO:		
Consortium (Ekofisk) cif Emden, Germany	3.75	3.60
United Kingdom	3.50	3.00
Consortium (Statpipe) cif Emden, Germany	(4.90)[b]	(4.40)[b]
ALGERIA TO:		
Italy	4.26	4.09
Belgium[c]	4.49	4.37
France[c]	4.34	4.22
Spain[c]	3.63	4.22

[a]Using quarterly average exchange rates from
OECD "Main Economic Indicators."

[b]For delivery October 1985.

[c]After allowing 20 cents regasification charge
and 20 cents freight (Spain), 25 cents freight
(France), 35 cents freight (Belgium).

a value to the buyer in terms of investments which must be made or which can be avoided depending on the flexibility available. Flexibility takes two forms; flexibility in the rate of build-up of deliveries to agreed plateau volumes, and flexibility in seasonal/daily rates of delivery. The latter form of flexibility itself changes in value to a particular buyer according to the terms of other contracts in the buyer's portfolio of supplies, and according to changes in the load factor which a transmission company must meet as its customers' aggregate seasonal and daily needs for gas change. In recent months and years, as transmission companies' overcommitment for the purchase of gas has required adjustment, flexibility in the build-up of supplies has been particulary valuable; Enagas of Spain, for example, was willing to concede a price increase from $2.95/MMBTU to $3.94/MMBTU to Sonatrach of Algeria as part of a package deal involving a stretching out of the build-up period for deliveries of Algerian LNG. In the future, if the highly seasonal residential and commercial space-heating market continues to increase in relative importance at the consumer end, as expected, then the second form of flexibility -- in seasonal and daily offtake -- will tend to become increasingly valuable.

Flexibility and other contract terms effectively adjust the meaning of a given BTU price for gas. There are also other external aspects to be taken into account which arise because of the dimension of international trade. Countertrade arrangements, and subsidized credit terms for countertrade purchases have been the most important external commercial aspects, and have been applied in deals between German, French and Italian companies, with both the Soviet Union and Algeria. It is meaningless to attempt to calculate the value of such arrangements in terms of discounts to or premia on the gas prices. For example, what appears, from the Western side, to have been a "low-interest" loan from Deutche Bank to the Soviet purchaser of Mannesmann steel pipe, which was associated with the 1981 (SGE-IV) purchase of gas from the Soviet Union by Ruhrgas and others, can equally be interpreted as a commercially-negotiated compromise between two economic systems

in one of which (the capitalist one) high interest
rates are temporarily prevalent and where in the
other (the Communist) low interest rates are a
structural feature of the system. Or again, French
government support for gas imports from and countertrade agreements with Algeria, can be assessed
in some way as part of a tied aid package to a
developing country with strong historical ties to
France.

In addition, there are more nebulous non-
commercial external aspects associated with gas
import contracts made at any given level of prices.
These are the political and foreign policy implications of long-lasting commercial ties which involve engineering and equipment suppliers (and
therefore employment) in the importing countries
as well as the importing gas companies themselves.
Gas trade in continental Europe, with its heavy
initial dependence on the Netherlands as a supplier, has for many years been an important feature
of integration between EC member countries. In
1985 it has provided a convenient vehicle for
symbolic promotion of the ECU (the European Currency Unit) in which gas trade between France and
the Netherlands will be denominated as a means
toward extending the commercialization of a common
currency in Europe. Further afield, gas purchases
from the Soviet Union have been seen as one element
of a bridge-building exercise in the era of detente; for all the much-vaunted independence of
German gas companies in negotiating for Soviet
supplies, a representative of the German Federal
Economics Ministry has nearly always been present
at important negotiating sessions. No further
imports are currently under consideration from
this source, which coincides well with the cooler
atmosphere in political relations with the Soviet
Union. The route is not necessarily closed, however, should the political winds change. With
respect to Algeria, resolution of details of gas
contracts have formed part of wider political
settlements with France (1982), Italy (1983) and
Spain (1985). None of these important factors show
up in a simple table of gas prices.

THE SUPPLY OF GAS -- A POLITICAL LIMIT?

In 1985 most of the supply side factors can be taken as pointers to a much larger role for natural gas in Western Europe's energy balance. Major additions to the infrastructure of supply have just been completed, which include the Statpipe system, the trans-Mediterranean pipeline, the transit line through Czechoslovakia linking Soviet export lines with the MEGAL line, the Morecambe Bay-Westfield Point line in the U.K., and the DONG and Swedegas Systems in Denmark and South Sweden. Extra compression and looping could add to supply capability on the Statpipe and, especially, trans-Med systems for relatively little additional investment. There is an immediate excess supply of contractually committed gas against expected demand over the next eighteen months. Recent settlements on build-up of deliveries of Algerian gas to Spain, France and Italy, and of Soviet gas to France, Germany and Italy have eased this imbalance; nevertheless, most transmission companies are likely to remain in a position to take only those volumes of gas from the Netherlands, their most flexible supplier, to which they are committed by minimum bill clauses in their contracts. Waiting in the wings for the long-term, new supplies of gas are under negotiation from Norway (from the massive Troll field among others). There are some indications that Algeria might be willing to make additional pipeline supplies available, and, while there have not yet been any discussions regarding a third tranche of Soviet gas, the awesome size of Soviet reserves and the existing capacity to bring gas at least as far as the Soviet frontier at Uzhgorod, suggest that the possibility is there -- if there is room in the market. Further afield there are new suppliers who would be anxious to break into the European market if commercially-viable projects could be successfully launched. Shell, Elf, and AGIP could bring LNG to European terminals from Nigeria's vast, disparate reserves; BP and CFP-Total are looking with the Qataris at markets east and west for gas from the giant North Dome field offshore Qatar.

In general, European gas transmission and distribution companies are rather better served

for guaranteed supplies under existing contracts
than are their counterparts, the major pipeline
companies in the United States. Existing commitments in international trade amount to between 222
BCF/D and 237 BCF/D, against current annual deliveries from the four major international suppliers
of about 9.7 BCF/D. The Netherlands has a total
committed 58 BCF/D from the beginning of 1985
through to the year 2010 in the case of some buyers.
The Soviet Union, under a series of contracts
signed between 1968 and 1984, will supply some 82
BCF/D to 96 BCF/D through to the early years of the
next century. Algeria has committed 22 BCF/D of
reserves, and the agreed slower rate of delivery to
Spain and Italy stretches supplies beyond 2000.
Norway has 11.5 BCF/D of reserves from specified
gas fields tied up in contracts even after allowing
for the reductions in volume agreed with buyers in
1985 because of problems with the Ekofisk field. In
addition to this, transmission companies in all
the major countries except Belgium have assured
supplies of indigenous gas -- sometimes from af-
filiated producers (as SNAM has with the Eni group
in Italy, or BGC from its own production in the
Morecambe Bay field and elsewhere) and sometimes
from long-term agreements, such as the arrangement
by which 50 percent of all gas discovered and
developed by major German producers is offered to
Ruhrgas. As an indication of the level of comfort
which European utilities like to have in terms of
committed reserves, consider a recent attempt by a
senior executive of the BGC to justify purchase of
the Sleipner field, by claiming that it would have
raised the contracted reserves from a level which
"will only keep us going for thirteen years" to a
reserves life indicators of seventeen years.[10] In
the terms of BGC's own experience these are indeed
short reserves life figures -- in 1974 the figure
stood at twenty seven years and in 1970 at forty
years. But compare this with the typical reserves
life ratio of U.S. pipeline companies at nine to
ten years, with the most conservative of the
thirteen companies at twenty years, and less than
a seven-year reserves life ratio for the company
with the lowest committed reserves.

In view of the supply position it may be
thought surprising, then, that the question of the

security of European gas supplies should ever have become an issue, or that it should be on the agenda at all for the next ten or fifteen years. It has only become a matter of concern because of the dimension of international trade, because of the relatively immature infrastructure for long distance supply, and because of the question of political amity with the Soviet Union which has been involved.

Trade and self-sufficiency in gas or anything else are not regarded with the same eyes in Europe as in the United States. Trade represents about a quarter of Europe's gross domestic product (imports were 27 percent of OECD Europe's GDP in 1984); less than one tenth of U.S. economic activity, by contrast, involves international trade (imports were 9 percent of U.S. GDP in 1984). Being dependent on international trade for the supply of vital commodities is neither new nor particularly shocking for European businessmen and governments. Nevertheless, the extra dimension which trade across national borders adds to the supply equation raises the threshold level of comfort which gas companies in Europe like to maintain in terms of reserves committed to contract.

It is the physical means by which gas is imported to Europe, rather than the fact of imports, which perhaps account for most of the justifiable anxiety about security of supply. Continental Europe's gas supply physically depends on pipelines and sets of pipelines which form six major transmission axes, shown in Table 4.3. These pipeline deliveries are supplemented by substantial deliveries of LNG to Fos-sur-Mer, Montoir-de-Bretagne (France) and Barcelona (Spain) for the French and Spanish markets in areas more remote from Europe's industrial heartlands. Smaller deliveries of LNG to Le Havre (France) and La Spezia (Italy) complete the picture. When LNG deliveries to Zeebrugge (Belgium) begin in 1987 there will be an additional supply source close to the heartland. This basic structure of North-South, East-West and South-North axes may be considered to have two basic strengths and two basic weaknesses in terms of physical supply security.

Table 4.3

Western European
Natural Gas Transmission Axes

Main Pipeline(s)	Direction	Conveying
SEGEO	North-Southwest	Dutch gas to Belgium and France
ETG, NETG, METG	North-South	Dutch gas to Germany
Norpipe, Statpipe	North-South	Norwegian gas to Germany, Netherlands, Belgium and France
TENP, Transitgas	North-South	Dutch gas to Italy and Switzerland
MEGAL, TAG	East-West	Soviet gas to Germany, France, Italy and Austria
TRANSMED	South-North	Algerian gas to Italy

The strengths are (1) the ability of the Dutch supply system to deliver for export in any one year more than double the current annual export volumes, and (2) the possibilities for exchange and displacement of gas from the major suppliers in northern and central Germany, the Low Countries and northern France. Exchange and displacement deals form part of the normal commercial arrangements between transmission companies, in order to minimize distribution costs. There are also, however, stand-by systems in place which would enable much larger scale switching so that low-calorific gas from the Netherlands (Groningen quality gas of 8400 kcals/m^3) could supply customers who normally use higher calorific value gas (9500 kcals/m^3). When a projected trunkline connection from near the Minerbio storage-field in northeast Italy (effectively the end-point of Algerian gas supplies through the trans-Med line) and Alessandria in northwest Italy is completed, further significant displacement possibilities will exist -- Dutch gas destined for Italy could be used further north, and more Algerian or Soviet gas delivered for use across the whole of north Italy.

The weaknesses of the system are focused in central Europe and southern Germany in less mature (but now rapidly growing) market areas. A scheme to convert a crude oil line from Genoa on the Mediterranean coast to Ingolstadt in Bavaria to natural gas fell through some years ago, with the collapse of a proposed purchase of Algerian gas by a consortium of, mainly German, transmission companies. The failure of this scheme leaves southern Germany, Austria and Switzerland exposed at the end of only one (in the case of Bavaria), or two, long-distance supply chains, supplemented by only relatively small quantities of local production. The second, related, weakness in the maturity of the supplying network lies in the lack of a major transmission line running north to south in the eastern part of West Germany -- which would complete a quadrilateral with the DETG, NETG and MEGAL transmission lines, and complete a ring configuration.

Finally there is the question of the political relationship with the Soviet Union. The history of Soviet gas supplies to Europe has from

the beginning been tied up with the political
stance of the West vis-a-vis the Soviet Union. The
first contract for the supply of Soviet gas to a
non-COMECON member country was to neutral Austria
in 1968. Negotiations took place through 1967, and
the contract involved part-payment of the gas with
the supply of large-diameter steel pipe rolled in
West Germany from Austrian steel. This was the
first time large-diameter steel pipe had been
delivered to the Soviet Bloc from a NATO country
following the lifting, in autumn 1966, of the NATO
embargo on the export of such materials. Eighteen
months after deliveries of Soviet gas began to
Austria in September 1968, the first contract for
the supply of 0.3 BCF/D (3 BCM per annum) was signed
with Ruhrgas of Germany. At the same time, the
steel and engineering group Mannesmann, one of
Ruhrgas' major shareholders, contracted to supply
1.2 million tons of steel pipe to the Soviet Union.
The example was thus set, shortly after the lifting
of NATO's restrictions, for what became a regular
pattern of reciprocal trade deals between West
European companies and the Soviet gas exporting
agency, Soyuzgazexport. Through the period of
political detente in the 1970s there were two more
contracts with German buyers, one with SNAM in
Italy, and two with Gaz de France. Technical
cooperation and exchange of views took place on a
growing scale, and Soyuzgazexport in effect became
involved in the exchange and optimization of supply within the West European transmission system
when Italy received extra supplies of Soviet gas
against a French contract in 1976 and France received a redirected equivalent amount from the
Italian's Dutch contract.

The political reversal of the policy of detente found West European buyers again involved in
negotiating new contracts with the Soviet Union
which would, when implemented, roughly double the
2.4 BCF/D of gas per year which had been imported
in total by West European buyers in the late 1970s.
These contracts, which Ruhrgas and Gaz de France
signed in spite of U.S. opposition, and which SNAM
and Eni in Italy signed after two years delay in
response to U.S. and Italian government pressure,
are now in the course of building up to full
volumes. The pipeline delivery systems within the

Soviet Union have more than enough capacity to fulfil these contracts, as their principal function is to supply the European parts of the U.S.S.R. and East European countries, as well as the West European buyers.

Two aspects of the business culture in the European gas industry contributed to the determination of the gas companies involved not to bow to U.S. pressure by backing out of these contracts when the political wind changed. In the first place, it remains the conventional wisdom that a healthy gas business intrinsically depends on long-term relationships, stability, and trust, because of long project lead times, fixed physical infrastructure, and the corresponding capital exposure. Secondly, in the case of German gas companies, who are the largest purchasers of gas from the Soviet Union, independence of government and government-interference is a source of particular pride. In all other major European gas industries governments have substantial direct involvement; in the FRG the industry is entirely a private sector affair. German gas companies are very conscious of the contrast between their own independence of operation and the extensive government involvement in the industry in neighboring countries. Resistance to pressure to change commercial relations for purely political reasons was therefore strong. German industry has never regarded the Soviet Union as in any sense an "unreliable" or "insecure" source of supplies of energy, and strongly maintains that their contracts enhance the security of energy supply since Soviet gas displaces oil which would otherwise come from OPEC countries. Within the ruling conservative Christian Democrat party in the Federal Republic of Germany there is an unresolved tension between support for the free market, no-government-interference line espoused by the gas industry and dislike of the existence of commercial contracts which contribute to improving the climate of relations with the Soviet Union.

In summary, the question of the "security" of European gas supplies, with particular reference to Soviet supplies, is not and never has been a question of physical security and reliability, but a question of the degree of political amity which the Western world wishes to develop or maintain with the Soviet Union. This tends to vary as political winds blow hot and cold, and in European gas industry culture variability is unacceptable to good commercial relations. At the same time, from the point of view of commercial security (and negotiating strength) it is not in the interest of the transmission companies to become overdependent on a single supplier of gas. The buyers of gas therefore do not show an inclination to increase their level of purchases of Soviet (or any other) gas to the point where there would be an imbalance in suppliers' market share. Even if short-term price advantages would tend to make Soviet gas more attractive, buyers do not believe they would serve their own or their customers' long-term best interests by increasing Soviet purchases and crowding out other suppliers. The same commitment to long-term relationships which led these companies to implement their agreements for additional Soviet gas in the early 1980s will tend to preserve the balance between suppliers for the future. Under such conditions, growth in the total market for gas is likely to be steady rather than dramatic, but constrained by the industry's structure and style rather than by political limitations.

NOTES

[1] In this essay Western Europe is taken to be the European members of the Organization for Economic Cooperation and Development (OECD), namely: Austria, Belgium, Denmark, Federal Republic of Germany, Finland, France, Greece, Iceland, Ireland, Italy, Luxembourg, Netherlands, Norway, Portugal, Spain, Sweden, Switzerland, Turkey, United Kingdom.

[2] See, for example, Malcolm W.H. Peebles "Evolution of the Gas Industry," Macmillan Press Ltd. 1980, p. 54.

[3]A result of a combination of Belgium's high average gas import costs and proximity to Europe's main oil refining centers.

[4]"Prospects for Natural Gas Through to the Year 2000," presentation by Malcolm W.H. Peebles, Shell International Gas Ltd. at 16th World Gas Conference, Mucich, June 1985.

[5]Commission of the European Communities Document COM(84)87, 88 and 120 final "communication from the Commission to the Council concerning Natural Gas."

[6]Background paper "Natural Gas Prospects" for meeting of IEA Governing Board at Ministerial Level, July 1985.

[7]Report of IGU Task Force "World Gas Supply and Demand" to 16th World Gas Conference, Munich, June 1985.

[8]H-H Rogner, A. Golovine, S. Messner, M. Stubagger "The IIASA International Gas Study," Lazenburg, Austria (June 1985).

[9]"Western Europe Natural Gas Industry Market and Economic Analysis to 2000," Purvin & Gertz, Inc., London (October 1982 and October 1984).

[10]C.W. Brierley, "U.K. Gas Prospects," paper presented at University of Surrey Conference on "International Gas" (April 1985).

5

Perspectives on the Role of Norwegian Gas

Janne Haaland Matlary

COMMENTARY

   We are now given a view of gas different from the earlier discussions which have been from the perspectives of significant gas importers. Norway does not consume any of its very large gas reserves; it exports all of its production. Norway is, as we know, an important oil exporter and, in that capacity, now meets the market price. But gas is still a different matter.
   Norwegian gas is costly to develop. In the several decades ahead, gas from its more northern areas will be very expensive at the "burner tip" compared to Dutch, Soviet, and possibly Algerian competition. Norway will be able to meet the market price from high-cost production only (1) if it, in effect, subsidizes the cost or (2) is able to charge European buyers a "security premium."
   Janne Haaland Matlary confronts these choices and discusses for us the issues and options which confront Norway as a producer whose export market is the United Kingdom or on the European continent; there are no other large opportunities. Dr. Matlary reargues the issue of security as did Simon A. Blakey -- but she does it from the Norwegian perspective. It has been the U.S. view since 1982 that Norwegian gas is an available, secure alternative to additional Soviet gas exports to Europe. The issue of expense has not been so directly addressed by the U.S. government. There is a case for a security premium without which the great gas reserves of northern offshore Norway may be too long delayed. The author warns us how much time is needed from an importer's decision to buy to the development of the fields and the logistic system. In short, a decision to recognize Norway's role in NATO, and as a secure gas

supplier would result in gas supplies a decade or longer hence. The availability now of Algerian and Soviet production to meet Europe's incremental gas needs emphasizes the need for what is, in effect, an alliance commitment. That has not yet been made.

-- Editor --

THE RESERVE SITUATION ON THE NORWEGIAN SHELF

The history of oil and gas exploration in Norway is a short one. It was not until 1975 that there was commercial production of oil. At that time, gas was relatively little discussed, as oil formed the main focus of attention. But with the start-up of production from the big Frigg gas field in 1977, Norway became a major exporter of gas to the United Kingdom (U.K.). The field delivers 1.5 BCF/D during the plateau production period, which is assumed to last until 1989. The gas is delivered via two pipelines to St. Fergus in Scotland. Gas also started to flow to Emden in Germany from the Norwegian Ekofisk-field in 1977.

Gradually Norwegian exports of oil and gas reached about 400 MB/o.e. with an approximate breakdown of 50 percent for each. In 1984, gas exports totaled 2.5 BCF/D. Exports to Britain made up almost 1.3 BCF/D, which amounted to 52 percent of total exports. The second major taker of gas was West Germany, with 0.6 BCF/D or 25 percent. France, the Netherlands, and Belgium took approximately 0.2 BCF/D each, which represented an 8 percent share of Norwegian exports for each country. The continental buyers form a consortium and do not individually buy gas from the producer.

Britain, then is, by far the most important buyer of Norwegian gas. It was therefore a major turning point in Norwegian gas history when the British government turned down the offer in 1985 of buying further quantities of Norwegian gas from the big Sleipner field. The Sleipner field, which could have started production in 1990, would have had a plateau production of approximately 1.3 BCF/D during the last part of the 1990s.

In addition to Sleipner, which seems to have been put on the back burner for the present, Norway's biggest challenge is to sell Troll field gas. Troll is a giant field with gas reserves of at least 46 TCF. One concept envisages a plateau production of 1.5 BCF/D from the mid-1990s. The field is situated in deep waters of about 300-350 meters, and this means that the development of Troll will be a pioneering effort. It also means that the gas from Troll will be expensive.

Apart from the two big gas fields, Sleipner and Troll, several smaller gas fields have been found. These are situated off mid- and north Norway, and will thus prove to be expensive to develop because of the need for extensive infra-structure.

In total, the estimated breakdown of proven reserves on the Norwegian shelf shows that they are made up of two thirds gas and one third oil. In addition it seems that the finds off the north Norwegian coast mainly consist of gas. (Apart from the Barents Sea, where the prospects mainly indi-cate oil. The government has recently passed a bill which makes exploration drilling possible in the southern part of the Barents Sea).[1]

The substantial part of Norwegian proven and possibly also probable reserves appears to be gas. In turn this implies it is of vital importance for the country to be able to sell gas if it is to exploit its sizable petroleum assets. Seen from this perspective, both the rejection of Sleipner gas by the British and the current limited pros-pects in the continental gas market illustrates the severity of Norway's situation. Moreover, from the standpoint of international security, Western Europe requires gas supply options from sources other than the Soviet Union. Norwegian supplies seen in this context are of potentially great importance.

THE MARKETS

Norway has two markets for gas, the U.K. and the Continent. After the rejection of the Sleipner deal, the United Kingdom as an immediate market for additional Norwegian gas is probably unrealistic. Yet Norway is aware that the U.K. gas market may become linked to, and thus be inseparable from, the Continental gas market. The European gas market might thus become thought of as one.

In this context, there are essentially five countries that are present and prospective takers of Norwegian gas: the U.K., West Germany, France, Belgium and possibly Italy. (The Dutch are also importers of Norwegian gas, partially because they will need gas imports in the future to cover domestic demand as the production from Groningen declines, but mainly because Groningen gas, which has a low calorific value, needs to be mixed with high calorific North Sea gas. The future demand for Norwegian gas may, however, be diminished as the Dutch increase their own offshore production.)

The future demand for Norwegian gas in the U.K. is very difficult to assess. The official reason for rejecting Sleipner was that the U.K. had enough indigenous reserves to cover domestic demand. These reserves were not specified, and doubts have been raised as to how realistic is the British postulate of self-sufficiency. This remains to be seen, but for imports, should the need arise, the British have the option of gas imports from the Continent with the construction of a cross-channel pipeline; Norway is not the only possible gas exporter to the U.K. The privatization of the British Gas Corporation, recently announced, may not make a difference with regard to export/import policy, as it seems certain that the government will want a strong hand in major decisions affecting U.K. gas need. Additional imports of Norwegian gas seem to depend on two main factors: one, whether a cross channel pipeline will be built and thus allow for Dutch and possibly Soviet imports, and second, whether the English are economically prepared to favor development of domestic reserves that may not be commercial by today's criteria. The future for Norwegian gas in the U.K. market is thus highly uncertain. This is particularly important for Norway since, as noted, the U.K. took as much as 52 percent of Norwegian gas exports in 1983. Present supplies to the U.K., mainly from the Frigg field, will have to be replaced to meet additional British needs, and that takes time to provide.

The second largest market for Norwegian gas is <u>West Germany</u> with a 25 percent share. While West German imports of gas rose during 1984 due to increases in deliveries from the U.S.S.R., (the latter exported about 1.3 BCF/D to West Germany in 1984, a rise of almost 24 percent), imports from the Netherlands dropped to 7.3 percent over the same period and Norwegian deliveries to about 0.6 BCF/D. The overall picture for gas, both domestic production and imported, had the Dutch deliver a 30 percent share of gas consumed in West Germany. Soviet suppliers provided 24.5 percent, with Norway's contribution about 14.5 percent.[2]

Net imports have represented about 60 percent of natural gas supply in West Germany. A major part of consumption is thus covered by domestic production. Domestic production will, however, probably decrease toward year 2000, from approximately 3.4 BCF/D in 1984 to about 2.8 BCF/D by the turn of the century. Total gas demand is expected to rise steadily but slowly toward year 2000 and reach about 4.8 BCF/D from 4.3 BCF/D in 1985. The growth rate for gas assumed in this projection is 1.3 percent.

With slowly declining domestic production and rising demand, West Germany will rely increasingly on imports. These will come from the Netherlands, the U.S.S.R. and Norway. Ruhrgas, the German gas buyer, has contracted additional deliveries of 0.2 BCF/D from Norway beyond Ekofisk gas supplies, which is to be slowly phased out in this decade. Gas from the big oil field Statfjord should start to flow this year. (Ruhrgas has recently asked for a renegotiation of the price terms of this gas, arguing that the price makes the gas unmarketable; the Norwegian response is not yet known.) Norwegian gas to Germany will have also to come from Troll and Sleipner, and Ruhrgas has expressed a clear interest in the former field. Competition from the Soviets and the Dutch to supply West Germany is, however, very keen. The share of Soviet gas in German supplies could clearly increase well beyond the present 24.5 percent, especially as the much discussed 30 percent limit of supply from the U.S.S.R. was never formally agreed to.

Potential increases in Soviet supplies will be linked to West German Ostpolitik. As energy is about the only commodity that Europe wants to buy from the U.S.S.R., an increase in East-West trade might, in all probability, entail further gas imports. There is no particular reason why a strict 30 percent limit on Soviet gas should be the rule. The number is not based on specific criteria, but is only a guide. Nevertheless, Soviet gas imports which exceed 30 percent will raise questions about security, enveloping gas trade into a political climate. Gas imports from other sources will have to be considered in light of political issues and the commercial aspect of diversification. Gas is, for the time being, not a controversial security topic with surplus in the West European market. Still, the security dimension is to be remembered.

Price will naturally be important with regard to the volume of imports. But price is only one factor among several. Gas trades increasingly involve wider considerations of economic trade between the gas buying and selling countries. The deals struck between European countries and two major suppliers of gas, the U.S.S.R. and Algeria, make this clear. With regard to these two suppliers, "balanced trade" possibilities and political questions play a predominant role in defining gas deals not price alone. Norway is limited in its ability to put other trade interests into a "balanced trade" with gas buyers.

The major competitor which Norway faces in the German market is the U.S.S.R. Although the Dutch have stepped up their production and intensified offshore exploration -- thus abandoning their former policy of conservation, they cannot offer the large quantities of gas that the German market will need from the mid-1990s onward.

The size of the share of Norwegian gas in future German supplies may therefore be determined largely by Germany's relationship with the U.S.S.R. This relationship is not a constant. It is difficult to predict how German Ostpolitik will develop, but it remains clear that trade with the East will remain of major importance to the West Germans for the East represents huge markets for industrial goods.[3] The political dimension in West Germany's relationship with East Germany is

thus of major importance with West Germany's policy to work toward a "reunification of the two
Germanies." Although the extent of trade between
West Germany and the East bloc in general depends
on the political climate between the two, German
trade with the U.S.S.R. has not depended on gov-
ernment-supported credits.[4] For instance, the Yamal pipeline project was financed on the Western
side by Deutsche Bank.[5]

During 1984, _France_ took approximately 0.2
BCF/D of Norwegian gas. Its major suppliers are
Algeria and the U.S.S.R. There is a political
commitment to buy at least one third of needed
supplies from Algeria, although gas trade with
Algeria is controversial. The present government
has especially cultivated a close relationship
with Algeria, made evident when the government
decided to pay a direct subsidy for gas from
Algeria. This decision was highly publicized and
much discussed,[6] for in the background was an
Algerian demand for higher gas prices, which was
opposed by Gaz de France. Consequently, the negotiations were between the French Ministry of Foreign Affairs and Sonatrach, the Algerian gas utility. The agreement was announced by the Ministry
thus making clear the political context in which
the negotiations took place, not the commercial.
The subsidization of Algerian gas was officially
presented as an export subsidy for French industrial goods of which Algeria promised to take
larger quantities in return for the gas subsidy.

The French emphasis on maintaining good commercial and political ties with Algeria is well-
known. The strength of the commitment to this is
tested by such situations as the one just described. A conservative government may possibly deal
differently with Algeria, but despite governments
it remains a fact that there exists the commitment
to strong Algerian-French relations, characteristic of any French regime, and gas is one of the
few commodities the French can use from Algeria.

The other main supplier of gas to France is
the U.S.S.R. where mutual trade arrangements are
an important factor. Recently, the French have
complained that the Soviets have not placed orders
with French industry as it was assumed -- or agreed
on -- would happen after the signing of the latest

gas contract. Gas imports from the U.S.S.R. have always received much political attention in France, and could exceed the 30 percent limit, if not soon. This means that Norway and Algeria remain competitors for the major part of remaining French needs in the mid-1990s and beyond. But the share of Algerian gas in the future may also change: While it may not be reduced, it may possibly increase. This will depend on Algerian gas policy, especially pricing policy; and also on what Norway can offer in competition. Algeria has a reputation of being a price hawk, and its record in gas negotiations is outstanding -- in a negative way -- in this respect. But two factors point to the need for treading more carefully in the future: First, domestic oil production is being reduced, and consequently, so also are oil exports. Second, LNG trade has been disappointing. Algeria, which depends for most of its revenues on petroleum exports, will have to rely increasingly on pipeline exports of natural gas to Europe. The pipeline to Italy testifies to this, as does the planned pipeline to Spain. But Algeria will have also to conduct itself more circumspectly if it is to gain gas market shares in Western Europe. While the French so far have viewed Algerian gas imports as something almost akin to a "necessary evil," however important politically, Algerian gas could become attractive for commercial reasons also. It is a possibility which the marketing of Norwegian gas has to consider.

Belgium's share of imports from Norway was 0.2 BCF/D, or 22 percent of total imports, in 1984. Algeria supplied 20 percent and the Dutch 58 percent of remaining imports that year. As Dutch supply is scheduled to decline, Belgium looks for other suppliers from the mid-1990s onward.[7] Imports from the U.S.S.R. are being considered. Demand is expected to rise gradually but slowly from approximately 1.2 BCF/D in 1990 to 1.5 BCF/D by the year 2000. Algerian deliveries are to go to the Zeebrugge terminal which is being built specifically for this contract. The terminal is to be completed in 1986. Imports from Algeria started to flow in 1982 and have been regasified at the Montoir terminal in France until the Belgian facility is completed. Algerian supplies to Belgium

will reach 0.5 BCF/D in 1985 and will continue to
flow at this level for another seventeen years.
But with the infrastructure for LNG in place it is
almost certain that further LNG imports will be
wanted afterwards.

If LNG keeps a constant share of Belgian gas
imports of 0.5 BCF/D, Norway's main competitors in
the Belgian gas market will be the U.S.S.R. and the
Dutch. The latter are again offering gas in the
market, and since Belgium does not require very
large quantities of gas, the Dutch may compete well
in this market. But the Soviets are in the market
as well for small as well as for large volume sales.
The Belgians will probably not want to rely too
heavily on Algerian plus Soviet supplies, and are
therefore likely to choose Dutch and/or Norwegian
supplies for reasons of diversification. But
Dutch supplies may, if available, be preferable.
After all, Belgium relied 100 percent on Dutch
supplies until the Dutch some years ago announced
a reversal of their gas export policy. It was the
unavailability of Dutch gas which forced the Belgians to look for other sources of supply.

Italy may be a potential purchaser of Norwegian gas although so far no supplies have been
contracted. The share of natural gas in Italy's
energy mixture has already reached the 20 percent
limit which was assigned to it in the national
energy plan. In 1984 Italy consumed 3 BCF/D gas,
of which 1.3 BCF/D was produced domestically.

From 1990, Italy is projected to import approximately 80 percent of its demand for gas. The
increase in demand, which by an independent consultant is estimated to grow from approximately 3
BCF/D in the 1980s to about 3.8 BCF/D in the 1990s,
will largely stem from the large-scale gasification project of the Italian South, the Mezzo-
giorno.[8] Generally, both GDP growth and energy
growth for Italy are forecast to be higher than the
European average: from 1980 to the year 2000,
average GDP growth is projected to be 2.4 percent,
and primary energy growth is estimated to be 1.7
percent.

Gas imports to Italy come from Algeria, Libya, the U.S.S.R., and Holland. Libyan LNG constituted 0.1 BCF/D of 1980 imports, but the contract
was suspended the same year when Libya ousted

foreign companies. In 1984 Dutch imports amounted to 0.5 BCF/D. Dutch deliveries started in 1974 with a twenty year span. The first Soviet contract started deliveries the same year and has a life of twenty six years. Another Soviet contract was concluded in 1984 for approximately 0.8 BCF/D and has a duration period of twenty five years. This contract was concluded as a "balanced trade" deal where the Soviets promised to spend the entire payment for gas sales on Italian goods and services. Italian industry complains, however, that the Soviets have so far placed few orders with Italian firms. There are, however, current talks in Moscow about the building of a plant for cars using methane as a fuel. Italy has the best developed expertise in this field. (Italy's trade deficit with the U.S.S.R. in 1984 was 4,300 billion lire, the highest with any country.)

Gas deliveries to Italy from Algeria have been a subject of controversy. The so-called Transmed pipeline was agreed on in 1973. It goes from Algeria to Tunisia, then across the straits of Messina and the Sicilian channel, to the Italian mainland. As a result of delays, construction only got underway in 1978, but by 1980 when the pipeline was over half completed, Sonatrach, the gas company of Algeria, raised its price demand for the gas from $3.50 MMBTU to $5.50 MMBTU. A further dispute came when Algerian firms allegedly hindered further work on important parts of the project.

When the project had been left idle for more than a year, SNAM, the Italian national gas company, was finally forced to ask the Italian government to intervene directly with Sonatrach. An agreement between the two gas companies was reached but made conditional upon the guarantee by the Italian government that it pay directly to Sonatrach the difference between SNAM's offer and what Sonatrach demanded. The Italian government finally agreed to do this and now pays a 12 percent differential directly out of the Treasury as a subsidy to the contract. The subsidy will, however, only last for the first three years of the contract period, which originally was for twenty five years, and for the amount of 0.9 BCF/D of gas. After this period, the contract will have to be renegotiated.

Norwegian gas may be desirable to the Italians from the mid-1990s onward for commercial reasons. Italy, like other gas importers, would not want to rely entirely on Soviet and Algerian imports. But the Italians express the need for "balanced trade" more clearly than other gas buying countries. They state officially that they will not be able to buy gas without a possibility of exporting goods and services to the gas selling country; such a "deal" would be difficult to strike for reasons of the Norwegian commitment to free trade.

THE "SECURITY" OF SUPPLY ISSUE

European considerations of gas supply security is the central reason why a need for alternative sources may provide opportunities for Norway whose gas may otherwise be too expensive to compete. Norway will have to argue its case in light of commercial and political (security) considerations. Europe's gas trade with the U.S.S.R. was made an issue in international politics when the U.S. administration in 1982 tried to prevent Western European exports of technology for the building of the Yamal pipeline by instituting an embargo on exports from American firms or their subsidiaries in Europe. The end of the embargo came in 1984 when it had become clear that Western European nations would not accept interference in their scheduled deliveries to the pipeline. However, American worry over the extent of Soviet supplies of gas to Western Europe resulted in prolonged debate over the issue of security of gas supplies. The International Energy Agency (IEA) took up the issue and made a study of possible damage in the event of interruptions in the gas flow from the East. The study concluded that present import levels of Soviet gas did not seriously threaten importing countries. It was, however, recommended that gas imports from any one source ought not to exceed about one third of supplies which is also prudent commercial practice.

This consideration is particularly important as gas contracting parties are bound for a considerable period, usually between twenty and thirty years. Because of this, it is extremely important not to cause irregularities in supply. The likelihood of interruptions in gas supplies is probably smaller the more important the long-term business relationship is to both parties. During the debate over gas supply security the point was often made that the Soviets were very unlikely to disrupt supplies as they needed the income in hard currency from gas sales very badly. This is correct, but the fear of supply interruption is tied to what might happen in a crisis not in a situation characterized by "business-as-usual."

From the record, Algeria, and not the U.S.S.R., is the country that has the reputation for the most irregularities in its gas exports. Time and again Algeria has not met its contractual obligations, and often demanded price rises for gas not envisaged in the contracts. Nevertheless, Algeria trades gas with France, Belgium, Italy, and Spain but security of supply is an extremely important issue, and no gas importer would like to rely too much on Algerian piped gas or LNG.

With regard to the security of supply of Norwegian gas, concern has been expressed in two main respects: One, the possibility of production setbacks due to labor strikes on platforms is a problem -- and, second, the possibility of supply disruptions due to sabotage on a North Sea pipeline although few have discussed this latter possibility in any detail. Production difficulties, which stem from technical factors, like the recent problem with the Ekofisk platforms which are sinking into the sea-bottom, are a third element.

Yet the problems -- actual or potential -- which surround Algerian and Norwegian gas -- are different from the security of supply issues connected with deliveries from the U.S.S.R. Soviet gas deliveries to Western Europe have an outstanding record of success and reliability, yet it remains a fact that all trade with the East bloc is part of a larger dimension of international security. Business with the East bloc can never be "business-as-usual" because the trading partners can only act within a framework that is defined by the international political climate between East and West. The East-West relation is never a constant, and it is usually beyond the powers of the trading partners to play a dominant role in influencing its direction. This makes East-West trade in energy so special as the parameters that define it can change rapidly and, to those involved, uncontrollably.

West European energy imports from the U.S.S.R. will probably never rise beyond a level that is acceptable to the IEA and to the Western countries' security concerns. Clearly NATO will play a role here if any one member approaches an import limit that may represent a danger in a crisis situation. Non-NATO countries do not seem to observe a specific limit of imports from the U.S.S.R. All imported Austrian gas comes from the U.S.S.R. The same is true for Finland.

If the security dimensions of natural gas seem to be relatively little discussed for the time being, they will continue to be an important element in international gas trade. Commercial considerations involved in diversification will have to take this into account also for the future. Nevertheless, it is by no means clear how far beyond the 30 percent "rule-of-thumb" limit for Soviet gas imports some importers may go. After all, each country acts alone in diversifying its gas imports, although a major increase in Soviet supply to a NATO country will not surely remain only a domestic concern. A major increase in supply to any West European country is, however, not very likely. A far more interesting factor is the likelihood of marginal increases in Soviet supply to Western Europe. Such increases will also affect the prospects for Norwegian gas in this market.

PERSPECTIVES ON THE ROLE OF NORWEGIAN GAS

Norway has more than plenty of gas, ready for the market in the mid-1990s, which is the time of renewed demand in Western Europe. Norwegian gas has a good market possibility in the U.K., West Germany, France, Italy, Belgium, and the Netherlands. Apart from these, there are long-term markets in Scandinavia, where parts of Sweden and Denmark are developing as natural gas markets. Finally, Spain may become an interesting if not large market in the long run. For Spain, however, Algeria already provides the gas imports needed into the 1990s. Scandinavia, apart from Finland, may in the long run be of interest, but this would be after the turn of this century.

ANTICIPATED WEST EUROPEAN DEMAND

Negotiations for gas to cover West European demand in the mid-1990s will have to be concluded within one to two years' time if the gas is to come from Norway due to the long lead time for bringing new offshore projects onstream. West European gas buyers will have to decide on whether they want Norwegian gas in the near future. What is their expected need for additional supplies and how may Norway best compete?

The following picture emerges: For France, the authorities recently published the preparatory work on energy for the 9th plan, 1984-88[9] with detailed analyses of all aspects of French needs. For gas, demand is projected to be:

1990	2000	BCF/D
2.8	2.6	Low scenario
2.9	2.9	High scenario

Reduced demand reflects the French policy of putting priority on the use of electricity.[10] It also reflects the decline of domestic production, which will only be about 0.1-0.2 BCF/D of gas in the mid-1990s. French demand in the mid-1990s should then lie approximately in the range 2.6-2.8 BCF/D. Imports needed will be in the order of 2.4-2.6 BCF/D. One third of these projected needs will come from Algeria, another third from probably U.S.S.R. leaving perhaps 0.7-0.9 BCF/D for Norwegian and Dutch suppliers.

West German gas demand in the mid-1990s is more difficult to assess as the Germans do not publish official demand projections. Gas represented 15.3 percent of primary energy demand in 1983 and 16 percent in 1984. Ruhrgas points out that its market philosophy is to increase gas penetration to approximately 18 percent.[11] Gas consumption in Germany was 4.2. BCF/D in 1983, of which 3 BCF/D was imported. Of this one BCF/D came from the U.S.S.R., 1.6 BCF/D from the Netherlands, and 0.5 BCF/D from Norway.[12] With Dutch demand gradually reduced toward the mid-1990s, Norwegian gas will have to compete with both Dutch and Soviet supply.

Italian gas demand in the mid-1990s will depend much on the success of the gasification projects in the south. But domestic production is declining, and this makes for a bigger import need. Norway faces competition from both the Dutch, the Soviets, and the Algerians in this market with Norway situated farthest of all from the Italian scene.

The United Kingdom will probably be in need of supplies by the mid-1990s. With existing infrastructure, supplies from the Norwegian North Sea are very likely. Yet the size of demand depends directly on future British depletion policy with regard to developing marginal gas field in the Southern Basin of the North Sea. This in turn depends much on the conflict between British Gas Corporation (BGC) interests and the companies on the shelf. The recently announced privatization of the BGC complicates the assessment of this question.

While Dutch and Belgian demand for Norwegian gas may be assumed to continue, it is limited in volume.

In sum, then, it seems certain that Norwegian natural gas will be in demand for deliveries from the mid-1990s onward. The question is basically how large this demand will be and/or how large a share of projected demand Norwegian gas will be able to secure. For reasons of diversification, buyers are almost certainly bound to take some Norwegian gas, but the interesting question is how much gas beyond a minimum they may be interested in taking. The answer to this depends on price, flexibility in Norwegian supplies, stability in deliveries, the quality of the gas -- but also on the development of East-West relations. Further, Norwegian gas may become more attractive if the Norwegians are able to offer some sort of trade reciprocity for a gas deal. Ideas that come to mind include less emphasis on the policy of "Norweg-ianization" on the shelf so that oil companies from gas buying countries may be invited to compete for a more significant role. The policy of "Norweg-

ianization" stipulates that Norwegian supplies of
offshore goods and services are to be preferred to
foreign supplies whenever competitive in terms of
price and quality. This also applies to the role
of foreign companies in deliveries of offshore
goods and services. Several gas importing countries naturally express the wish to see such a
change of policy. On the Norwegian side, such a
change may become necessary to sell more gas. In
other words, the Norwegian licensing policy and
the policy for goods and services may have to be
viewed and possibly reviewed in light of the opportunities in the gas market which a change in
these policies may entail. The options in the
current policy of Norwegianization may entail
costs which will perhaps be most visible in the
natural gas market. Norway cannot -- unlike the
U.S.S.R. and Algeria -- offer large markets for
industrial and other goods from gas buying nations. Norway cannot offer trade deals like those
of other gas sellers. Moreover, that free trade
commitment of a Western country like Norway militates against such arrangements. This very important fact makes it even more important that the
policy of "Norwegianization" on the shelf is considered in light of the gas market. The object is
not to develop a shelf policy characterized by
preference for gas buying nations' goods and services and their oil companies, but rather to develop further toward a "free market situation."
The charge of protectionism has been launched
against Norwegian firms when foreigners claimed to
have offered the lowest bids. The point is however
not whether this be correct or not, but simply that
less emphasis on "Norwegianization" on the shelf
may now be necessary to compete with gas sellers
that offer "balanced trade" opportunities to gas
buyers.

It is clear that Norway needs to be more
attentive to the significant changes that have
taken place in the gas market in view of its
expressed aim to sell much gas in the future.
Issues that need consideration at present include
the price issue, the issue of supply flexibility,
and the issue of "reciprocity" which has been
discussed briefly above. Yet another issue facing
Norway is that of downstream integration in the

West European market, particularly in the West German market.

The issue of price centers on the question of whether Norway wants to try to sell much gas more cheaply and possibly aid in the expansion of demand in the market, or rely on the position of a more marginal supplier. The difficulty in selling "cheap gas" seems to lie in the fact that the U.S.S.R. is able to meet any reduction in price. Yet it is an open question whether buyers would not prefer Norwegian gas to Soviet gas for reasons other than price even if the price were lowered.

The issue of supply flexibility is being widely discussed: Cooperation with the Netherlands, with possible gas storage in Groningen, in an arrangement where the Dutch sell the "swing" and Norway sells the volume. Other ideas center on the storage of Norwegian gas in abandoned mines in Northern Europe.

The issue of downstream integration requires a bolder and more offensive gas selling strategy on the part of Norway than has hitherto been the case. The means for such integration are readily available as Norway has petroleum revenue reserves of a very considerable size which could be invested abroad. The question is the effect of integration on the demand for Norwegian gas.

Since major decisions regarding gas sales for the mid-1990s will have to be made during 1986 with the lead time for field development in the North Sea of ten and often fifteen years, decisions of vital importance to Norway's gas future will be made this year and next. In the final analysis, Norway's share in the Western European gas market depends perhaps as much on Norwegian choices as on gas demand from the buyers. The need seems to be for a more aggressive Norwegian strategy to sell gas than the more cautious attitude characteristic of Norwegian behavior in gas sales.

While this characterization may be an exaggeration of the Norwegian attitude, it remains a fact that Norwegian choices will influence greatly its share of the Western European market. But influencing buyers' decisions requires forthright marketing: The challenge is to meet still Soviet, Dutch, and Algerian competition, and not to wait for the market share "left over" after contracts with these suppliers have been closed.

NOTES

[1]"Om lete- og basevirksomhet m.v." St.meld. nr. 79 (1984-85)("On exploration activities and supply bases,") government paper presented to Parliament on April 16, 1985. The area in the Barents Sea which is being opened up for exploration drilling is in the southern part of the Bear Island basin, and represents a north and eastward extension of existing licenses in the Tromsø path.

[2]World Gas Report, February 18, 1985.

[3]A.F. Ewing, "Energy and East-West Cooperation," Journal of Trade Law, Vol. 15, No. 3, May-June 1981. This article provides a good overview of East-West trade with particular emphasis on energy.

[4]A. Lebahn, "The Yamal Gas Pipeline from the U.S.S.R. to Western Europe in the East-West Conflict," Aussenpolitik, Vol. 34, No. 3, 1983. The author is the director of foreign credit in Deutsche Bank and was responsible for the financing of the Yamal gas pipeline. He was then Director of the Moscow office of Deutsche Bank. His article discusses most aspects of the American-European conflict over the extent of U.S.S.R. gas imports.

[5]Ibid.

[6]See e.g., Le Monde, January 4, 1983, September 20, 1984, February 3, 1982, February 4, 1982, February 10, 1982, February 16, 1982, March 7, 1982, March 24, 1982, May 28, 1982. All the articles deal with French-Algerian gas trade.

[7]D. Traversin, Director of Distrigaz, "Natural Gas in Belgium: Supply and Demand," paper presented at the Financial Times European Gas Conference, Vienna, December 11, 1984.

[8]See e.g., the European Energy Report, February 8, 1985 and the International Gas Report, February 1, 1985.

[9]Rapport du groupe long terme, Energie Vols. 1 and 2, Commissariat General du Plan, Preparation du IXe plan 1984-1988.

[10]For a discussion of the emphasis on electricity in the plan in English, see European Energy Report, January 11, 1985 and "Gas Fights for Its Place in French Homes," in International Energy Report, March 1, 1985.

[11]"Erdgas heute und Morgen," publication by Ruhrgas, Essen, October 1984.

[12]"Petroleum Intelligence Weekly," March 4, 1985, Special Supplement.

6

Gas in Eastern Europe and the U.S.S.R.

Balint Balkay and Sandor Sipos

COMMENTARY

Since the 1960s there have been impressive additions to natural gas supplies in North America, Western Europe and the Soviet Union. These additions have been made possible by large investments into development of fields, transmission and preparation of markets to receive them. But nowhere has the effort reached the magnitude of the U.S.S.R. undertaking. It is an extraordinary achievement. It is held that every eighteen months the Soviet Union completes a gas investment equivalent to the size of the enormous project required to bring Alaskan gas to the U.S. market; the point is that the Alaskan investment was postponed. The Soviet Union continues to place very high priority on the fullest possible use of its gas reserves for domestic consumption and into international trade, including both Eastern and Western Europe.

The authors of this chapter bring the gas effort into perspective both as to the needs and the importance of the U.S.S.R. as the gas supplier to Eastern Europe, and as a very major source for Western Europe. The volumes involved and the price arrangements are set forth in lucid expositions. Not enough is yet known of the U.S.S.R. role in natural gas and the following contribution helps significantly to enlarge upon our understanding of one of the great energy revolutions of our time.

-- Editor --

OVERVIEW

Today, gas is the uncontested growth fuel of the European CMEA.[1] It is all set to retain this role to the year 2000 and beyond.

In the 1960s, a surge in petroleum production and the construction of the necessary pipelines made petroleum the dominant fuel in the CMEA, relegating coal to the second plan. In the 1970s, however, the gathering problems of the Soviet petroleum industry, combined with the U.S.S.R.'s rising dependence on the hard currency income of its petroleum exports to the world markets, blocked the expansion of its supplies of petroleum and petroleum products to the other CMEA member countries. On the other hand, only the recipients' absorptive capacity growth seems to limit the expansion of the U.S.S.R.'s exports of natural gas to the CMEA Six and to Western Europe: In fact, the blueprints of such expansion are being elaborated and implemented. Electricity exports too are slated to grow, intra-CMEA above all, but the transportation of gas is much cheaper over the distances involved.

By 1984, the CMEA region had become the world's greatest producer and consumer and also the greatest exporter of gaseous fuels; of all the world regions, its production, consumption and exports have been rising fastest in absolute terms (albeit not in percentage terms). However, the CMEA region proper falls into two very different parts: (1) the Asian part of the U.S.S.R., extremely rich in gas reserves, which produces a big and fast-growing gas surplus, and (2) the European U.S.S.R. and the CMEA Six which are, despite a not inconsiderable gas production of their own, characterized by a large and growing gas deficit. In fact, the bulk of gas exported to outside the CMEA region is increasingly originating in the Asian part of the U.S.S.R., physically as well as statistically. The development of the huge gas reserves in the remote and inhospitable areas of the Asian U.S.S.R. and the construction of the infrastructure needed to take it to market is one of the main burdens on the U.S.S.R.'s energy economy.

THE CMEA SIX: SOME GAS ECONOMY FEATURES

RESERVES (See Table 6.1)

The CMEA Six's natural gas reserves amount to between one half and one percent of world reserves or to about one tenth of Western European gas reserves.

PRODUCTION (See Table 6.2)

The CMEA Six's natural gas production, at around 4 percent of world production, considerably exceeds their share of world reserves. Yet, thanks to a considerable drilling effort, they have in recent years been able to maintain the lives of their gas reserves constant, more or less. This includes Rumania, whose reserve situation appears the most precarious at a first glance. The gas economy of the CMEA Six with the exception of Rumania is based on imports from the U.S.S.R. The flow of these is kept level as far as possible, so as to use the transportation facilities to the full. Domestic gas therefore plays a growing role in buffering the daily and seasonal fluctuations of demand. Keeping up this buffering function as long as possible is a major preoccupation of domestic reserve depletion policy. Rumania in particular plans to reduce domestic production to somewhere around 2.4 BCF/D.

EXPLORATION PROSPECTS

Drilling in the Baltic may turn up interesting reserves for the German Democratic Republic (GDR) and Poland, and drilling in the Black Sea for Bulgaria and Rumania. For Czechoslovakia and Hungary, deep drilling to 7,000-8,000 meters (m) may turn up some gas when the current shallower prospects have been exhausted. None of these undertakings is expected to change the reserve picture in any dramatic way.

SELF-SUFFICIENCY (See Table 6.3)

While Rumania is practically self-sufficient in natural gas and is promoting imports of Soviet

Table 6.1

CMEA Seven's Reserves of Natural Gas
Compared with Those of Three OECD Countries
(TCF)

	January 1970 TCF	January 1985 TCF	January 1985 % World Reserves	Life* on 1/1/85
Bulgaria	1.12	.2	n	50
Czechoslovakia	.56	.4	n	14
Germany, Democratic Republic (GDR)	.56	4.6	.1	9
Hungary	4.76	4.8	.1	17
Poland	.36	4.4	.1	18
Rumania	6.8	8.4	.3	6
U.S.S.R.	365	1500	39.0	64
Austria	.44	.72	n	14
Germany, Federal Republic (FRG)	11.6	7.6	.2	10
United States	311.6	226.8	5.9	12
World	1524	3848	00.0	

*"Life" is reserve on 1/1/85 over production in 1984.

Source: Author's calculations based on Petroleum Economist's World Gas Surveys, 1970 and 1985. Remarks: n = negligible (less than 0.05 percent). Reserves mainly proven ones.

Table 6.2

Natural Gas Production in the CMEA Seven Countries
and in Three Countries of the OECD Group shown for Comparison

	Commercial Output (BCF/D)			Change %/Year 1979-84	Life of Reserves*	
	1978	1983	1984		1978	1984
Bulgaria	.002	.01	.01	30.8	250	50
Czechoslovakia	.105	.06	.08	-5.7	15	14
Germany, Dem.Rep.	.93	.83	1.35	6.5	9	9
Hungary	.80	.71	.75	-1.5	18	17
Poland	.87	.60	.65	-4.7	17	18
Rumania	3.17	4.3	4.15	5.2	5	6
U.S.S.R.	40.8	58.7	64.32	7.9	75	64
Austria	.23	.13	0.14	-8.1	6	14
Germany, Fed.Rep.	2.22	1.94	2.03	-5.1	9	10
United States	62.0	49.3	53.42	-2.5	10	12
CMEA 7 Total	46.7	65.3	71.34	7.3		
- as world %	29.8	38.5	38.6			
U.S.S.R. as world %	26.0	34.6	34.8			

*Reserves over last year's output.

Source: Petroluem Economist, London, August 1985 and August 1985. Remark: Excluding flared or reinjected; mainly excluding field usage.

Table 6.3

The CMEA Seven and Selected OECD Countries;
Self-sufficiency in Gaseous Fuel

Domestic Production as % of Domestic Consumption

	1970	1975	1980	1981	1982
Bulgaria					
All gases	100.0	36.4	16.5	14.0	11.9
Natural gas	100.0	8.6	4.5	3.0	1.6
Czechoslovakia					
All gases	84.2	66.3	47.1	47.0	45.6
Natural gas	47.5	20.5	7.1	7.7	7.3
Germany, Democratic Republic					
All gases	97.9	67.0	55.3	54.6	53.8
Natural gas	100.0	45.8	34.9	35.4	34.5
Hungary					
All gases	94.9	88.5	69.9	67.3	70.5
Natural gas	94.6	86.2	65.0	62.5	66.2
Poland					
All gases	91.7	83.3	71.9	70.0	65.8
Natural gas	83.8	70.8	53.2	52.6	46.4
Rumania					
All gases	100.8	100.6	96.9	97.0	96.1
Natural gas	100.8	100.7	96.6	96.8	96.4

Table 6.3 (continued)

The CMEA Seven and Selected OECD Countries;
Self-sufficiency in Gaseous Fuel

Domestic Production as % of Domestic Consumption

	1970	1975	1980	1981	1982
U.S.S.R.					
All gases	100.8	103.9	112.6	111.9	111.9
Natural gas	100.9	104.6	114.7	113.9	113.7
Austria					
All gases	79.2	68.9	53.2	46.4	47.7
Natural gas	66.8	57.4	40.2	31.9	32.7
Germany, Federal Republic					
All gases	93.4	60.1	52.1	53.7	51.9
Natural gas	84.0	41.9	32.1	34.8	32.6
United States					
All gases	98.6	97.4	95.0	96.5	95.6
Natural gas	98.3	97.3	94.9	97.0	96.4

Source: UN, 1982 Energy Statistics Yearbook, ST/ESA/STAT/Ser.J/26, New York, 1984.

gas mainly in order to lengthen the life of its domestic reserves, Bulgaria's and Czechoslovakia's domestic production of natural gas is insignificant. Hungary, Poland and the GDR are in-between these extremes.

COAL GASES

Poland and Czechoslovakia are major hard coal producers. The GDR is the greatest lignite producer in the world, and Czechoslovakia follows not far behind. The other countries also produce modest quantities of coal. Each country can therefore produce a great deal of coal gas (gasworks gas, coke-oven gas, blast-furnace gas). In 1982, these plus other gases (such as LPG, refinery tail gases, etc.) contributed almost 40 percent to self-sufficiency in gaseous fuels in Czechoslovakia, almost 20 percent in the GDR and Poland and slightly more than 10 percent in Bulgaria; only in the case of Hungary and Rumania was their contribution rather insignificant (see Table 6.3)

Polish hard coal mining produces a significant quantity of methane by the preventive degassing of coal seams.

In Table 6.3, Austria, the Federal Republic of Germany (FRG), and the United States are also presented for comparison.

THE CMEA SEVEN: CONSUMPTION PATTERNS

Rumania is in a class of its own in that gases cover more than half of its primary energy consumption. The GDR and Poland, at less than 10 percent, constitute the other extreme.

The GDR's gas percentage increased from almost nil in 1970 to almost 10 percent in 1982; Poland's, on the other hand, has been stagnating about 7 percent. Hungary's fast-rising gas percentage passed the 30 percent mark in 1980 (and so did that of the U.S.S.R., too). In the same year, Bulgaria and Czechoslovakia passed 10 percent. In each country, gas consumption is rising in both absolute and percentage terms, albeit at rather widely different rates.

As to per capita consumption, Rumania at about 78 gigajoules (GJ) was approximately equal to the U.S. in 1983. The U.S.S.R. topped 60 GJ/cap in 1983, rising fast. Hungary comes next at slightly less than 40 GJ/cap. Bulgaria, Czechoslovakia and the GDR form a fourth echelon at 20 GJ/cap; Poland brings up the rear with 10 GJ/cap. Clearly, the Rumanian energy economy is locked into gas (not on to petroleum, as is widely believed, and this despite its efforts to conserve gas reserves), and the Polish energy economy into coal; the other countries have all been shifting into natural gas, mainly into imports from the U.S.S.R., both for interfuel substitution and for covering new demand.

Per capita consumption is about the same in Austria as in Bulgaria, Czechoslovakia and the GDR; the FRG is halfway between these and the Hungarian examples.

As to the sectoral distribution of consumption (see Table 6.4), consumption by energy-producing industry plus conversion to other forms of energy consume roughly the same percentages in the countries shown, except for the very low Polish figure[2] and the rather high Austrian one. Electricity generation (largely in peak-load and emergency operation) uses rather more gas in the CMEA member countries than in the three OECD countries shown, and its share has been rising. The very low Polish figure reflects the emphasis on open-cast lignite in electricity generation. The high Hungarian percentage is due to the substitution for residual fuel oil in dual-fired power stations (the residual fuel oil saved is fed to a cat cracker).

Losses in transport and distribution seem statistically incomparable and are insignificant in any case.

For the rest, there seems to be a vague tendency for industrial use to decline toward a stabilization level of about 35 percent and for "other" consumption (the bulk of which is household use) to rise toward a saturation level of about 25 percentage in the CMEA Seven.[3] The sig-

Table 6.4

Breakdown of Fuel Gas Consumption (%) in 7 CMEA and 3 OECD Countries

Country	CSSR	GDR	Hun-gary	Po-land	Rum-ania	USSR	Aus-tria	FRG	U.S.
Year	1982	1983	1983	1983	1970	1980	1983	1983	1980
Conversion in & consumption by energy industry	33.8	35.6	33.9	23.2	35.8	30.8	39.5	29.0	31.7
Losses in transportation & distribution	1.5	4.0	.2	4.0	.2	1.9	1.4	–	.0
Consumption by non-energy industry including feedstock	39.3	35.0	44.1	56.5	42.9	54.1	41.0	43.8	22.1
Other consumption*	25.4	22.8**	21.8	16.8	11.1	12.9	18.2	30.7	35.1

* Households, agriculture, forestry, trade, catering, communal, transportation, storage and other minor uses.

** Includes "transfers" (9%), an item that is insignificant in the case of all the other countries shown.

Source: Authors' calculations based on UN ECE, Annual Bulletin of Gas Statistics of Europe, 1983, New York 1984, sales number E/F/R.84.II.E.28, and previous volumes of the same.

Remark: Given the prolixity of country notes and exceptions to the definitions in the source, the above figures should be considered as indicative only; for the details, see the source. "Year" is the latest year for which the source provides data.

nificantly lower "other" percentages of Poland, Rumania and the U.S.S.R. indicate a considerable potential for growth in this sector. The out-standing percentage of the U.S. is, of course, due to the widespread use of gas in space heating; the FGR also seems to be tending that way.

NATURAL GAS TRADE INTRA-CMEA

Table 6.5 shows the U.S.S.R.'s gas exports and imports in recent years. Apart from minor volumes exported by the GDR to the FRG and, until recently, by Rumania to Hungary, the U.S.S.R. is the only exporter in the CMEA group. Its most important customer at present is the FRG, followed by Czechoslovakia and Italy. The share-out of Soviet exports between the CMEA Six and Western Europe has been roughly half-and-half since 1976.

The pipeline system by which Soviet natural gas reaches the CMEA Six is shown in Figure 6.1.

The Brotherhood (Bratstvo) pipeline, of 720 mm diameter, takes Soviet gas from the border near Uzhgorod to Czechoslovakia and the GDR. It branches off into Hungary and Austria. The basic facility came onstream in 1967, but its throughput has been expanded greatly since by several addi-tions and new branches.

The Transit pipeline system is the Czecho-slovak section of the transport system taking Soviet gas to both Western Europe and some CMEA member countries. Between Velke Kapusany near the Soviet border and Plavecky Peter near the Austria border, it is a double string of 1220 mm pipe of 417 km length, operated at 75 kg/cm^2 pressure. From Plavecky Peter, a branch passes through Vysoka and Baumgarten into Austria. Between Plavecky Peter and Zlonice near Prague, there is a double string of 900 mm pipe of 340 km length, operated at 61 kg/cm^2 pressure. At Zlonice, the system splits into a branch to the GDR, and one to the FGR, through Rozvadov and Baumgarten. The total throughput of the Transit system was 3.9 BCF/D in 1983, including .39 BCF/D for Czechoslovakia. A third line has been added recently, to take Urengoy gas to the west, and a fourth one is being laid.

Table 6.5

U.S.S.R.'s Foreign Trade in Natural Gas (Thousand Terajoules)

	1975	1979	1980	1981	1982	1983	1984
Exports to other CMEA Member Countries							
Bulgaria		110.4	141.2	155.7	195.0*	190.0*	
Czechoslovakia		249.4	284.8	293.5	275.4	300.0*	
Germany, Dem.Rep.		150.0	209.5	221.0	216.7	217.2	
Hungary		95.1	132.0	133.1	130.1	135.7	
Poland		140.1	169.9	168.3	192.8	206.0	
Rumania		50.0*	60.0*	60.0*	60.0*	90.0*	
Subtotal		795.0	997.4	1031.6	1070.0*	1138.9*	
Exports to outside the CMEA							
Austria		118.2	122.9	160.0	119.6	98.6	161
Finland		38.2	35.9	28.5	26.9	26.1	28
France		94.3	138.4	161.7	143.2	140.6	174
Germany, Fed.Rep.		352.6	379.2	414.8	370.0*	383.0*	479
Italy		217.1	236.4	211.6	344.4	290.0*	295

Table 6.5 (continued)

U.S.S.R.'s Foreign Trade in Natural Gas (Thousand Terajoules)

	1975	1979	1980	1981	1982	1983	1984
Exports to outside the CMEA (continued)							
Yugoslavia		27.7	56.9	71.7	84.4	99.7	96
Subtotal		848.1	969.7	1048.3	1088.8	1038.3	1233
Total, exports	674	1643.1	1967.1	2079.9	2159.0*	2177.0*	
Imports							
Afghanistan		85.1	98.5	91.9	90.0*	90.0*	90*
Iran		210.7	8.6	-	-	-	-
Total, imports	433	295.8	107.1	101.8	96.7	90.0*	90*

*Estimates. Sources: UN, 1982 Energy Statistics Yearbook, ST/ESA/STAT/SER.J/26, New York 1984; UN ECE, Annual Bulletin of Gas Statistics for Europe, 1983, Sales No. E/F/R.84.II.E.28, New York 1984; Klaus Brendow, East-West Co-Operation in the Field of Energy: Facts, Factors, Perspectives, Internationale Tagung "Energie, Umwelt und Zusammenarbeit in Europa," Ottenstein, Austria, November 11-14, 1985.

Figure 6.1

Schematic diagram of pipelines taking Soviet natural
gas from the U.S.S.R. to the CMEA Six and to some
Western European countries

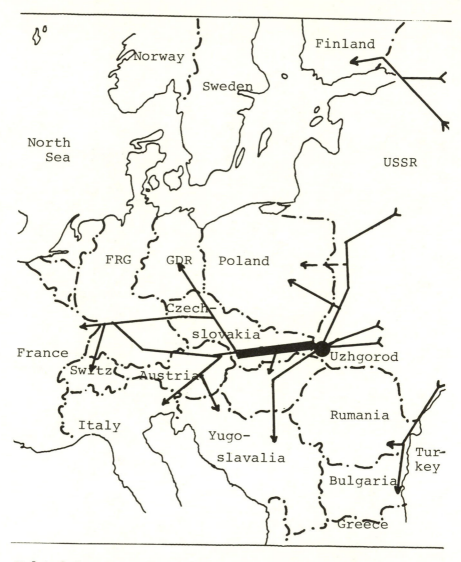

Updated from Izvestiya, Moscow, April 19, 1982, p. 1.

The Brotherhood and Transit lines have turned Czechoslovakia into the greatest gas transiter of the world. She also receives a great deal of gas in the form of transit and service fees and in repayment of her investment into line construction.

The Union (Soyuz or Orenburg) gas pipeline, of 1420 mm diameter and 76 kg/cm^2 operating pressure, connects in a length of 2677 km, the greatest natural gas and gas condensate deposit of the European U.S.S.R. at Orenburg, with the western border of the U.S.S.R. near Uzhgorod in the Soviet Carpathians. Its engineering was initiated in 1974. Construction began in 1977; the system came onstream in 1979. Its branches take .30 BCF/D a year of Orenburg gas each to Bulgaria, Czechoslovakia, the GDR, Hungary and Poland, and .16 BCF/D a year to Rumania.

A pipeline on the Union system's pattern, to be named Progress, is being contemplated from Yamburg to a point in the neighborhood of Uzhgorod. It would have about twice the length of the Union line and would double its supply capacity. Its deliveries to the CMEA Six may start in 1988 at the earliest.

INVESTMENT CONTRIBUTIONS

The Union pipeline system has so far been the most important joint construction project involving all the countries of the CMEA Seven. Its contractual and financial structure has a number of features sui generis, which distinguish it both from the normal run of joint venture and from the "gas-against-pipes" contracts that the U.S.S.R. concludes with the Western European countries.[4]

An investment contribution deal comes about when a supplier of a good within the CMEA declares itself ready to supply incremental quantities to those member countries which will import that good, but only on condition that the importers prefinance the facilities needed to generate/ transport the incremental output, by contributing capital goods, engineering, services of construction and installation, materials, etc. The would-be importers can either supply these goods and/or services themselves, or if they are loath or unable to do so, they may purchase them from other parties inside or outside the CMEA group. They may also extend credits in goods not directly related to the project, if the future host country agrees.

Investment contributions, then, are a specific form of international capital movement. They help to finance a certain form of joint undertaking based on the participating countries' community of interests, but they do not typically give rise to any joint ownership, either of assets or of equity. In this, they resemble credit flows rather than equity flows. They also guarantee supplies from the output of the facility to which the investment contribution has been made, typically for fifteen to twenty years; but then, any long-term mineral supply agreement worthy of the name does just that. Investment contributions help to maintain or indeed to boost the supplier country's propensity to export "hard" (dollar-worthy) goods against non-convertible currencies. They are thus to be regarded primarily as raw materials prepayments rather than as any other form of transaction.

Joint extractive-investment projects, such as the union pipeline, demand as a rule massive imports of goods and technology (pipe and compressors, to name just two) from the West, typically on credit of one form or another. In the Hungarian case, e.g., the direct dollar content of investment contributions extended to the other CMEA member countries (to the U.S.S.R. in their bulk) exceeded 50 percent in the 1970s.[5] These investment credits are repaid in transferable rubles (the common currency of the CMEA), over twelve years at 2 percent interest; by contrast, the normative rate of return on the same sort of investment in Hungary would be 10-12 percent, and its dollar content would be significantly lower. These drawbacks are offset partly only by the "counter-credits" that may be granted in other spheres by the country which has absorbed the investment contributions. Perhaps the most important point, however, is that the product of the project is typically delivered to the contributing partners at sliding-clause ("Moscow-formula") prices, whereas the investment contributions proper are non-floating-rate loans.

What the transaction boils down to, then, is that the importing country pays, to all intents and purposes, a preferential price in a mixture of hard and soft currencies (goods). Of course, the importing country greatly prefers doing so to paying the full world market price in some convertible currency: This is why the prophecies of the CMEA Six diverting increasing volumes of their purchases of fuels and raw materials to the developing countries or to the open markets have failed to come true.

PRICES

Gas deliveries by the U.S.S.R. to the CMEA Six are priced according to the comprehensive intra-CMEA pricing formula. Expressed in a much simplified way[6], the intra-CMEA price is the arithmetic average over five past years of a suitably identified world market price. This is the "Bucharest principle." Up to 1975, the "five past years" were typically the five years of the preceding Five-year Plan period, and the price thus averaged was changed once per five years, at the beginning of each new Five-year Plan period. Since 1975, the price is changed each year, and the "five past years" are simply the five years preceding the year of reckoning. This is the "sliding-price" or "Moscow" formula. By and large, the Moscow formula lags prices by two and a half years (assuming a uniform price rise rate). It therefore benefits the buyer in a rising market and the seller in a falling one.

The price of Hungarian imports of natural gas from the U.S.S.R. is related in Table 6.6 to the price of petroleum imports (a) from the same source and (b) from OPEC countries. The ratio of the two Soviet prices corresponds to the calorific-value ratio of the two fuels, by and large, and with fluctuations; the ratio of the Soviet gas price to the OPEC petroleum price, on the other hand, reveals how cheap, relatively speaking, the deliveries of Soviet gas come to Hungary.

Table 6.6

Pricing of Soviet Gas Supplies to Hungary
(annual averages, cif, as related to the prices of petroleum supplies
(annual averages, cif) by the U.S.S.R. and by non-CMEA sources)

	1976	1977	1978	1979	1980	1981	1982	1983	1984
Soviet crude (ton) to Soviet gas, thousand cu. m	1.52	1.56	1.57	1.64	1.25	1.32	1.25	1.25	1.44
OPEC crude (ton) to Soviet gas, thousand cu. m	3.21	3.00	2.49	3.16	4.64	4.38	3.58	3.21	3.43
Soviet gas price, forint* per cu. m	1.16	1.28	1.41	1.58	1.62	2.03	2.47	2.92	3.04

*Hungarian currency.

Source: Author's calculations based on Kozponti Statisztikai Hivatal, Budapest, Kulkereskedelmi Statisztikai Evkonyv (Yearbook of Foreign Trade Statistics), the relevant issues.
Remark: The movements of these figures reflect also the variations of the Hungarian exchange rates.

The third row of Table 6.6 reveals how, under the lagging influence of the Moscow formula, the Soviet gas price (and the petroleum price, for that matter) rose gently with no abrupt shocks but kept rising when the world market price had started to decline.

NATURAL GAS IN THE U.S.S.R.

RESERVES

The overall proven reserves of the U.S.S.R. (see Table 6.1) amounted to 39 percent of world proven reserves as of January 1985. Their statistical life (proven reserves over last year's production) was sixty four years at the time.

Proven and probable reserves as of 1983[7] totalled 1925 trillion (million million) cubic feet in the following distribution:

Urengoy	321	TCF
Yamburg	190	"
Bovanenkovskoye	166	"
Zapolyarnoye	104	"
Orenburg	64	"
Medvezhye	38	"
Other fields in Asian U.S.S.R.	799	"
Other European fields	243	"

At present, Urengoy is the biggest gas deposit in the world; its reserves exceed the entire proven North American reserves. The bulk of the reserves is in Western Siberia and, to a lesser extent, Soviet Central Asia (Kazakhstan, Uzbekistan, Turkmenistan). Orenburg and the "other European fields," of which those of the Komi region (Vuktyl and others of the same group) are the most important, make up just 16 percent of the total. The most important fields are identified in Figure 6.2.

Estimates of proven and possible natural gas reserves range from 2400 to 5200 trillion cu.ft.; geologic reserves have been estimated at 8000 trillion cu.ft. This, however, is not the last word. Soviet gas reserves increased more than fourfold between 1970 and 1985. Recently, too, reserves have been increasing satisfactorily. The two most hopeful groups of deposits are those of Astrakhan and Karachaganak, both close to Orenburg on the European border of the Asian U.S.S.R.

Also, the prospection of the Yamal, Gydansk and Taimyr peninsulas is far from achieved; subsequently, the Barents and Kara Seas and zones on- and offshore in the Eastern Siberian Arctic and on- and off-Sakhalin Island are also hopeful, even though their exploration and development will be a major challenge.

DEVELOPMENT, PRODUCTION

The production of natural gas and gas accompanying crude petroleum evolved as follows:

1960	1965	1970	1975	1980	1985 (Est.)
		Billion Cubic Feet/D			
4.62	13.03	20.21	29.58	44.45	70.13
Increment	8.41	7.17	9.36	14.86	25.68

In addition to the systems shown in Figure 6.2, there are a few minor ones further East; the system supplying the Norilsk mining complex in North Central Siberia, the one supplying the Yakutsk region in Eastern Siberia, the line, now being built, that is to take gas from Okha on Sakhalin Island in the Pacific to Komsomolsk-na Amure on the mainland, and the LNG terminal of .41 BCF/D capacity, now being built with Japanese cooperation, which is to come onstream in 1988.

At an estimate, in 1985, some 40.54 BCF/D will have come from Western Siberia, with the Urengoy deposit flowing at its name-plate capacity of about 22 BCF/D one year before the deadline. Soviet Central Asia as a whole contributes another 13.15 BCF/D or so, three quarters of it from Turkmenistan (mainly Sovetabad-Dauletabad-Donmez). The rest of the U.S.S.R.'s output comes from the Volga-Urals region (mainly Orenburg), from Komi (mainly Vuktyl) and several other minor producing areas.

The period 1981-85 saw the construction of 48,000 km of gas trunkline, typically 56-in.; at end-1985, the U.S.S.R.'s gas trunkline system will have a total length of almost 180,000 km. The basic pattern, shown in Figure 6.2, is made up of an outward-radiating center in Northwestern Siberia and an absorptive center in the Moscow region. It is a fairly straightforward system with few loops. The figure also emphasizes the very considerable importance of the Uzhgorod export node, which handles practically all the U.S.S.R.'s westerly exports, except those of Finland and the Balkans, and some of those to Poland.

Despite the favorable prospects of areas like Sovetabag, Karachaganak, Astrakhan, etc., and the longer-term hopes of Eastern Siberia, the Soviet Far East and the shelves, the key to gas development in the U.S.S.R. is clearly Western Siberia, at least up to the turn of the century and very probably beyond. Fortified by the consistent over-fulfillment of plans for gas production in this region, the Soviet government has prescribed a future escalation of production to 1990 and beyond, based on a program of "Siberian acceleration."[8]

In 1981-85, six 56-in. gas trunklines were built from Urengoy to the European U.S.S.R. Their fitting out with compressor stations is proceeding with some lag, but consumption at the delivery ends also takes time to build-up. Another six 56-in. gas trunklines from Yamburg this time, figure in the plan for 1986-90; in fact, however, the first of these, the Yamburg-Yelets line, will be more than half-completed by end-1985. One of the other five is to be the Progress line by which gas exports to the CMEA Six are to be boosted. Yamburg is to attain its design capacity of 21.7 BCF/D in 1990.

WESTERN SIBERIA: PROGRESS AND PROBLEMS

Gas production in Western Siberia began in 1966 at the deposits of Punga and Berezovo, and thence proceeded East to Vyngapur and North to

Figure 6.2

Schematic diagram of U.S.S.R.'s internal gas supply system
Updated from Izvestiya, Moscow, April 29, 1982, p.1.

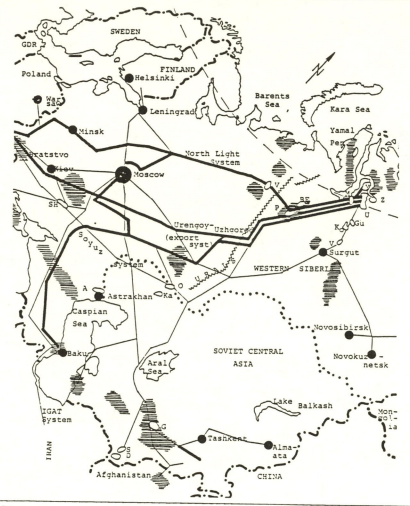

〃〃〃 Concentration of gas fields. Area is no indication of reserve size.

◯ Major or otherwise important gas field.

Pipelines built in 1981 through 1985. One bold line typically denotes a pair of 56-in. gas lines, although some sections are single-line.

Pipelines built pre-1981; typically less than 56-in. in diameter, although some sections, including the entire Soyuz system, are 56-in.

Symbols of individual gas fields. A = Astrkhan, BE = Berezovka, BO = Bovanenkovskoye, D = Dauletabad-Donmez, G = Gazli, GU = Gubkin, KA = Karachaganak, KO = Komsomolskoye, M = Medvezhye, O = Orenburg, P = Punga, SH = Shebelinka, S = Shatlyk plus Severo-Urengoy, Z = Zapolyarnoye, V = Vyngapur, Y = Yamburg.

Medvezhye, brought onstream in 1972, and Urengoy, already part way beyond the Arctic Circle. In addition to permafrost, impassable snows, and temperatures of minus 60°C in the winter and a plague of insects in the summer, which are standard fare in any Arctic region, development in Northwestern Siberia has to contend with most of the region being a waterlogged lowland swamp along two of the world's major rivers, the Irtysh and the Ob'. Here, gas has to be chilled or cooled after compression or otherwise the pipe will thaw out the permafrost and sink, and pipelines have to be weighed down as otherwise they will float up to the swamp surface when not under pressure. These are some of the reasons why infrastructure in the region used to be practically non-existent before the gasmen arrived, and natural population density is extremely low.

One of the Siberian problems is an embarras de richesse. The huge reserves demand -- and warrant -- a huge investment effort into gas and petroleum extraction and transportation. In fact, a considerable amount of gas is being produced in the petroleum regions; most of it is being flared, which is considered intolerable in the longer run. The gas wells produce a considerable amount of condensate (a condensate pipeline is being built from Urengoy to Surgut and Yuzhnyy Balyk). There is a considerable likelihood of sizeable petroleum reserves beneath the big gas deposits of Northwestern Siberia, etc. Given all this, plus the problems of access and egress, the region is oversaturated with projects; in other words, if the need for fast rising volumes of fuels were not so pressing, it would presumably be reasonable to develop Western Siberia at a more sedate pace.

In recent years, productivity growth in the fuel sectors of the European CMEA member countries in general has shown a marked decrease. After Poland, it is in the U.S.S.R. that the decrease has been the most striking.[9] Even though the specialist press in the U.S.S.R. tends to ascribe this, among other things, to inadequate coordination among the ministries involved in fuel production and backup activities.[10] the quality of management is unlikely to be significantly inferior in this sector, the less so since the leadership attributes such a strategic importance to fuels and energy. A greater part of the decline should in our view be attributed to the gathering natural (climatic and geographic) difficulties, not amenable to mitigation by any economic policy levers. Yet, clearly, the deterioration is certainly not altogether independent of the economic mechanism and of the ways and means of management. And it is precisely at this point that, by a confrontation of the petroleum sector's difficulties with the relative ease which which the gas industry fulfills and over-fulfills its plans, in the face of the very real and very considerable hardships enumerated above, one realizes <u>what an enormous natural windfall the Northwestern Siberian gas province is</u>.

Nevertheless, the decline of labor productivity is highly undesirable in a period when the labor force is growing very slowly overall, and when a great deal of new development is centered in regions with a profound shortage of labor, in Siberia and the Soviet Far East above all. Wage costs are further increased by the fact that, with the low sophistication of the social-cultural and physical infrastructure making these areas insufficiently attractive for settlement, there is a widespread practice of shifting personnel in and out at comparatively short intervals, with many workers spending only a season at a time at the most remote locations.

Even in the late 1970s, <u>the capital-output ratio</u> in the fuel and energy sector of the U.S.S.R. was forecast to double by 1990:[11] In view of the inhospitability of the environment and the growing geographic distance between the centers of production and consumption, this may well turn out to be too optimistic. And, even despite the new important finds in Soviet Central Asia close to the European U.S.S.R., the growing distance seems to be an inescapable fact of life: By the year 2000, more than 70 percent of the U.S.S.R.'s natural gas output is to come from Siberia and points east. On the other hand, taking fuel-guzzling industry to the sources of fuel runs the risk of being even more capital-intensive, even though it may well take some of the pressure off transportation infrastructure development.

In 1982, 40 percent of all industrial investment and 15 percent of all investment in the country was absorbed by the fuel sector. Capital demand rises at present by 5-6 percent per year on average for petroleum and by 3-4 percent for natural gas. Yet, between 1975 and 1985, extensive pipeline building turned gas into the most capital-intensive fuel.[12]

The growth of the capital intensity of direct extractive investment constrains the finance available for infrastructure even more. Between 1976 and 1980, e.g., in rapidly developing Western Siberia, non-productive investment made up just 19 percent of all investment, way below the U.S.S.R.-wide average.[13]

The Transportation infrastructure in the regions involved is seriously overloaded even though, between 1976 and 1980, investment into transportation increased by a factor of 2.5 over the preceding five years, and the Plan for 1981-85 envisaged a further fivefold increase. The focal idea of current development is getting the gas to the consumers and to the export markets as fast as possible. This is why, in Western Siberia for example, 80 percent of the investment into transportation is being spent on pipeline construction, with the building of compressor stations lagging behind. Moreover, in the northern part of the Tyumen region, the center of gravity of gas development, the cost of pipeline construction is 1.8 - - two times the cost in the European U.S.S.R. Given all this, investment into roads and railroads has remained inadequate. Optimally, roads should reach a gas field one year before its coming onstream. Today, more often than not, output has risen close to the peak rate by the time the road reaches the field. Machinery and materials are brought in in complicated ways, often by river routes involving repeated transshipments.[14]

These inadequacies tend to hamper the most rational, most intensive extraction especially of the deposits with several pay horizons. The in-

frastructural problem thus helps perpetuate a
creaming-off-type, low-efficiency extraction.
Reserve-wise, a development program proceeding
from South to North may permit this type of extraction to be sustained over many years still, but a
more deliberate program of extraction at higher
overall rates of recovery should likely significantly improve the returns on this enormous investment.

The inadequacy of infrastructure combines
with the other adverse factors to prolong construction; fixed assets brought onstream as a
percentage of funds spent had declined to 59 percent by 1980 as against 94 percent in 1975.[15]

All in all, infrastructure is at the same time
one of the principal villains and the principal
victims of the deteriorating efficiency and growing capital intensity of extractive industry, and
appears liable to remain the principal neuralgic
point of such industry in the U.S.S.R.

These inadequacies are further exacerbated by
an insufficiency of coordination especially harm-
ful in a region where most deposits contain natural
gas, condensates and petroleum. According to E.F.
Kozlov, the Party secretary of Urengoy town,
"There is no program as yet for the extraction of
all these deposits under a self-consistent program. No decision has been taken as to the complex
management of these tasks...at Urengoy, each of
the products gas, condensate and petroleum is
under different control, although the tasks concerning them are closely linked together."[16]

The symptoms of all this are painful enough:
shortages of energy in the big hydrocarbon regions, recurring particularly in the springtime,
an unreliable electricity supply, an inadequate,
remote and costly R&M base and, above all, a
shortage of dwellings and an insufficiency of
social and cultural infrastructure. These in turn
feed back into a reduced labor productivity, which
is mitigated by massive injections of assets; in
fact, the fixed asset renewal rate has been faster
in the fuel and energy sector than the industrial
average, especially in regard to machinery and
equipment.

The program for the complex development of petroleum and natural gas in Western Siberia in 1986-90,[17] which fits into the U.S.S.R.'s energy program up to the year 2000, is well aware of these problems. It prescribes that construction and installation in the petroleum and gas sector in Western Siberia is to be increased by a factor of 1.6 against the 1981-85 period. A considerable effort should render electric power supply more reliable. A broad-based program of construction of transportation infrastructure is scheduled, including the opening of the Novy Urengoy-Yamburg railroad in 1986. All this is to be backed up by an enhanced output of modern machinery and equipment for petroleum and natural gas development and production, a boost to dwelling construction and to the development of the social-cultural base.

* * * * *

The attitude of the Soviet government to Western Siberia was presented in some detail in First Secretary M.S. Gorbachev's speech at Tyumen.[18] Mr. Gorbachev stated that, in the Party's economic strategy, the development of this region was assigned an extreme importance. Accelerating the growth of the Soviet economy is predicated on the availability of the necessary volumes of petroleum and natural gas. This is why the accelerated growth of the forces of production in Siberia overall and in the Soviet Far East is so important an element of economic strategy. The efficiency and reliability of the country's fuel base is to be greatly increased, mainly by the intensification of the facilities available and by the deployment of modern science and technology. Huge sums and vast resources are to be made available for the purpose because a sufficiency of fuels and energy strengthens the country and accelerates its progress, whereas an insufficiency is like an illness.

In the Soviet gas industry, Mr. Gorbachev said, things were not going badly overall. Yet even here, lags are common in the bringing onstream of new facilities; the R&M base is inadequate, and so is road building; the overall production plan is

often fulfilled by over-producing the existing
wells. The lags in capital construction hamper the
solution of many a crucial task. Huge cost overruns in the "firefighting mode" have to be approved. Electric power supply to the region is not
reliable enough, nor is some of the machinery and
equipment introduced into the region. The scien-
tific base of the gas sector comes in for a good
deal of the blame. Although even in the 1981-85
Five-year Plan period, the construction of dwellings and social infrastructure has been faster
than elsewhere in the U.S.S.R., and wages have been
increased by appropriate multipliers, many who had
moved to the region have moved out again. "Siberia
must become more to the people than just a gigantic
construction site and workshop. If we cannot
render this region attractive, then all our plans
will remain so much paper" -- Mr. Gorbachev said.
    The personnel now engaged in the Siberian
development effort includes oil men from Tatariya
and Bashkiriya, builders from Georgia, Azerbaidz-
han, Moldavia, Armenia and Turkmenia working on
dwellings, social and cultural infrastructure and
roads. More than 150,000 members of the Komsomol,
the Party's youth organization, are working in the
region; students have performed work worth more
than 1.5 billion rubles. These forms of mobilization and participation are to be expanded further.
In Siberia more than anywhere else in the U.S.S.R.,
labor saving through more extensive electrifica-
tion and by the deployment of the most advanced
technology and the best machinery is crucial. By
the year 2000, construction volume in Siberia will
have doubled. The key thereto is a technical and
organizational overhaul of the material base of
construction.
    Mr. Gorbachev restated with some emphasis a
concept that had apparently been given up in recent
years, notably that energy-intensive production -
- metallurgy, the chemical industry, petrochemicals above all, microbiology (sic), pulp and
paper and the manufacturing of certain construction materials are to be relocated in Siberia and
the Soviet Far East, where raw materials and fuels
abound. Engineering in the region is to be re-
oriented: it should not be made to produce comparatively labor-intensive goods little related to

the needs of the region.   Raw materials are to
undergo a deep complex processing in the proximity
of the deposits.   The aim of industry siting is to
set up a network of mutually interdependent systems of production.   Highly efficient territorial
productive complexes of this sort permit savings
of 15-20 percent on investment capital and also
reduce operating costs.   To realize the importance
of all this, it should be recalled that fuels and
raw and basic materials contribute more than half
to the costs of social production in the country,
and that extractive industry is highly capital-
and labor-intensive. This is also why a transition
to an active policy of conservation is so crucial
for the growth of society as a whole.

TECHNOLOGY

The construction of these pipelines is not
just a pressing infrastructural problem.   It also
demands a substantial hike in technological sophistication in the backstopping industries, especially as regards the adaptation of drilling and
production equipment to the inhospitable or down-
right hostile conditions in which the new gas
deposits and the upstream segments of the pipelines are to be located. An engineering industry
that cannot keep up with the necessary (and
planned) development of new technology is unable
to offset the deterioration in environmental conditions.

Thereby hangs one of the widespread misunder-
standings connected with they hydrocarbons program
of the U.S.S.R., the issue of technological
dependence on the West.   The fact of the case is
that the Soviet factories can turn out first-rate
or good second-rate equipment for practically all
the needs of thehydrocarbon program; in fact, at
any time in the recent past, the demands of the
program have invariably exceeded the volume of
equipment purchased in the West, often by a wide
margin.   Yet business opportunities for Western
makers can confidently be predicted to persist,
among other things for line pipe, enhanced grades
above all, pipelaying equipment, compressors,
automation, pipe-manufacturing equipment, equipment for the handling of sour gas, etc.

GAS EXPORTS TO THE WEST

Gas exports from the U.S.S.R. to the countries of Western Europe were initially byproducts of the development of the intra-CMEA Brotherhood network, onstream in 1967. In fact, the first taker was Austria in 1968; only in 1973 was Austria followed by the FRG. Today, on the other hand, supplies of gas to Western Europe are a major commercial venture in their own right, although the supply systems to the CMEA Six on the one hand and to Western Europe on the other are to some extent interconnected and can serve as mutual backups.

The volumes contracted for by the Western European customers are as follows (in BCF/D):

| | pre-Urengoy[*] | from Urengoy[**] | |
		firm	optional
FRG	1.20	1.15	
Berlin/West		.07	
Italy	.77	.65	.22
France	.44	.93	
Yugoslavia	.33		
Austria	.27	.16	.11
Finland	.10		
Switzerland		.04	
TOTAL	3.11	3.0	.33

[*] Until 2000
[**] Until 2008

All these contracts (excluding the options, of course) are being executed.

The above-listed volumes of gas are delivered at just two transfer points, Baumgarten on the Austrian border of Czechoslovakia and Waidhaus on her border with the FRG. As the transiter of all this gas, Czechoslovakia is responsible to the U.S.S.R.

Yugoslavia has another contract running with the gas being transited through Hungary.

The pricing of Soviet gas is straight commodity type (that is, the price per unit of gas at the transfer point includes no separate fixed-cost and variable-cost components). Volumes taken are payable ex-post, with no take-or-pay provision, on a cif basis. The contracts include escalation clauses; apart from that, they have been renegotiated on ocasion.

The early contracts used to involve initial periods, typically seven years, over which supplies of equipment on credit to the U.S.S.R. (typically gas line pipe and gas and petroleum production equipment) were offset by a volume of gas at a price fixed ex ante. In a period of rising energy prices, this cost the U.S.S.R. some loss in windfall profits and was abandoned in favor of pricing with escalation clauses. At present, supplier credits extended by the Western suppliers of pipe and equipment are contractually independent of the Soviet deliveries of gas.

As to the reliability of the U.S.S.R. as a gas supplier, let us cite a Western view:[19]

"The U.S.S.R. has for many years been supplying volumes of natural gas to the FRG, France, Italy, Austria, Finland, and Yugoslavia. The U.S.S.R. has so far proved a responsible contractual partner as good as its word. The technical level of the Soviet gas economy, which today produces and distributes more natural gas than even the U.S., makes the technical risks appear minimal. Furthermore, the supply system consists of a number of parallel lines with hookups to a vast system of production and distribution within the U.S.S.R.

"This does not of course permit one to disregard the issue of a hypothetical stoppage of supplies. Yet even in the case of one, the situation can be brought under control:

• by exploiting the flexibility of existing import contracts with other suppliers,

• by exploiting the flexibility of domestic production and by resorting to buffer storage facilities, and

• by diverting dual-fired consumers to other fuels.

"It was found by a European Community study that, in the period 1985-90, a 25 percent drop in supplies, tantamount to the total failure of a natural gas source of the size of the Soviet supply component over a period of six months in the winter half of the year would cause no grave supply problems. An analogous study by the International Energy Agency gave a similar result."

In any case, since any stoppage of gas deliveries would entail a stoppage of payments as a matter of course, the U.S.S.R. would be hit as hard as its Western customers, and arguably even harder.

As to the U.S.S.R.'s role in satisfying future Western European gas demand, we agree that

(1) "incremental needs over and above current contracts and extensions will amount to between 3.28 BCF/D and 5.45 BCF/D by the year 2000,"[20] and

(2) the Netherlands is going to assume the role of swing producer to the Western European markets, making gas available under its flexible export contracts, to supplement cheaper baseload supplies at times of high winter demand, with today's exports in the 3.8 BCF/D range declining to 2.19 BCF/D by 2000; Norway is to be a high-cost high-price supplier of stagnating volumes, with the U.S.S.R. (possibly together with Algeria) increasingly becoming the baseload supplier at competitive prices, going for market share rather than high prices on limited volumes.[21]

The market is, in fact, liable to be constrained by demand growth rather than by a shortage of supplies on offer. In any case, demand growth from the view of the U.S.S.R. is limited by the notion that the NATO members' dependence on Soviet gas is to be held within "acceptable" limits, usually construed to mean 30 percent. There is, of course, no such limitation in the case of Austria, Switzerland, Finland, or Sweden. The main prospects for future Soviet gas sales are seen in (1) the deals currently being negotiated with Greece and Turkey; (2) penetration of the Swedish, Spanish, and possibly even the Netherlands, Belgian and

U.K. markets, and (3) most importantly of all, an expansion of sales to its current customers should a change of attitude permit a raising of the 30 percent limit. As to the technical feasibility of catering to such incremental demand, should the U.S.S.R. obtain the contracts for the entire upper-limit incremental demand of 5.4 BCF/D by the year 2000 cited above, it would have to build just another pair of 56-in. pipelines which, by the record of the Urengoy-Western Europe line, certainly is eminently feasible.

The issue of Soviet gas supplies to Japan and to Southeast Asia in general is a separate issue; any such demand will certainly not be satisfied from Western Siberia or Soviet Central Asia. Although supplies to Japan have so far been considered largely in LNG terms, a pipeline from, say, Sakhalin Island should be feasible despite the earthquake hazard. Supplies to South Korea should present no technical problem, either. The political issues, including right-of-way through North Korea and the four controversial islands held by the U.S.S.R., appear more potent than in Europe. Yet, given a new wave of detente, another 1.64-3.28 BCF/D market for Soviet gas may well develop in this region by the year 2000.

PRICE COMPETIVENESS OF SOVIET GAS

The two possible approaches are (1) theoretical, and (2) pragmatic. Theoretically, competitiveness is a major factor if the gas supplier stands or falls by the profits/losses of his contracted-for deliveries, and the impact of his exports on his profits/losses is readily ascertained thanks to the convertibility of the currencies involved. Neither of these conditions holds for the U.S.S.R.'s gas sales. The gas supplier is isolated from the export market by the foreign trade organization Soyuzgazexport, and his future depends largely on the plan targets it is given to fulfil; to no significant extent does it depend on the export proceeds of the gas sales. The task of Soyuzgazexport in its turn is to generate a cash flow in convertible currency, rather than just profits. In any case, since it is the profitability (more precisely, the terms of trade) of the entire convertible-currency-demoninated foreign trade of the U.S.S.R. that is at stake, it is not the export prices at large that matter but the import prices as well. In other words, there is a "U.S.S.R. Inc." effect just as much or more than a "Japan Inc." effect.

On the pragmatic side, the U.S.S.R.'s hydro-carbon sales have invariably been reasonably priced, following what the market could bear both upward and downward, with due regard to the volumes available for export, and with sustained export proceeds rather than short-term windfalls being regarded as the more important. It is therefore only logical to presume that Soyuzgazexport will continue to offer -- and, given sufficient reason, renegotiate -- prices and terms attractive enough to give it all the market share not foreclosed by political considerations.

PROSPECTS OF GAS IN THE U.S.S.R.

The 12th Five-year Plan (1986-90) and the long-term development plan up to the year 2000[22] afford some important insights into the changes that are to take place in the energy sector as a whole and in the gas sector in particular.

The targets for the 12th Five-year Plan (1986-90) include raising the output of fuels and raw materials by only 11-13 percent over the five years, as against a 25-28 percent increase in manufacturing output. The energy demand of growth is to be satisfied by strict conservation plus the accelerated development of nuclear energy, natural gas production and open-cast coal mining. By 1990, 200-230 million tonnes coal equivalent (MMTCE) of fossil fuels are to be saved as compared with 1985; of that, 75-90 MMTCE is to be replaced by nuclear energy. By 1990, electricity generation is to attain at least 1840-1880 billion kilowatts (kWh): at least 290 billion kWh is to come from nuclear power stations (an increase of about 25 percent for electricity overall and 160 percent for nuclear).

After a plan target of only 617 MMTCE for 1986, petroleum production is to attain 630-640 MMTCE by 1990 -- a quasi-stagnation, but the decline is to stop. After 73.64 BCF/D in 1986, gas production is to attain 91.5-93.15 BCF/D, up by 32-34 percent over the five years, or, in volume terms, by as much as between 1981 and 1985. New output is to come mainly from Yamburg, Karachaganak and Astrakhan; development is to focus on the Yamal peninsula; in the Caspian depression, the discovered deposits are to be brought into production mainly for feedstock purposes. The flaring of gas accompanying petroleum is to be reduced to 10 percent from the current 25-40 percent.

Coal production is to attain 780-800 MMT, up by 10-12 percent. In addition to the Kuznetsk, Ekibastuz and Kansk-Achinsk regions, some of the increase is to come from Eastern Siberia and the Soviet Far East.

The most important figure in the outline plan up to the year 2000 is that energy consumption per unit of national income produced (= net material product) is to be reduced to about 70 percent of today's figure, with conservation reducing unit demand by 20-25 percent. Nuclear power generation is to increase by a factor of 5-7; gas production, by a factor of 1.6-1.8. The use of renewable energy is to expand.

What does this spell for natural gas? A rough calculation gives till the year 2000 an aggregate production of about 14 trillion cubic meters, taking the upper limits given in both cases; 70 percent of that is to come from Western Siberia in the year 2000. Given these premises, the reserves of just Urengoy, Yamburg, and Medvezhye are to last till 2006 and, plainly, other deposits in Northwestern Siberia will also be developed in the meantime. Hence, the reserve base of gas development well into the next century is firmly in hand.

The flexible gas volume that is to be available can be calculated in a rough-and-ready manner on some simple assumptions. By flexible gas we mean the volume that can be freely used either for exportation, for freeing petroleum and petroleum products for export, or for reducing the expansion targets of other fuels. The assumptions in question are as follows:

•   Petroleum and product exports stagnate at the 1985 level.

•   Net coal exports stagnate.

•   Electricity exports remain negligible despite a growth of about 4 percent a year.

•   The committed gas export volume is roughly 9.86 BCF/D as of end-1985.

•   National income is to grow by 3.5-4.1 percent a year.

•   Energy consumption is to grow by 2.5-2.9 percent a year.

This calculation gives a flexible gas volume of 16.43 BCF/D by 1990. But even if the energy consumption of the given national income growth is to be 3.2-3.2 percent a year, the flexible gas volume will be 9.86 BCF/D by 1990. That is, the availability of further Soviet gas for export exceeds the likely growth in the market share open to the U.S.S.R. by a wide margin, even given that an estimated 2.19-2.74 BCF/D is earmarked for the CMEA Six, through the Progress pipeline to be built and possibly through other channels.

Let us underscore with some emphasis that the calculation which has led to the above results is a very simple one and should be regarded as an order-of-magnitude estimate only.

What it does make clear, however, is that the growth of the U.S.S.R.'s exportable fuel base will depend crucially on the success of the conservation effort.

It would be irresponsible as yet to attempt any calculation along similar lines up to the year 2000. It may, however, be confidently predicted that, provided import demands materialize, the Soviet gas industry will have sufficient flexibility to cater to it. This confidence is based not so much on sheer output growth, however impressive it is, as on the very considerable backup reserves and on the fact that a single pipeline can deliver up to 3.6 BCF/D today and may well be able to deliver 5.48 BCF/D in the 1990s. These figures are commensurate with expected demand growth in Western Europe up to the year 2000, and beyond.

NOTES

[1]The European member countries of the CMEA or Comecon group are Bulgaria, Czechoslovakia, the German Democratic Republic, Hungary, Poland, Rumania and the U.S.S.R. We shall call this grouping the CMEA Seven; the term CMEA Six shall mean these countries minus the U.S.S.R.

[2]Given the very low overall gas consumption of Poland, the idiosyncrasies of its distribution percentages are of little significance.

[3]The high percentage of the U.S.S.R. is surmised to be due to the statistical convention of exports also being carried under this item. Without them, the industry figure would be about 40 percent.

[4]The reader interested in the details of these transactions is referred to Tompe, Istvan, "On the economic nature of investment contributions between CMEA-countries, Acta Oeconomica, Budapest, Vol. 21, No. 4, pp. 313-323, and Balkay, Balint, Some macroeconomic aspects of the CMEA countries' mineral economy, Research Report No 105 of the Vienna Institute for Comparative Economic Studies, Vienna, April 1985.

[5]Cf e.g., Csaba, Laszlo, "A szocialista nemzetkozi penzugyi rendszer nehany kerdese" (Some issues of the socialist international monetary system), Penzugyi Szemle, Budapest, No. 4, 1979, p. 309.

[6]The reader interested in the details should peruse Balkay, B., op. cit.

[7]Spravochnik Gazovyye i Gazokondenzatnye Mestorozhdeniya (Directory of Gas and Gas Condensate Deposits), Nedra Publishers, Moscow, 1983.

[8] "Sibirskoye uskoreniye" (Siberian acceleration), Pravda, Moscow, October 7, 1982, p. 2.

[9] UN ECE, Economic Survey of Europe in 1981, sales number E.82.II.E.1, New York, 1982, p. 136.

[10] Shadrin, L.N., "Neftyanaya i gazovaya promyshlennost: ne pora li obedinitsya?" (Petroleum and gas industry: isn't it time they united)?, EKO, Novosibirsk, 1983, No. 1, pp. 44-51.

[11] UN ECE, Energy Investments Prospects to 1990 in the ECE Region, EC.AD.(XVII)/R.5, September 18, 1980, p. 27.

[12] Kononov, J.D., "Toplivno-energeticheskiy komplex v systeme narodnokhozyaystvennykh svyazey (The fuel-energy complex in the sytem of national economy links), EKO, Novosibirsk, 1983, No. 4, pp. 17-32.

[13] Ageeva, S., B. Orlov: "Nekotorye cherty investitsionnogo protsessa v zapadno-sibirskom neftegazovom komplekse" (Some features of the investment process in the Western Siberian petroleum-gas complex), Izvestiya Sibirskogo Otdeleniya Akademii Nauk SSSR, Novosibirsk, 1982, No. 11, pp. 85-89.

[14] "Tsena golubogo zolota" (Price of the blue gold), a roundtable discussion, EKO, Novosibirsk, 1983, No. 5, pp. 44-80.

[15] Ageeva-Orlov, op. cit., p. 87.

[16] "Tsena goluboga zolata," EKO, l.c.

[17] "V politbyuro CK KPSS" (In the Politburo of the CPSU's Central Committee), Pravda, Moscow, August 9, 1985, p. 1.

[18] "Razvitiye zapadno-sibirskogo kompleksa - obshchenarodnoe delo" (The growth of the West Siberian complex is a nation-wide matter), speech reported in Pravda, Moscow, September 7, 1985, pp. 1-2.

[19] Safoschnik, Rudolf, "Die Erdgasexporte der Sowjetunion und ihre Bedeutung fur Europa," The Financial Times European Gas Conference, Vienna, December 11-12, 1984, pp. 9.1-9.8.

[20]Gault, John C., "European Gas - the Salient Issues," Financial Times European Gas Conference, December 11-12, 1984, Vienna, pp. 1.1-1.10.

[21]Quinlan, Martin, "West Europe: Gas Market Poised for Further Growth," Petroleum Economist, London, February 1985, pp. 45-48.

[22]"Proekt - Osnovniye napravleniya ekonomicheskogo i sotsial'nogo razvitiya SSSR na 1986-1990 gody i na period do 2000 goda" (Draft outline of the U.S.S.R.'s economic and social development in the years 1986-1990 and to the year 2000), Pravda, Moscow, November 9, 1985.

7

Present and Future Problems
of Japan's LNG

Toyoaki Ikuta and Norio Tanaka

COMMENTARY

Japan's experience with gas is both important and instructive. The nation is wholly dependent on imports of oil and gas, and of coal. It has long had a set of energy policies which have had three objectives:

(1) To diversify fuels by type and by source to limit damage to itself from supply disruptions;

(2) to obtain fuels at the lowest possible cost, and

(3) to pursue programs of improved energy efficiencies and to deal with the environmental effect of fuels.

In each of these, natural gas has been important. The special situation of Japan without pipeline links to suppliers forced the nation to look to LNG supplies to meet its gas needs (against the three guidelines noted above). The authors make clear the reasons why LNG had been an attractive fuel. They then make very clear that LNG's price has to be renegotiated in light of reduced demand and lower prices for competing fuels, matters which were principal ingredients in the earlier chapter by Gerald B. Greenwald.

In coping with this problem, Japan has one unique advantage: It is still the sole buyer of LNG from all sources around the Pacific Basin and the only likely major buyer of LNG from the Middle East Gulf. Without that Japanese market, where else could LNG suppliers turn? In the next period, other buyers are expected to emerge: Hong Kong, Taiwan, South Korea but these, cumulatively, will not come close to matching the Japanese market. Only if China

(PRC) should import LNG for certain coastal needs might Japan find its rival.

The authors then take up a theme expressed in the chapters dealing with the European and U.S. gas markets, and with all suppliers of piped gas and LNG: The emergence of intense price competition between fuels and the necessity of gas suppliers remaining more than competitive with oil and gas. This is a new phenomenon and the warning that Japan expects present and prospective LNG suppliers to take notice has to be taken with great seriousness. If it is not, then the possibility of additional supplies from Alaska, or the beginning of LNG exports from Canada, to take two examples, disappears.

Periodically, mention is made of the possibility of an eventual Soviet gas supply piped to Japan from Siberian reserves. These gas assets are not yet sufficiently developed to be surplus to Soviet needs, but some day they will. And when they do, Japan will have some very difficult decisions to make, probably against U.S. views. U.S.S.R. gas could, if the Soviets wished to, be the most economically attractive alternative to LNG. That time is not now but even the possibility should give added reasons to LNG suppliers' thinking about the price (and front end capital costs) of their LNG delivered to Japan.

-- Editor --

BACKGROUND OF LNG GROWTH IN JAPAN

Japan began importing LNG in 1969 and the volume of LNG consumption has grown steadily since then (see Table 7.1). In 1984, these imports accounted for 60 percent of all international LNG trade. At 3.7 BCF/D of imports of LNG in 1984, these had come to account for 8.7 percent of Japan's total primary energy. But as shown in Table 7.2 this LNG share in Japan's primary energy is very low compared with the gas used in the United States and Western Europe. The main reasons for the growth in Japan's use of LNG are to be found in many causes.

After shifting into high gear in the mid-1960s, Japan's economy recorded an average annual growth of 9.5 percent until the first oil crisis of

185

Table 7.1

Japan's LNG Imports
(unit: 106 CF/D)

Name of Project F. Year	Alaska	Brunei	Abu Dhabi	Indonesia	Malaysia	Total
1969	26	--	--	--	--	26
1970	138	--	--	--	--	138
1971	137	--	--	--	--	137
1972	123	28	--	--	--	151
1973	139	194	--	--	--	333
1974	135	397	--	--	--	532
1975	143	555	--	--	--	699
1976	132	701	--	--	--	832
1977	143	742	100	178	--	1,163
1978	135	747	167	599	--	1,648
1979	135	782	206	972	--	2,095
1980	123	764	282	1,223	--	2,392
1981	142	727	284	1,243	--	2,397
1982	143	733	305	1,299	15	2,495
1983	147	752	256	1,502	253	2,910
1984	139	735	298	2,057	536	3,765

Source: "The Summary Report, Trade of Japan," by Japan Tariff Association.

Table 7.2

Share of Natural Gas in Total Primary Energy Consumption
(unit: %)

	1955	1965	1970	1975	1976	1979	1980	1981	1982	1983	1984
Natural gas produced in Japan	0.4	1.2	0.9	0.7	0.7	0.6	0.6	0.6	0.6	0.6	0.6
Imported LNG	-	-	0.4	1.8	4.0	4.9	5.5	5.7	6.4	7.2	8.7
Total	0.4	1.2	1.3	2.5	4.7	5.5	6.1	6.3	7.0	7.8	9.3
U.S.			31	30	30	30	27	28	27	25	24
West Germany			17	18	20	20	17	16	15	15	16
United Kingdom			18	20	20	21	22	21	22	24	25

Source: Agency of Natural Resources and Energy, etc.

1973. During this period of rapid growth, the demand for primary energy had expanded at an astonishing annual rate of 11.0 percent. Similarly, electric utilities realized 11.8 percent annual gains in their market, while the demand for city gas grew 10.5 percent a year. It was primarily this steep increase in the overall demand for energy that stimulated the demand for LNG and the launching of projects to obtain it. However, LNG demand was also given a boost by the superior economy this fuel demonstrated at electric power plants and gas production plants, especially after 1973, as shown in Table 7.3.

Persuaded that LNG was cheaper, cleaner, and more reliably available than the petroleum fuels (crude oil, naphtha, residual heavy oil) which they were burning for the bulk of their power generation, electric utilities began switching over to LNG in earnest. It is also very significant that city gas utilities found the manufacturing cost of gas derived from LNG to be lower than that of manufactured gas using naphtha or LPG. They tried, therefore, to convert to the former.

In the past, LNG simply proved itself able to produce cheaper electricity and cheaper city gas than was possible burning oil. This was enough for LNG to be seen as economically superior to oil (see Table 7.3.)

Thus, by 1984, about 94 percent of Japan's 4 BCF/D of natural gas consumption was met by importing LNG. The electric utilities share of LNG consumption was 76.7 percent, and town gas' share was 21.2 percent in 1984, as shown in Table 7.4. (These percentages are compared with those of other industrialized countries as in Table 7.2 and Figure 7.1.)

MITI's EVALUATION OF LNG

An excerpt of MITI's interpretation of LNG policy is as follows:

(1) In the past, LNG has been imported mainly because of its convenience and supply stability both for electric and gas utilities, and for being economical, especially for gas utilities.

188

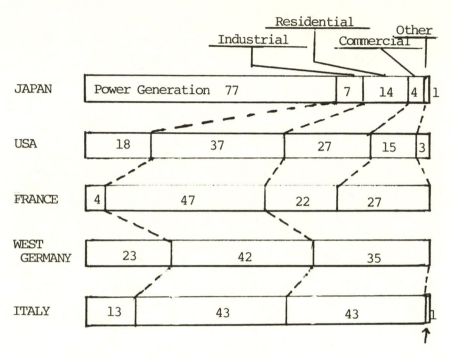

Figure 7.1

Natural Gas Demand by End-Use Sector
of Japan, United States & European Countries
(Unit: %)

Note: Residential sector for West Germany
and Italy includes commercial sector.

Source: OECD, Annual Oil & Gas Statistics, 1983.

Table 7.3

Prices of LNG and Crude Oil in Japan

Fiscal Year	LNG $/10^6$BTU	CRUDE OIL $/B	CRUDE OIL 10^6BTU	LNG / CRUDE OIL
1969	0.52	1.8	0.31	168
1970	0.52	1.8	0.31	168
1971	0.52	2.6	0.44	118
1972	0.55	2.6	0.44	125
1973	0.70	4.8	0.82	85
1974	1.49	11.5	1.97	76
1975	1.71	12.0	2.05	83
1976	1.89	12.7	2.17	87
1977	2.16	13.7	2.34	92
1978	2.41	13.9	2.38	101
1979	3.30	23.1	3.95	84
1980	5.57	34.6	5.91	94
1981	5.87	34.6	5.91	99
1982	5.75	34.1	5.83	99
1983	4.96	29.7	5.08	98
1984	4.93	29.1	4.97	99

Calculated by 13.000 Kcal/kg for LNG and 9.270 Kcal/kg for crude oil.

(2) Looking at the current situation, LNG pricing seems to continue to be equivalent to the price of crude oil on a thermal basis; however, pricing in the future will depend, to some extent, on the Japanese attitude toward gas negotiations, since Japan currently accounts for about 60 percent of the world LNG trade.

(3) Gas utilities should continue to switch from burning petroleum products to LNG.

(4) As for the electric utilities, it is realistic to expect only a slight increase in LNG demand, as long as LNG cannot assert a price advantage.

(5) In the foreseeable future, supply of LNG will be paced in accordance with demand forecasts. There are two fundamental tasks for LNG development; one is to review the existing rigid pricing formula which links LNG prices to crude oil prices; the other is to modify the supply condition, which now requires a "take or pay" clause.

ATTITUDE TOWARD LNG OF THE TWO TYPES OF UTILITIES

ELECTRIC UTILITIES

Recently, electric utilities have taken less interest in LNG. The following may explain the reasons:

a. Expected demand for electricity has been revised downward year by year.

b. Rigid LNG supply conditions cannot meet seasonal demand fluctuations.

c. The advantages of LNG, such as stability of supply and cleanliness, have significantly been reduced because of lessened apprehension about the adequacy of energy supplies and the progress being made in environmental protection technology.

d. LNG-burning generating plants have already been established in almost all

Table 7.4

LNG Consumption in Japan for Each Use
(Unit: 106 CF/D)

	1977	1978	1979	1980	1981	1982	1983	1984	Share in 1984 (%)
Town Gas	340	380	435	472	480	527	680	797	21.2
Electric Power Generation	807	1,214	1,530	1,820	1,824	1,887	2,141	2,886	76.7
Industrial	13	30	89	73	80	81	81	79	2.1
Total	1,160	1,624	2,054	2,365	2,384	2,495	2,902	3,762	100.0

Source: Agency of Natural Resources and Energy MITI.

places requiring clean energy, such as Tokyo, Osaka, and Chubu Electric Utilities.

e.   The electric utilities, together with MITI, estimate nuclear power and coal to be less expensive than LNG. MITI's cost estimates in 1984 are shown in Table 7.5.

Table 7.5

Costs of Generating Power Plants in Japan

	Construction Cost (Thousand Yen/kW)	Generating Cost (Yen/kWh)
Hydro	630	21
Residual oil	140	17 (75)*
LNG	190	17 (65)
Coal	240	14 (40)
Nuclear	310	13 (25)

*Figures in parentheses indicate % of fuel costs.

f.   The Japanese electric utilities have the goal of establishing the "best mix" of fuel for power generation in which LNG-burning plants are expected to be built for medium load requirements. It is most likely, therefore, that further construction of LNG-fueled plants will be curbed in the near future (see Table 7.6).

Therefore, the electric utilities in Japan are not expected to change their key strategy, shown in Table 7.6, of heavy dependence on nuclear power and coal for planned increases in power generation capacity, unless LNG suppliers can demonstrate a greater incentive to use LNG.

Table 7.6

Electricity Supply Target
(Unit: billion kWh)

	1982	1990	1995	2000
Nuclear	101.8 (19.5)	190 (28)	285 (35)	370 (39)
Coal	35.5 (6.8)	65 (10)	95 (12)	140 (15)
LNG	79.2 (15.2)	165 (24)	170 (21)	170 (18)
Hydro	77.4 (14.8)	92 (13)	101 (13)	110 (12)
Geothermal	1.0 (0.2)	4 (0.6)	10 (1)	20 (2)
LPG	5.9 (1.1)	10 (2)	10 (1)	
Petroleum	203.9 (39.0)	140 (20)	115 (14)	115 (14)
Others	17.8 (3.4)	19 (3)	19 (2)	25 (2)
Total	522.5 (100.0)	685 (100.0)	805 (100)	950 (100)

GAS UTILITIES

As for gas utilities, the following limitation on supply capacity should be remembered. Only Tokyo, Osaka, and Toho Gas Co. can handle LNG, while other local utilities lack the technology, gas demand, and supply systems appropriate to receiving LNG. So that only local utilities which are located in the vicinity of the above "big three" can be provided with gas derived from LNG mainly by way of the large utilities' trunk lines. The 1983 total gas volume supplied by the big three was .874 BCF/D and the volume of LNG imported by the three in 1984 was .790 BCF/D. The ultimate supply capacity of the big three is expected to be equivalent to 2.1-2.1 BCF/D. Of that capacity, however, at most 80 percent (1.6-1.8 BCF/D) will be supplied by LNG, because of the rigidity of LNG supply arrangements and the other policy of diversification of fuels.

Note that this discussion is based on the existing limited domestic pipeline networks and regasification sites. It should also be noted that the gas utilities have contracted to import one BCF/D of LNG from the U.S., Brunei, Indonesia, and Australia. Thus, the additional required capability of gas utilities to receive these new LNG supplies is calculated to be in the range of 0.6-0.7 BCF/D.

FORECAST OF NATURAL GAS SUPPLY-DEMAND BALANCE

SUPPLY SIDE

Japan's comparative shopping for LNG around the world is almost at an end, at least for forecast demand by 1990. Total supply by 1990 is to be 35.39 million tons (MT) as shown in Table 7.7. It consists (1) of the operating units of Alaska .14 BCF/D (0.96 MT), Brunei .67 BCF/D (5.14 MT), Abu Dhabi 0.3 BCF/D (2.06 MT), Indonesia 2 BCF/D (14.00 MT), and Malaysia 0.8 BCF/D (6.00 MT). (2) The planning projects of Australia .56 BCF/D (5.84 MT) and Canada 0.3 BCF/D (2.35 MT) are also included in this volume. As shown in Table 7.8, such other sources as Qatar 0.8 BCF/D (6.00 MT), Thailand 0.4

Table 7.7

LNG Projects Operated or Planned by Japan
(As of April 1984) (Unit: 1,000 tons)

	Source	Contract Volume (per year)	Date When Import Started	Contract Period (year)	1980	1985	1990	Remarks
Projects Now Operating	Alaska	960	11/69	15+5	872	960	--	Extended by 5 Yr.
	Brunei	5,140	12/72	20	5,418	5,140	5,140	
	Abu Dhabi	2,060	5/77	20	2,001	2,060	2,060	
	Indonesia	7,500	8/77	20	8,674	7,500	7,500	
	Malaysia (Sarawak)	6,000	1/83	20	---	4,500	6,000	
	Indonesia (Badak)	3,200	9/83	20		3,200	3,200	
	Indonesia (Arun)	3,300	1/84	20		3,300	3,300	
Sub Total (A)		28,160			16,965	26,660	27,200	
Projects Being Planned	Canada	2,350	7/89	20			2,350	Under Negotiation
	Australia	5,840	10/89	19			5,840	Tempor. Signed
Sub Total (B)		8,190					8,190	
Total (A) & (B)		36,350			16,965	26,660	35,390	
(In terms of BCF/D)		4.8			2.3	3.5	4.7	

Table 7.8

Newcomers: Planned LNG Project not Committed by Users
(Unit: 1,000 ton)

	Source	Contract Volume	Date When Imports Start	Contract Period			1990s	Remarks
Projects Available	U.S.S.R. (Sakhalin)	3,000	Early	20			(3,000)	
	Thailand	2,000–3,000	Early 1990s	20			(2,000–3,000)	LESS
	Qatar	6,000	Early 1990s	20			(6,000)	CERTAIN
	Alaska (Prudoe Bay)	1,500–10,000	Early 1990s	Undecided			(1,500–10,000)	
Total							(12,000–23,500)	Subject to Future Developmt.

BCF/D (3.00 MT), Alaska 2 BCF/D (14.00 MT) and Sakhalin 0.4 BCF/D (3.00 MT) are under negotiation or in the earlier stage of prefeasibility studies.

DEMAND SIDE

The demand of electric utilities for LNG is expected to almost level off after 1990 as shown in Table 7.9. A steady increase in LNG demand by gas utilities is expected even after 1990, due mainly to the exceptional upsurge in the industrial sector demand. But the share of natural gas in the industrial sector was only 7 percent in 1983, compared with 37 percent in the U.S. and about 40 percent in Western Europe in 1983 shown in Figure 7.1 and Table 7.6 summarizes a forecast investigation conducted by the Electric Utility Deliberative Committee in November, 1983.

Table 7.9

LNG Demand Forecast
(Unit: BCF/D)

	1984	(mt)	1990	(mt)	1995	(mt)	2000	(mt)
Electric Utilities	2.74	(19.4)	4.09	(29.0)	4.23	(30.0)	4.23	(30.0)
Gas Utilities	0.79	(5.6)	1.02	(7.2)	1.35	(9.6)	1.56	(11.1)
Other Industry	0.03	(0.2)	0.04	(0.3)	0.06	(0.4)	0.06	(0.4)
Total	3.56	(25.2)	5.15	(36.5)	5.64	(40.0)	5.85	(41.5)

FORECASTS

Japan's energy market has drastically changed since the two oil crises. Japan's LNG projects, after having followed a straight path of steady expansion, are now at a turning point. Annual economic growth in terms of GNP has fallen off to an average of 3.9 percent since the 1973 oil

crisis. Total demand for primary energy has lev-
eled off in the same period essentially to zero
growth. Moreover, growth in demand for city gas
and electricity has slowed dramatically to 5.5
percent and 2.4 percent, respectively. Thus it is
impossible to avoid the feeling that Japan's energy needs is destined for a period of decelerating
growth rates.

THE PROBLEM OF LNG PRICING

Looking back over the fifteen years as shown
in Table 7.3 and Figure 7.2, prices of LNG shipped
to Japan, tightly linked with crude oil prices on
a CIF basis, have been much higher than those in the
U.S. and Western Europe.

However, this record does not imply that the
Japanese market is willing to continue receiving
LNG tagged at a high price. The more the share of
LNG climbs, the more the so-called premium market
disappears.

For instance, in the case of the Japanese city
gas industry, substitution of LNG for petroleum
products had been advantageous to gas-making because regasification of LNG requires only negligible energy, while a 15 percent energy loss is
inevitable in the gasification of petroleum products. This advantageous aspect of LNG has declined as the share of LNG has grown. In addition,
one of the other relative advantages of LNG --
cleanliness -- has been reduced because of the
progress being made in environmental protection
technology.

In the field of gas marketing, LNG price
conditions have become tougher in accordance with
the expansion of the gas share. Most "premium
markets" have already been converted from petroleum to city gas derived from LNG.

In sum, it should be noted that even though
Japan has imported LNG on terms more expensive than
the international standard, the past willingness
to do so can't be taken as a signal for the future.

Note that gas demand for industrial use is
expected by MITI to climb at an annual rate of 6.6
percent during the period 1982-95, compared with
4.1 percent and slightly more than 2 percent for

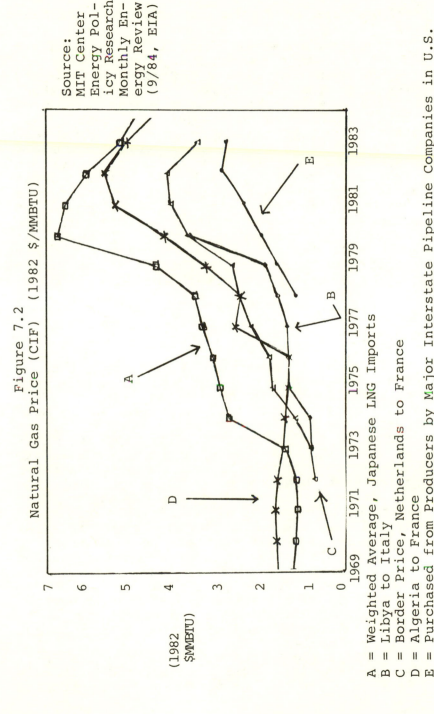

Figure 7.2
Natural Gas Price (CIF) (1982 $/MMBTU)

Source:
MIT Center
Energy Pol-
icy Research
Monthly En-
ergy Review
(9/84, EIA)

A = Weighted Average, Japanese LNG Imports
B = Libya to Italy
C = Border Price, Netherlands to France
D = Algeria to France
E = Purchased from Producers by Major Interstate Pipeline Companies in U.S.

total gas demand and total primary energy, respectively.

In the case where crude oil is imported at $28/BBL and market prices for petroleum products are set on a cost basis, LNG priced below 103 percent of crude oil prices looks to be about competitive with kerosine in the industrial market. It should be noted, however, that actual market prices of petroleum products have been below a cost basis because of the slack oil market. Thus, LNG salesmen have found themselves in a tough situation. The decline in crude oil prices, as most energy experts expect, will put LNG prices under even greater strain. LNG priced at 98 percent of crude oil prices can theoretically penetrate the petroleum market. However, it should also be acknowledged that when the net calorific value is applied, LNG pricing is the loser by about 5 percentage points.

THE KEY FACTOR -- HOW TO CURB THE COST OF NEW LNG PROJECTS

In order to present LNG pricing mechanisms suitable for penetrating the Japanese energy market, attention has to be given to trends in the capital costs of the LNG business. While some experts have been paying much attention to cost overruns of nuclear plants, stressing the five-fold real increase in the average per kilowatt construction cost from 1971 to the 1980's another nightmare has been emerging in the field of LNG.

Before the first oil crisis, the capital cost per one million tons of LNG was in the vicinity of $100 million, whereas a project completed after the second oil crisis cost around five times as much. What is worse, the projects being planned require more than ten times as much capital cost as one completed in the early 1970s.

As a matter of course, a cost overrun narrows the profit for the exporter and widens the gap in prices between LNG and competing energy in the importer's market.

Finally these trends will make new LNG business impossible. This circumstance will have greater force in the face of sluggish energy demand

and declining oil prices. The only conclusion is
that the key to a brighter future for LNG trade with
Japan lies in all-out efforts to slash the capital
cost of these projects.

8

Canadian Natural Gas Trade with the United States: A Case Study

Daniel E. Gibson and Mason Willrich
With the substantial assistance of Thomas Wander, Senior Resource Analyst,
Fuels Policy Planning and Analysis Department, Pacific Gas and Electric Company

COMMENTARY

A common feature in appraisals of natural gas is the general perspective of the private sector. What follows is, however, a highly unusual and specific account about gas as experienced by one of the largest U.S. utilities -- the Pacific Gas and Electric Company which is also the single largest U.S. importer, by far, of Canadian gas. It is one matter to think of gas in market generalities, it is another to view the fuel from "within," as it were.

Several points about the chapter deserve emphasis. First, there is explicit reference to the extent that changing national energy policies in both the United States and Canada have greatly affected PGandE. These changes have not been evolutionary but cyclical which has given problems to all buyers and suppliers. With abrupt reversals of public policy it is extremely difficult to make long-term investments into this crucial fuel, and long-term commitments are vital.

Second, there is explicit reference to the revolutionary impact upon gas pricing and prices as a consequence of levels of energy demand, competition between fuels and suppliers and the need to relate short-term phenomena to long-term supply needs. That revolution is by no means over for the United States. A crucial question remains: When (and if) the so-called U.S. gas "bubble" disappears, and supply is deemed short, will the public policy of the United States change once again, returning to the regulation of prices, apportionment of supplies, and changes in the roles of gas companies -- both suppliers and buyers?

-- Editor --

INTRODUCTION

Canadian natural gas exports to the United States comprise only about 5 percent of total U.S. natural gas consumption. Nevertheless, it is a vital portion of the gas supply to those parts of the U.S. it serves -- in particular, California, the upper middle west, and certain areas in the northeast -- and its role in those regions has been shaped by market and regulatory forces in both Canada and the U.S.

The international and national events which have affected Canadian gas exports have been reviewed in many publications. This chapter focuses on the role of Canadian gas in California which has been, and presently remains, the largest export market presently for Canadian gas exports. The emphasis is on the period from the mid-1970s to 1985. This period saw profound and continual changes in world, Canadian, and U.S. energy supply, price and market conditions, and in the government actions responding to them. The account shows how Canadian gas exports have gone full swing from contracts with terms and prices which were negotiated in response to market conditions, to government-imposed terms and prices, to again, by the end of 1985, market responsive prices. But the market of the mid-1980s is far different from that of the early 1970s.

In this chapter, the market for natural gas in northern and central California and Pacific Gas and Electric's (PGandE's) role in supplying that market are briefly summarized. Next, the construction of the Alberta-California Pipeline Project is described. This was the first large international gas pipeline that opened the way for U.S.-Canadian natural gas trade and it remains a vital element in the planning of future Canadian frontier, as well as Alaskan, gas resources. Thereafter, the effects on PGandE's gas market of the U.S. natural gas shortage experienced during the late 1970s and the role of Canadian gas in mitigating these effects is discussed. Canada has proven itself to be a reliable supply source. The energy price shock and the regulation of the Canadian border price is then reviewed, focusing on the U.S. regulatory response and the cumulative effects of this interaction on PGandE's Canadian gas purchase contracts and purchasing policies. The market response and actions the Canadian government and gas producers took to remain competitive in the declining and increasingly price sensitive market in the U.S. are then outlined. Finally, it is concluded that Canadian, as well as U.S., natural gas suppliers must remain competitive if they are going to retain their position in the marketplace -- at least in the California markets served by PGandE.

PGandE's NATURAL GAS MARKET AND SUPPLY STRATEGY

PGandE is a combination gas and electric utility serving customers throughout northern and central California. The San Francisco Bay Area and central Sacramento-San Joaquin valleys are the heart of PGandE's service territory which covers most of northern and central California, an area of 94,000 square miles encompassing a population of ten million people. Natural gas is sold directly to over three million retail and wholesale customers. Furthermore, large quantities of gas are used in PGandE's own oil/gas-fired power plants to generate electricity for PGandE's 3.7 million electric customers.

Historical data for 1973-84 concerning PGandE's natural gas market are shown in Table 8.1. For 1983-84, 67 percent of PGandE's total gas deliveries, averaging 1180 million cubic feet per day (MMCF/D), were direct sales to customers, apart from the Company's own power plants. Thirty one percent, or 540 MMCF/D, were residential customers. The remaining 36 percent were sales to commercial, industrial, and wholesale customers. PGandE's Gas Department sales to the Electric Department for use in power plants and other uses, such as compression fuel, accounted for the remaining 33 percent of deliveries. As indicated in Table 8.1, PGandE's interdepartmental use can swing dramatically from year to year as a result, primarily, of the availability of hydroelectric power generation, e.g., in 1983.

Table 8.1 shows a dramatic decline in sales to customers, from 708.7 BCF in 1973 to 430.6 BCF in 1984 -- a 39 percent decrease over the eleven year

Table 8.1

PGandE's Natural Gas Market in BCF Per Year[1]

Year	Interdepartmental[2]	Sales to Customers	Non-Residential[3] Sales
1973	272.4	708.7	453.3
1974	161.5	671.6	429.9
1975	189.3	670.9	408.5
1976	221.2	610.9	367.6
1977	235.0	557.9	334.2
1978	163.2	513.1	293.0
1979	237.3	600.2	365.9
1980	219.7	558.2	342.0
1981	299.3	531.3	335.7
1982	223.3	482.5	269.5
1983	179.4	433.3	232.5
1984	248.8	430.6	235.5
1985 (est)	257.3	499.0	284.4

[1]Source for 1973-1984 is PGandE's Annual Financial and Statistical Report.
[2]Consists of PGandE's own gas use, primarily power plant fuel use.
[3]Consists of commercial, industrial, and wholesale sales.

Table 8.1 (Continued)

PGandE's Natural Gas Market in BCF Per Year

Year	Residential Sales	Average Annual Residential Consumption in MCF	Residential Cost as Percent of Average Customer Cost
1973	255.4	113	137
1974	241.7	105	129
1975	262.4	111	112
1976	243.3	101	98
1977	223.7	91	89
1978	220.1	87	89
1979	234.3	90	92
1980	216.2	82	91
1981	195.6	73	89
1982	213.0	78	89
1983	200.8	73	91
1984	195.1	70	96
1985 (est)	214.6	N/A	N/A

period. This trend began to change during 1985 as the market responded to lower rates and sales to the new cogeneration and enhanced oil recovery (EOR) markets develop. Nevertheless, PGandE's direct gas market today is only 70 percent of what it was in 1973, at the start of the energy shortages and price shocks that reverberated throughout the U.S. and the world energy industry.

Historically, about 20 percent of PGandE's natural gas supplies have been purchased from producers in California, about 40 percent from El Paso Natural Gas Company (El Paso) which has acquired its supplies principally from gas fields in New Mexico and Texas, and about 40 percent from gas produced in the Province of Alberta, Canada. In fact, PGandE is the largest single market for Canadian gas in the United States, representing about 23 percent of Canada's authorized flowing exports. Since the latter 1970s, PGandE also has purchased relatively small volumes of gas from producers in the Rocky Mountains, amounting to 1-2 percent of its total annual purchases.

Originally, PGandE depended solely upon production areas within the state of California for all of its natural gas supplies. However, the tremendous economic boom following World War II forced PGandE to look farther afield for additional gas supplies. In the late 1940s and early 1950s, El Paso constructed its long distance pipeline from Texas to the California border. Within a few years, it became clear that even more gas supply was necessary to meet the demand fostered by the rapid population growth and economic development in northern and central California. To obtain greater supply diversity and to avoid being too heavily dependent on any one major source of natural gas supply, PGandE conceived the Alberta-California Pipeline Project to transport Canadian gas from gas fields in Alberta to PGandE's customers.

PGandE's basic strategy to develop and maintain diverse resource options consistent with supplying customers reliable and least-cost natural gas supply has been a continuing theme in the Company's gas supply planning and operations. PGandE has sought to offer suppliers a large attractive market for their competitively priced gas, thus providing suppliers with substantial incentives to develop new gas reserves and to commit their gas to PGandE. With its diverse resources and large market, PGandE has sought to foster price competition among its suppliers, to achieve contract terms with sufficient flexibility to respond to changing market conditions, and to treat equitably all major suppliers so they will be willing and able to participate in serving PGandE's future needs.

How these goals have been implemented and achieved over the years has varied in response to changing market and regulatory circumstances. In fact, as with many other aspects of U.S.-Canadian trade relations, the history of PGandE's Canadian gas purchases has not been without conflict as PGandE and Canadian producers have sought to adapt their relations to changing regulatory and market circumstances. In fact, the history of PGandE's purchases of Canadian gas provides a case study of how the economic and political forces influencing the natural gas trade between Canada and the United States as a whole have affected a single consumer market.

THE ALBERTA-CALIFORNIA PIPELINE PROJECT

The link between PGandE's gas customers and Canadian producers is the Alberta-California Pipeline Project. Its construction and initial operation essentially marks the beginning of large volume U.S.-Canadian natural gas trade. The Project was international in character and its successful operation continues to be based upon the conviction, shared by participants on both sides of the border, that the distinct economic interests, and the differing legal and regulatory concepts, of the U.S. and Canada must be respected and accommodated in all dealings with each other.

As planning for the Alberta-California Pipeline Project began in the late 1950s, PGandE established separate corporate entities responsible for the various distinct tasks involved in the pipeline's construction and future operation. Pacific Gas Transmission Company (PGT) was formed as a PGandE subsidiary company to build and operate the U.S. interstate portion of the pipeline from the Canadian border in northern Idaho to the California-Oregon border. Alberta Natural Gas Company, Ltd. (ANG), was formed as a Canadian affiliate of PGT, and given the task of building and operating the British Columbia pipeline segment from Alberta to the international border. Alberta and Southern Gas Co. Ltd. (A&S), was formed as a Canadian subsidiary of PGandE, and was assigned the responsibility of purchasing gas from Alberta producers and arranging for its transportation within Canada to the international border. The transportation pipeline facilities within Alberta were built and operated by NOVA AN ALBERTA CORPORATION, a company unaffiliated with PGandE. PGandE's Canadian affiliates, ANG and A&S, are staffed and run by Canadian citizens. The majority of shares in ANG are Canadian-owned and are traded on various Canadian exchanges.

The several distinct corporate entities were established to mirror the several regulatory jurisdictions involved, each to monitor and protect some aspect of the public interest in the U.S., Canada, and in each province and state along the way. The Canadian companies are subject to various Alberta authorities and the price and volume of natural gas exports at the international border are subject to the jurisdiction of the Canadian National Energy Board (NEB). PGT is subject to the jurisdiction of the U.S. Economic Regulatory Administration (ERA) regarding import authorizations and to the Federal Energy Regulatory Commission (FERC) which has jurisdiction regarding PGT's facilities, and sales and transportation rates. PGandE is subject to the jurisdiction of the California Public Utilities Commission (CPUC) regarding virtually every aspect of its public utility activities, including the rates, terms, and conditions under which gas may be offered for sale to ultimate consumers.

Planning and development of the Alberta-California Pipeline Project also included a significant undertaking on the part of Alberta gas producers to develop the required pipeline quality gas supplies and deliverability. In addition to their investment in the exploration and development of the gas purchased by A&S, the producers also made a significant investment in gas processing facilities. The purchasers (A&S, PGT, and PGandE) contractually committed and received regulatory approval, to take the gas at a fairly high constant volume in order to assure that the processing facilities could operate and that the producers' investment in the production and processing facilities could be recovered.

In addition, the initial $340 million investment to construct the Alberta-California Pipeline Project, which was a very large investment in the early 1960s, had to be financed. A measure of the degree of international cooperation -- both corporate and regulatory -- that was involved in the huge undertaking is that lenders found the project so secure, despite its international scope and size, that they were willing to finance it solely on a "project-financing" basis, without recourse to PGandE. In total, 1500 miles of new pipeline were financed and built to carry gas from Alberta to PGandE's California market.

Construction of the initial facilities began in 1960 and was completed in late 1961. PGandE began purchasing approximately 400 MMCF/D of natural gas from producers in Alberta. Subsequently, the capacity of the system has been expanded on three occasions to increase deliverability to meet growing gas demand in PGandE's service area. Each of the three expensions required modifications or additions to the overall pipeline system, and cooperative regulatory actions on both sides of the international border. In total, A&S now holds licenses issued by the NEB permitting the export of approximately one billion cubic feet of gas per day (BCF/D) for sale to PGT at the Kingsgate, British Columbia export point.

More recently in 1981, the Alberta-California pipeline was expanded as a precursor of its future role in the overall system to carry gas from Alaska's North Slope to markets in the Lower 48 states. It is planned that as part of the Alaska Natural Gas Transportation Systems (ANGTS), approved by President Carter and the Congress in 1977, the U.S. and Canadian segments of the Alberta-California pipeline wll be expanded by the installation of a parallel pipeline to form the so-called "Western Leg" of the ANGTS, thus providing California and other western states with direct pipeline access to the 26 trillion cubic feet (TCF) of proved gas reserves at Prudhoe Bay, Alaska, and other Alaskan gas resources yet-to-be-discovered.

In order to spread out the financing and construction of the mammoth ANGTS projects, and to provide an outlet for some surplus Canadian gas, it was decided to "prebuild" certain southern portions of the ANGTS in advance of the construction of the remaining segments of the system and of the time that Alaskan gas could flow. As part of this "prebuild" project, which was constructed during 1980-81, the ANG line through British Columbia was fully paralleled, and 160 miles of parallel line at a cost of $176 million, were also installed on the PGT system, thus making it possible by connection with other U.S. pipelines to deliver over 200 MMCF/D of new Canadian gas supplies to Southern California Gas Company for sale to gas consumers in southern California.

Finally, it should be noted that utility customers in California are not the only consumers who have benefited from the Project. Some gas deliveries are made from the ANG pipeline in British Columbia, thereby benefiting Canadian gas consumers, and Canadian gas is also transported for Northwest Pipeline Corporation (NPC) to a number of points within Idaho, Oregon, and Washington for delivery to various communities.

THE U.S. NATURAL GAS SHORTAGE

Since 1961, Canadian gas has been PGandE's most stable, reliable and secure source of natural gas supply. The pipeline has performed well, and Alberta's gas supplies have remained ample. Perhaps most important of all, no governmental authority, executive, regulatory, or legislative, has ever intervened to decrease the flow of Canadian gas to PGandE. This admirable record over nearly a quarter of a century is made all the more remarkable when viewed against the backdrop of the worldwide oil crisis, the severe U.S. natural gas shortage, and massive government intervention in energy markets, all of which occurred during the 1970s. PGandE's other major gas sources did not perform so dependably during this period, and were it not for the stable, secure Canadian gas supply,

northern and central California customers would
have suffered much more from energy shortages than
they did.

California's natural gas production capability and reserves are not adequate to make up for the
loss of either of PGandE's other two major supply
sources. El Paso is dependent on interstate gas
production and its gas purchases are subject to
federal regulations. Starting in the late 1950s,
U.S. federal wellhead price regulation set gas
prices at an unrealistically low level, choking
off exploration for new gas reserves. A shortage
was inevitable and it came at the worst possible
time. Coincident with the oil crisis in the Middle
East, El Paso and other interstate pipelines were
caught in the crunch with inadequate supplies to
meet all their customers' requirements. U.S.
Federal regulators, therefore, established pipeline "curtailment" or rationing schemes. Despite
the fact that El Paso had a firm contractual
obligation to serve PGandE, El Paso's deliveries
to PGandE were sharply reduced.

The impact on PGandE and its customers was
severe, mandatory conservation measures were put
into effect, curtailment priorities were set by
the CPUC, gas was not longer made available to
large new industrial customers, and existing industrial customers were forced to scramble for
fuel oil or try to convert to coal, if they could.
Additionally, PGandE's own oil/gas-fired power
plants, which had previously used predominantly
clean burning natural gas as fuel, had to switch to
low-sulfur fuel oil. The switch was forced at a
time when low-sulfur fuel oil costs were substantially higher than natural gas, security of supply
was dubious and environmental controls were increasingly stringent.

Fortunately for California's economy, PG-
andE's Canadian gas supplies remained steady, and
rose to almost 50 percent of the Company's total
available gas supply. Canada, too, was a net
importer of energy, and was beginning to see the
shape of a potential future gas shortage. A bleak
report issued by the NEB in 1974 foresaw the need
to take a more cautious approach to gas exports in
the future to assure that Canada's own domestic
needs for gas could be met. The NEB refused to

grant A&S an application for additional export volume levels. But the NEB did not move to restrict the existing authorized exports. Consequently, during the darkest days of the U.S. energy crisis, gas continued to flow from Alberta to California at an average rate of about one BCF/D. PGandE's supply diversity strategy adopted in the late 1950s paid off.

Additionally, as a result of the shortages, and taking account of the 1974 NEB report and refusal to grant even higher levels of export volumes, PGandE undertook to develop several new gas supply options for the future. PGT formed a subsidiary company, Pacific Transmission Supply Company (PTS), to explore for and develop new gas supplies in the Rocky Mountains. PGandE, too, established a special ratepayer-funded program, with the approval of the CPUC, to explore for and develop new gas reserves in the Rocky Mountains and California. Another PGandE subsidiary became a partner in the development of the ANGTS in Alaska, and as discussed above, PGT was assigned the responsiblity to construct the Western Leg of the system. Finally, PGandE and subsidiary companies became partners in liquefied natural gas (LNG) projects to bring LNG to California from Cook Inlet, Alaska, and Indonesia.

THE PRICE SHOCK

In the early 1970s, many in Canada were coming to the realization that the price for natural gas was unrealistically low, and was contributing to the prospects of a future gas shortage. In 1973, Alberta producers were receiving a contractually negotiated wellhead price of about 20 cents per thousand cubic feet (U.S.$.20/MCF) for the gas destined for California, a price about the same as that received by U.S. producers at the time, but far below the real market value of the gas. As the worldwide energy shortage began to emerge, and especially when oil prices began to jump upwards, Canadian authorities became alarmed at the fact that their natural gas was being exported from the country at a price below market value, and below equivalent prices that Canada would have to pay to import oil for its own people.

In 1975, the Canadian government imposed a uniform border price for exported natural gas regardless of the differing transport costs to each export point and regardless of differing conditions in each U.S. market. (Initially, there were some minor variations allowed for certain markets, but those were later ended.) This uniform price was initially based on Canada's perception of the "commodity value" of natural gas in the U.S., i.e., the value of the alternate fuel, such as oil, for which gas could be substituted. Subsequently, because it is a net importer of energy, the NEB adopted the view that Canada should not be expected to export gas at a lower price than the BTU-equivalent cost of imported oil. The "substitution value" concept became the basis for setting the uniform border price for gas. In 1980, Canadian Energy Minister LaLonde and U.S. Energy Secretary Duncan formally -- and belatedly as it turned out -- adopted the substitution value pricing concept. At its highest, the Duncan-LaLonde formula raised the border price in 1981 to $4.94 per million British thermal unit (U.S.$4.94/MMBTU).

Beginning in 1981, however, the world energy picture dramatically changed. Deep worldwide recession (caused in part by energy price shocks) continued structural change in industrial countries toward less energy intensive and more service oriented economies, and energy conservation (both priced induced and government mandated) combined to cause a dramatic decrease in energy consumption growth rates. Moreover, on the supply side, with the advent of higher gas prices for U.S. gas production as a result of the Natural Gas Policy Act (NGPA) of 1978, domestic natural gas production turned around. Once again, oil and gas supplies were relatively abundant, and what had previously been a strong seller's market rapidly shifted to a buyers' market.

Under the Canadian government-mandated uniform border price scheme, the price of Canadian gas to California and other U.S. markets rose rapidly as shown in Table 8.2. The impact on PGandE and its Canadian gas imports was two-fold -- PGandE's regulators became much more active in their oversight roles and PGandE's customers began to reduce

Table 8.2

Canadian Regulated Export Gas Prices in $/MMBTU

Date Established	Price
January 1, 1975	$1.00
August 1, 1975	1.40
November 1, 1975	1.60
October 10, 1976	1.80
January 1, 1977	1.94
September 21, 1977	2.16
May 1, 1979	2.30
November 3, 1979	3.45
February 17, 1980	4.47
April 1, 1981	4.94
April 11, 1983	4.40
July 6, 1983	4.40 and 3.40 for volumes above 50 percent of annual contract amount (Volume Related Incentive Price).
November 1, 1984	Negotiated market pricing subject to Toronto wholesale price floor.
November 1, 1985	Negotiated market pricing subject to adjacent zone price floor.

their gas purchases. U.S. regulatory authorities, concerned over rapidly escalating prices, questioned whether Canadian gas imports to California and other U.S. markets would continue to be in the public interest. The Federal Power Commission (FERC's predecessor) held a special investigation and in 1974 revised PGT's tariff to assert the authority to disapprove the reflection of future Canadian gas price increases in PGT's rates in the event the price became too high. (That authority has never been exercised. Despite the rise in prices it became clear that Canadian gas was irreplaceable in the gas supply mix available to California.) In 1983, the FERC initiated a special inquiry into PGT's purchase policies for Canadian gas as part of a consolidated review of interstate pipeline tariff provisions to California utilities. That inquiry was later terminated after significant changes in the terms of the contracts for PGandE/PGT's Canadian gas purchases were concluded with Alberta's producers and approved by Canadian and U.S. government authorities.

The CPUC, also concerned over Canada's high gas costs, established gas sequencing guidelines by which PGandE's gas purchases would be evaluated for purposes of their reasonableness. These guidelines are reviewed semi-annually and have been changed from time to time to reflect the changing price relationships between Canadian and U.S. gas supplies. These guidelines have now developed into detailed sequence steps and are reflected in PGandE's own gas purchase policies. Generally, gas supplies priced within a "price window" are purchased on a percentage of availability equivalent basis. Canadian gas now must maintain a closely competitive price or be exposed to the risk of substantial substitution of less costly gas supplies. The CPUC also instituted value-of-service rates and established a baseline rate structure for residential customers. While not done solely in response to Canadian gas prices, the weight of Canadian price increases contributed to the rapid rise in PGandE's overall price acquisition cost and was an important factor in leading to the new rate structure. Under a value-of-service rate structure, the CPUC set residential rates at about 90 percent of the average cost per customer, while setting rates for commerical, industrial and power plant gas uses to make up the remainder of the revenue requirement. Furthermore, the CPUC set those rates at the value of the alternative fuel (for example, low sulfur No. 6 fuel oil in the case of power plants). In effect, other gas customers, including PGandE's electric customers, were paying for costs that under a cost-of-service rate structure would have been borne by residential customers. As indicated in Table 8.1, by 1984, the non-residential gas market had become too competitive to maintain the 90 percent residential cost target and residential customers began to assume a greater portion of their total cost of service.

THE MARKET RESPONSE

Table 8.1 shows PGandE's sales to customers beginning from 1973 to the present. Similar to the trend across the U.S., as a result of the gas supply shortfalls and rapidly rising gas prices of the 1970s, PGandE's gas customers began reducing their gas purchases. Total sales fell 40 percent from 1973 through 1983, led by a 49 percent decline in sales to commercial and industrial customers as their rates rose even faster than the cost of gas import because of the value-of-service rate design. Annual average residential gas consumption also declined, from 113.4 MCF in 1973 to 73 MCF in 1983, for a 36 percent decline. While the oil price shock in 1979 provided a momentary relief from the falling markets, the decline in oil prices which occurred thereafter, the continuing climb in U.S. gas prices under the NGPA and the increase in Canadian export prices, as evidenced in Table 8.3, once again caused PGandE's gas customers to reduce their purchases and to continue their shift to other fuels and conservation.

PGandE's response to the market erosion and rapid price increases was to find ways, including negotiated contract revisions, which would allow it the flexibility to reduce its gas purchases, if prices were not competitive. PGandE also developed a concerted program through its gas purchase policies of encouraging competition among its

Table 8.3

PGandE's Purchases of Canadian Gas and Cost of Gas[1]

Year	Canadian Purchases in BCF Per Year	Annual Average Acquisition Cost of Gas in $ Per MCF	
		Canadian	Average
1973	373.6	.44	.42
1974	346.0	.65	.57
1975	365.4	1.37	.97
1976	375.8	1.92	1.34
1977	373.2	2.18	1.61
1978	333.4	2.40	1.89
1979	375.6	2.79	2.23
1980	307.0	4.56	3.18
1981	256.3	5.07	3.35
1982	249.5	5.24	4.07
1983	244.4	4.56	4.09
1984	228.6	4.22	3.96

[1]Source is PGandE's Annual Financial and Statistical Report.

long-term gas suppliers with a commitment to equitably treat suppliers on a percentage of availability basis, if their prices were competitive. Canadian gas purchases were reduced in response to the declining market, and reduced even more by the substitution of less costly U.S. gas supplies. For example, by 1979-80 the Canadian gas price was 150 percent above the average acquisition cost of PGandE's gas supplies and comprised almost 60 percent of PGandE's gas costs, although accounting for only 42 percent of gas purchases. Furthermore, PGandE began seeking changes in the interrelated chain of contracts from the Alberta wellhead to PGandE at the California border in order to reduce its purchase obligations from the high levels originally agreed upon for financing the construction and the expansions of the Alberta-California pipeline. These reductions and other contract changes, which eventually were successfully negotiated with Canadian producers and approved by the Canadian and U.S. federal governments, had become essential to provide the flexibility needed for Canadian gas to meet the needs of PGandE's rapidly changing and competitive market and were instrumental in sending market signals to Canada. PGandE's purchases of Canadian gas fell from almost 376 BCF in the mid-1970s, when domestic supplies were declining, to 249.5 BCF in 1982 and continued at low levels into 1983. Purchases by other U.S. importers of Canadian gas also were reduced. By early 1983, it was evident to all that significant new measures were needed if Canada was to maintain its gas markets in the U.S.

In April 1983, the government of Canada announced an 11 percent reduction in the border price, down to U.S.$4.40 per MMBTU. This price reduction saved customers in PGandE's service area approximately $144 million on an annual basis. Then, in July 1983, yet another price revision was announced, this time with the adoption of a so-called Volume Related Incentive Price (VRIP) scheme. The VRIP provided a sharply lower "incentive price" of $3.40 per MMBTU for volumes which exceeded 50 percent of the annual authorized volume in an export license year. PGandE was able almost immediately to take advantage of this incentive price. Nevertheless, with a base price of

$4.40 per MMBTU, average Canadian gas prices remained above the cost of gas available from other sources and PGandE continued to substitute less costly domestic sources for the higher cost Canadian supplies.

The VRIP represented an attempt by the Canadian government to move toward a competitive position in the market. The new gas market in the U.S. and in PGandE's service area is characterized by increasing competition. This competition comes not just from continuing conservation and fuel oil, but now gas competing against gas from alternative suppliers. The VRIP was insufficiently flexible to enable Canadian suppliers to respond to strong price competition from U.S. suppliers with growing deliverability in a still shrinking market. Gas prices had stabilized and begun to decrease, and PGandE was actively continuing to foster price competition among its suppliers through its gas purchase policy.

Thus again in mid-1984, the Canadian government announced a new export pricing policy that allowed, within certain guidelines, for negotiated prices between Canadian suppliers and U.S. purchasers. Among the guidelines was that the export price could not be lower than the Toronto "city gate" or wholesale price in Canada. This benchmark was about U.S.$3.00 per MMBTU. This policy became effective on November 1, 1984. PGandE promptly undertook negotiations with Canadian suppliers and was able to pass through to customers cost reductions of $176 million on an annualized basis. With Canadian producers once again able to economically compete for PGandE's market, domestic suppliers responded by reducing their prices, resulting in even further gas cost savings to PGandE's customers.

The response by PGandE's customers to declining gas prices was positive. As gas once again became competitive with alternate fuels, PGandE was able to reduce rates to a point where sales increases began in most customer classes during 1985, especially in the industrial sector. Of course, the resumption of economic growth, as well as lower gas prices, contributed to these increases in the demand for natural gas. The de-

crease in gas costs also benefited electric customers, since PGandE's rate for gas used in its own
power plants was reduced significantly.

The 1984 Canadian gas export policy might
have been sufficient to allow Canadian producers
to remain competitive in their U.S. markets if it
had not been for the U.S. "gas bubble," the very
rapid growth of a spot market for natural gas, and
the increased interstate transportation of customer-owned gas. The "bubble," or excess deliverability, resulted from new gas discoveries stimulated by deregulation of wellhead prices of such
new gas and the expected continued marketability
of high priced gas, coupled with shrinking gas
markets across the U.S. The spot market evolved as
a means of selling gas at discount prices in a
market with excess deliverability, as well as a
means for interstate pipelines to seek relief from
high cost gas purchase contracts. Direct interstate transportation of customer-owned gas first
became significant in the latter 1970s. It was
initially a means for local distribution companies
and large end-use customers to purchase and transport gas, which the interstate pipelines were
denied access to because of price controls. By the
mid-1980s, however, it has become a means for
producers to market gas to customers other than the
interstate pipelines and for distributors and
large end-use customers to bypass their interstate
pipeline suppliers. Transportation service appears to be a major new business within the evolving structure of the natural gas industry.

The combined effect of these developments is
that natural gas prices have continued to decline
thus far. Furthermore, the advent of deregulation
for most gas supplies on January 1, 1985 meant that
natural gas will now have to be marketable against
other gas supplies in order to be sold.

The emerging U.S. gas "spot" market also
created another source of competition for Canadian
gas. PGandE began purchasing spot market gas in
the summer of 1985. An innovative program for
allowing Canadian producers to match the spot
market prices and be purchased on an equitable
basis with U.S. suppliers' spot gas was developed
by PGandE and received the necessary regulatory
approvals. Under this policy, if Canadian sup-

pliers met the spot market price competition, their discounted gas would be purchased on an equitable basis subject to certain relative ceilings.

By the middle of 1985, it had become apparent that another, still more market oriented and price competitive policy for overall exports would be necessary for Canadian gas to maintain market share in the increasingly competitive U.S. gas market. Price competition by El Paso to retain its position in its California markets, including PGandE as a major purchaser, resulted in a significant rate reduction effective October 1985. This caused PGandE to seek a corresponding reduction in Canadian gas prices to a level below the Toronto wholesale minimum price in order to allow Canadian gas to retain its relative position as a supplier to PGandE.

The Canadian government responded to the pressure on the minimum price floor by authorizing, effective November 1, 1985, pricing terms freely negotiated between Seller and Purchaser. Certain conditions were established, including one that the "export contracts must contain provisions which permit adjustments to reflect changing market conditions over the life of the contract." Additionally, the floor price cannot be less than the price charged Canadians for similar types of service in the area adjacent to the export point. This assures that Canadian producers receive at least the Canadian market value for their gas.

THE NEW GAS MARKET

In 1985, Canadian gas export regulation and pricing had come full circle from the early 1970s -- from negotiated prices, to regulated prices, to negotiated prices. But in the interim, the market had changed. As reflected by PGandE, the market is both leaner and more competitive. Intrastate transportation of customer-owned gas will soon be a new source of competition in PGandE's service area. The vigor with which PGandE will be able to compete to maintain its customers and market attractiveness for Canadian producers will be directly related to the continued market responsiveness of Canadian gas supplies. With contract flexibility and price sensitivity, Canadian gas producers can have a vital continuing role in meeting the energy needs of PGandE's customers and they can maintain that role well into the future.

In looking to the future, PGandE will continue to pursue its least-cost strategy for meeting customers' needs for economic and reliable gas service. PGandE maintains its participation in a number of potential future gas supply options, some of which may require PGandE investment, such as ANGTS, Mexican gas, Rocky Mountain gas, deep gas resources, and LNG imports from Alaska and other nations on the Pacific rim. The timing of such developments and their roles in the market will be greatly influenced by the extent to which Canadian gas maintains its historical supply reliability and its renewed price competitiveness.

PGandE's California market for natural gas is not without the potential for substantial growth under appropriate conditions, but it is also affected by large uncertainties. Operation of PGandE's Diablo Canyon nuclear power plant will significantly reduce gas use in PGandE's own oil/gas-fired power plants. Total gas demands in PGandE's markets could increase at about a 2 percent per year compound growth rate over the next twenty years, or the total could be quite flat or even decline. Cogeneration of electricity by industrial gas customers and by the developers of EOR projects could significantly increase gas demand. For example, PGandE's long-term planning indicates a potential gas demand of 75 BCF/year in 1990 for cogeneration, up from 8 BCF/year in 1985. Also the emerging EOR market, apart from cogeneration, could add another 127 BCF/year to PGandE's market by 1990.

The development of these new markets will be very dependent on price and on the future meshing of federal and state policies as they affect California gas markets. The EOR market is drawing attention from suppliers all across Canada and the U.S. PGandE's competitiveness for this market, in part, will be determined by the willingness of Canadian suppliers to support PGandE in its aggressive pursuit of these new markets.

9

The Canadian Natural Gas Industry: Road to Deregulation

Arnold J. Lowenstein and Shane S. Streifel

COMMENTARY

The point that Canada is the only significant supplier of natural gas to the U.S. market -- but contributes no more than 5 percent of U.S. consumption -- should not mislead us as to the importance of that Canadian supply. For certain sections of the United States, in the north and northwest, and in California, Canadian gas is a highly important addition to domestic U.S. supplies.

This essay on the Canadian gas scene emphasizes two vital considerations: The cyclical changes in the U.S. and Canadian gas policies which are caused, essentially, by changes in philosophy -- the degree to which open markets should define prices and volumes -- and by the energy circumstances in which each country finds itself. The same point emerges from the chapter by Daniel E. Gibson and Mason Willrich in their perspective from the vantage point of a U.S. utility concerned about Canadian gas supplies. But our Canadian contributors move the discussion forward to a new level in their closing paragraph when they ask if what we are watching in gas may be the early stage of a continental or North American market. The economic and political ramifications from such an evolution would be profound. But unless Canada should decide (once again) to limit export volumes, the only question is when the continental context will be understood and dealt with by similar and consistent energy policies on both sides of the border.

-- Editor --

INTRODUCTION

After decades of regulation in the natural gas industry, Canada is moving toward deregulation. Markets will be largely freed up November 1, 1986, but concerns remain over transportation, export volumes, and export pricing. The implications of deregulation are extensive and complex, and are intricately tied into the movement toward deregulation in the United States. In this paper we review the history and structure of the Canadian natural gas industry, the road to deregulation, and the new Agreement on Natural Gas Markets and Prices. We conclude by outlining some of the issues and problems that lie in the wake of deregulation.

HISTORY OF THE CANADIAN NATURAL GAS INDUSTRY TO 1984

Ironically, the first Canadian natural gas exports to the United States were from Ontario nearly a century ago. However, the large basins were to be found not in eastern Canada but in the west. Natural gas was first discovered in Alberta in 1883. In 1913, a major gas field was found near Turner Valley southwest of Calgary. This area remained the center of the gas industry until the discovery of the Leduc field in 1947. The industry subsequently expanded and many new fields have since been discovered.

Until the 1950s, most of the gas was consumed locally within the province of Alberta. By 1955, reserves stood at over 11 TCF and new markets were actively being sought. After a great deal of controversy, it was decided to build an all Canadian pipeline to eastern Canada. In 1958 Alberta gas began flowing to consumers in Toronto and Montreal through the TransCanada PipeLines (TCPL) system. A year earlier, Westcoast Transmission had connected the northern fields of British Columbia with Pacific Northwest Pipeline's transportation system in Washington and Oregon, and gas exports commenced to the U.S. In 1960, the TransCanada system was linked up to Midwestern Pipeline through Emerson, Manitoba and gas shipments to the United States mid-west began. The following year a pipeline was completed by Pacific Gas Transmission from the Alberta border to California. In order to expand sales to eastern Canadian markets and also reach major markets in Chicago and Detroit, the Great Lakes Pipeline loop was built passing south of Lake Superior and through Michigan reconnecting with TransCanada at St. Clair, Michigan. In a few short years, western Canadian gas had found its way to markets in eastern Canada, California, the northwest and mid-west United States.

The next pipeline construction project was not until 1977 when Canada and the United States agreed to construct the Alaska Highway Natural Gas Pipeline. Difficulties with both the economics and financing led to considerable delay in the project. However, U.S. natural gas curtailments in the late 1970s raised the possibility of persistent long-term natural gas shortages such that it was decided to build the southern portion of the line first with the assurances that the entire Alaska Highway Natural Gas Pipeline would be constructed. In 1982, the 1500-mile prebuild section was completed and Canadian gas began flowing south to the U.S. mid-west via the east leg and to southern California via the west leg. About this time the U.S. natural gas market was undergoing dramatic changes and greatly impacted upon this newly completed system. A few months after exports commenced, contracted volumes through the eastern leg of the prebuild, Northern Border Pipeline, had fallen to less than one third. Needless to say, the remainder of the Alaska Highway Natural Gas Pipeline has yet to be built.

In 1983, Dome Petroleum, former leader of the Japan LNG project, was granted Canada's first LNG export license of 2.2 TCF to be shipped over a fifteen year period. This project has been delayed awaiting completion of financial arrangements and permit from provincial authorities to remove the gas. The concern from the producing provinces is that in the early years of the project the netback to the producers may be less than that received from exporting gas to the U.S. On the other hand, a price guarantee to the producers may leave the delivered price in Japan uncompetitive. Continuing delays make the likelihood of Canadian LNG reaching Japan by the early 1990s increasingly doubtful.

SUPPLY AND DEMAND

In 1983 the Geological Survey of Canada estimated Canada's known natural gas reserves to be 106 TCF (see Table 9.1). Their average expectation of undiscovered reserves is 335 TCF, with speculative estimates approaching 650 TCF. The potential is balanced somewhat evenly between the four major regions -- Western Sedimentary Basin, Beaufort Sea-Mackenzie Delta, Arctic Islands and Eastern Offshore. Other eastern and western basins are likely to be much less prolific. Naturally the frontier areas face high development, operating and transportation costs as well as technological and environmental obstacles. However the reserve base is sufficiently large to ensure that Canada will have large volumes of gas in excess of domestic requirements for a considerable number of years. Current Western Sedimentary Basin reserves alone represent over forty years of current domestic demand.

Canada's known reserves are distributed less evenly. Two thirds of the reserves are in the province of Alberta, while about 8.5 percent are located in British Columbia. Approximately 15 percent of the country's established reserves are in the Arctic Islands and another 8 percent are situated in the Mackenzie Delta/Beaufort Sea. To date none of the gas found off the east coast has been officially booked by the Canadian Petroleum Association.

As shown in Figure 9.1, Canada's production rose by 44 percent in the 1970s, peaking at 9.31 BCF/D in 1979. Production slipped in the early 1980s, mainly due to lower exports, but rebounded in 1984 on the strength of higher domestic demand. Approximately 88 percent of Canada's production originates in Alberta. British Columbia accounts for about 9 percent, while the only other significant producing province, Saskatchewan, is around 2 percent of total Canadian output. As yet no gas is produced from the frontier regions.

Domestic consumption has risen steadily since 1970 with 1984 sales at 4.59 BCF/D, an increase of

Table 9.1

Conventional Gas Resources of Canada
(TCF)

	Reserves and Discovered Resources	Potential		
		High Confidence	Average Expectation	Speculative Estimates
Western Canada Sedimentary Basin	74.5	54.5	88.4	174.0
Cordilleran Basins	—	1.4	9.5	26.8
Beaufort Sea-MacKenzie Delta	10.1	30.7	65.8	144.8
Arctic Islands	12.7	38.8	79.7	129.3
Eastern Canada Offshore	8.7	25.6	85.5	166.7
Paleozoic Basins-Eastern Canada	0.3	1.6	6.7	23.3
Total*	106.4	153.3	335.7	645.5

*These numbers do not add arithmetically but must be summed using statistical techniques.

Source: Geological Survey of Canada, Oil and Natural Gas Resources of Canada 1983.

230

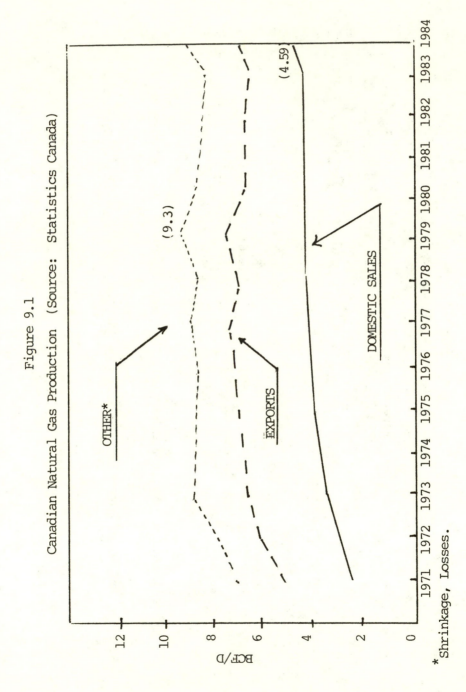

Figure 9.1

Canadian Natural Gas Production   (Source: Statistics Canada)

*Shrinkage, Losses.

83 percent over the period. Consumption flattened out in the early 1980s due to higher prices, recession and conservation efforts. Losses in the industrial and commercial sectors were offset by gains in the residential sector. All sectors rebounded in 1984 due to extension of the gas distribution system in Quebec and from generally improved economic conditions.

Usage is divided almost in half between eastern and western Canada. The two largest consuming provinces are Ontario and Alberta, with 1984 shares of total domestic consumption of 40 percent and 32 percent respectively. Of total Canadian demand, shares for the residential, commercial, and industrial sectors were 25.5 percent, 21.2 percent and 53.3 percent respectively in 1984. Shares have not changed all that much since 1970, except for a slight increase in the residential share at the expense of industrial's share.

EXPORTS

Natural gas exports peaked in 1973 at 2.81 BCF/D and averaged slightly below this rate throughout the 1970s. In 1979 exports were still 2.74 BCF/D but began to decline in 1980. Exports fell some 20 percent that year and slipped to 1.95 BCF/D in 1983, its lowest level since the 1960s. Actual 1983 exports were only 43 percent of authorized volumes. To understand this serious reduction in Canada's gas exports, we must examine developments in the U.S. gas market at that time.

On the regulatory side, the inception of the Natural Gas Policy Act (NGPA) in 1978 set in motion a series of events. The NGPA began a regulated series of increases in U.S. gas prices which allowed natural gas producers higher wellhead prices. Most important to Canada, the NGPA distinguished between old regulated gas and new unregulated gas, the latter which would have price ceilings. In brief, higher priced new gas was averaged together with cheaper old gas. Canadian exporters, therefore, were able to sell gas into the U.S. at a high price and take advantage of the low priced old-gas cushion. Canada, therefore, saw a growth in exports despite uncompetitive prices, due to the peculiarity of the U.S. regulatory environment.

In 1982, two major events transpired which began to dramatically change the U.S. gas industry and hence Canadian exports:

1.   the U.S. suffered a recession more severe than any experienced since the great depression, and

2.   crude oil prices halted their upward climb and began to come under downward pressure.

As a result, U.S. gas sales suffered since natural gas prices continued to rise in total disregard to surrounding events in the market. Canadian natural gas exports, a high-priced source (U.S.$4.94 /MMBTU), became increasingly uncompetitive.

In the last two years, the U.S. natural gas industry has undergone sweeping changes which made Canadian export policy increasingly outdated. In 1984, the Federal Energy Regulatory Commission (FERC) implemented Decision 380 which effectively nullified take-or-pay clauses in all contracts with interstate pipelines. Canadian gas exporters, whose gas was already overpriced, needed to respond if export sales were not to erode further. In July 1984, the Federal Government announced the move toward freely negotiated export contracts subject to the major caveat that the export price could not extend below the Toronto City Gate wholesale price of gas at each Canadian border crossing. By November 1984, most Canadian export contracts had been renegotiated, effectively lowering prices by nearly U.S.$1/MMBTU to about U.S. $3.25/MMBTU.

However, this change was not sufficient to allow Canadian gas to take a significant and growing role in the U.S. natural gas market. As U.S. wellhead natural gas prices continued to decline, Canadian gas started to again become uncompetitive. To complicate matters, FERC instituted further profound changes with the Notice of Proposed Rule Making (NOPR). While the NOPR is yet to be fully played out as to its final effects, the simple message is that the U.S. gas market is rapidly becoming competitive.

With regard to Canadian exports, two other structural issues are worth noting. First, the maximum volume of gas that Canada may export is determined through a "reserve test" by the National Energy Board (NEB). Under its reserve formula, established reserves must be 25 times the current year's Canadian requirements. The excess is deemed Canada's exportable surplus. The reserve formula was modified in 1982 to include estimates of future reserve additions rather than only established reserve figures. Under the new formula, the NEB in 1983 determined that 17.4 TCF was surplus to Canadian requirements.

Second, with regard to exports to the U.S. from Alberta, all producers presently share in the revenues from export sales, regardless of whether their production reaches the U.S. market. The export flowback, i.e., the difference between the export price and the Alberta border price net of transportation charges and Market Development Incentive Payments, is distributed to all Alberta gas producers on a pro-rata basis. The producer must be onstream to share in the export flowback.

STRUCTURE OF THE CANADIAN NATURAL GAS INDUSTRY

Within Alberta, NOVA AN ALBERTA CORPORATION, transports gas for local consumption and for removal from the province. NOVA delivers gas to the TCPL system for shipments to eastern Canada and to the U.S. border. To the west, NOVA delivers gas to the Westcoast Transmission system, which transports mainly British Columbia gas for provincial consumption and for export into the Northwest Pipeline system. In the southwest corner of the province, the Alberta Natural Gas Pipeline Co. line extends from Coleman, Alberta to the U.S. border at Kingsgate, British Columbia for shipment to the U.S. Also to the south, both the eastern and western legs of the Alaska Highway Natural Gas Pipeline prebuild system deliver gas to the U.S. In addition, small volumes are exported into Montana.

TransCanada PipeLines Limited is the major carrier of gas to eastern Canada and to U.S. systems serving the mid-west. In the early 1980s, TCPL had to reduce payments for contracted gas not taken because of an over-supply situation that had developed. The latter was a result of area pur-chase contracts that allowed producers to raise their gas sales volume as they increased reserves within a specified area. Coincidently, TCPL ex-port sales began to decline while domestic sales weakened with the recession. This situation re-sulted in the TOPGAS agreement in which a consor-tium of banks made prepayments to producers to cover take-or-pay obligations for the 1980-81 and 1981-82 contract years. In return, the producers agreed to reduce TCPLs take-or-pay obligations to 60 percent of minimum contract volumes until take-or-pay payments were repaid. Weak markets led to the TOPGAS TWO program in which payments were made to producers for the 1982-83 contract year in exchange for reducing the 1983-84 prepayment to 50 percent of the 1980-81 minimum obligations. In addition, prepayment levels for the years sub-sequent to 1983-84 were to lie between 50 percent and 60 percent of minimum 1981-82 obligations. As will be discussed, the TOPGAS agreement is a major factor in any attempt to totally deregulate the Canadian natural gas industry.

There are six major distribution companies in Canada that dominate the gas consuming provinces of Canada. B.C. Hydro and Saskatchewan Power are both provincial crown corporations and are the largest distributors in their respective provinces of British Columbia and Saskatchewan. In Alberta, the major distributor is Canadian Utilities Ltd. that distributes gas through two utilities. In Ontario, two companies dominate the market -- Consumers Gas Company Ltd. and Union Gas Limited. The other major distributor is ICG Utilities which delivers gas to consumers in British Columbia, Alberta and Manitoba. In addition, it is the major shareholder of Gaz Inter-Cite Quebec and also distributes nominal volumes in New Brunswick. Smaller distribution companies are scattered across the country.

The NEB is the Federal regulatory body that oversees interprovincial and international move-ments of natural gas. Its main duties with respect to gas are to license exports, set domestic inter-provincial pipeline rates, and ensure that an adequate surplus of gas is maintained for Canadian requirements before exports are allowed.

The Federal Government and the governments of the producing provinces have been the dominant players in the determination of gas prices. However, that role ends November 1, 1986 as the industry becomes largely deregulated. Before we examine present plans to deregulate the gas industry, we need to look at regulation as it exists in Canada today.

REGULATION AND PRICING

Domestic.

Government has long been involved in regulation of natural gas prices dating back to the late 1940s when the industry really began to grow. As with other energy sources, Canadian natural gas prices remained very low until the 1970s. Even prior to the upheaval in energy markets in the early part of that decade, the Alberta Government was seeking to raise the value of the field price for natural gas, which at the time was about C$0.20/MMBTU. Prices subsequently started escalating and are represented in Table 9.2. On January 1, 1975 the export price rose to C$1.00/MMBTU. In November of that year, the Toronto City Gate wholesale price for gas was set at C$1.25/MMBTU which at the time was 85 percent of the value of crude oil on a BTU equivalent basis. The government decided to set gas prices with each rise in the price of crude, with the intention of ultimately closing the 15 percent gap with oil. In 1975, the average well head price for gas in Alberta was C$0.37/MMBTU.

In October 1980, the Federal Government introduced the National Energy Program (NEP). With the rapid increase in international crude oil prices, the government decided to let natural gas prices rise less rapidly than the price of oil in order to create an incentive for consumers to substitute away from oil to gas. Gas was now to be priced at 65 percent of the BTU equivalent of oil. Under the Federal/Alberta pricing agreement, the Alberta border price (the price paid to producers less transportation costs within the province)

Table 9.2

Canadian Natural Gas Prices
(Cdn$/MCF)[a]

	Toronto City Gate Wholesale Price	Export Price
April 1, 1974	0.62	
November 1,1974	0.82	
January 1, 1975		1.00
August 1, 1975		1.40
November 1, 1975	1.25	1.60
July 1, 1976	1.405	
September 10, 1976		1.80
January 1, 1977	1.505	1.94
August 1, 1977	1.68	
September 20, 1977		2.16[b]
February 1, 1978	1.85	
August 1, 1978	2.00	
May 1, 1979		2.30[b]
August 1, 1979	2.15	
August 11, 1979		2.80[b]
November 4, 1979		3.45[b]
February 1, 1980	2.30	
February 17, 1980		4.47[b]
September 1, 1980	2.60	
April 1, 1981		4.94[b]
July 1, 1981	3.20	
February 1, 1982	3.70	
August 1, 1982	4.10	
February 1, 1983	4.15	
April 1, 1983		4.40[b]
August 1, 1983	4.07	
February 1, 1984	4.14	

[a]1 MCF - 1000 BTU

[b]Beginning with September 1977, export prices of
natural gas are listed in U.S. rather than Canadian dollars.

Source: Various sources.

was to rise by C$0.25/MMBTU every six months for the life of the five-year agreement. With falling oil prices and the 65 percent oil parity ratio, the last partial increase was in February 1984, setting the Alberta border price at around C$3.00/MMBTU.

Export.

In 1976, the U.S. government requested a uniform border price to avoid discriminatory pricing in individual states. The following year the Canadian government introduced a uniform border price and linked export prices to the cost of Canadian oil imports. This substitution value concept was formalized in 1980 by U.S. Secretary of Energy Charles Duncan and Canadian Minister of Energy Marc Lalonde with the "Duncan-Lalonde" formula. Export prices reached their highest level on April 1, 1981, at U.S.$4.95/MMBTU. U.S. purchasers were very critical of the price resulting from the Duncan-Lalonde formula even though no further escalation occurred after April 1981. With the downturn in U.S. markets, the export price was lowered to U.S.$4.40/MMBTU on April 12, 1983. On July 6, 1983, the Federal Government introduced the Volume Related Incentive Pricing Program to stimulate exports. Under the program, volumes sold in excess of contracted volumes were sold at the incentive price of U.S.$3.40/MMBTU. On November 1, 1984 the Canadian Government allowed buyers and sellers to negotiate contracts subject to guidelines in the Natural Gas Export Pricing Policy statement. The main criteria were that the export price must at least be equal to competitive energy prices in the market in question, and that the price be greater than the Toronto City Gate wholesale price.

With respect to domestic pricing, the Alberta border price has been set by joint federal/provincial agreement. All producers receive this price less cost of service. In Saskatchewan, the government sets two prices for producers, one for oil gas and one for new gas. Gas is sold to the Saskatchewan Power Corporation, the provincial government's gas and electric utility. In British Columbia, the government historically regulated its own prices for old and new gas as well as for gas sold to local utilities. Under its system, gas was purchased by the crown corporation British Columbia Petroleum Corporation and sold directly to Westcoast Transmission. Producers did not pay royalties, processing or transportation charges. In 1985, British Columbia modified its pricing regime to resemble that of Alberta.

THE ROAD TO DEREGULATION

The background to the deregulation of the Canadian natural gas industry is a long and multi-faceted story. In this section we will briefly examine the following key segments:

1. domestic natural gas sales;

2. direct gas sales in domestic markets;

3. export volume constraints;

4. export pricing, and

5. export licensing and contracts.

As mentioned, domestic natural gas sales are dominated by TransCanada PipeLines. TCPL both transports gas from Alberta to Ontario and Quebec, and is also the largest seller of Alberta gas. Therefore TransCanada has the largest reserves of natural gas dedicated to it to serve their markets in both Canada and the United States. In addition, TCPL has contracts with four major Canadian gas distributors -- Consumers Gas, Union Gas, Inter City Gas and Gaz Metropolitan.

Given this dominance of the Canadian gas industry by TCPL in supply, marketing and trans-portation, deregulation can only take place if this central position is reduced. However, there exists one major impediment to deregulation and that is the large take-or-pay liabilities to which TCPL is obligated (TOPGAS). That is, if other companies, including producers and brokers, are to gain access to eastern markets, then TCPL would be subject to competition. These liabilities amount to near C$2.1 billion and are critical since loss of its domestic market to direct sales would mean that TCPL would be unable to meet their obliga-tions.

Direct gas sales are defined as sales between producers or gas marketers and end user or distribution companies. If they are to proceed, TCPL would act as a carrier of the gas and not at any time take title to the gas. Direct sales are thought to offer advantages to both buyers and sellers:

1. it offers the seller another sales option in addition to traditional methods;

2. it offers sellers not selling gas to the domestic market an opportunity to do so, and

3. it offers the buyer another option to purchase by negotiating for its gas supplies directly with gas producers or marketers in addition to the traditional distribution company.

If buyer and seller can freely negotiate a sales contract, then each could stand to gain. But as mentioned, the major road block to this occurring is that TCPL could find part of their market displaced, and hence, the take-or-pay liability problem with its present suppliers would worsen. From the existing TCPL suppliers' perspective, direct sales represent a threat to their domestic sales. There is also no clear means by which these producers is able to compete with direct sales. The direct sale issue is further complicated by transportation issues including whether TCPL or the distributors will transport the gas. Even if gas is transported competitively, terms for the movement of gas need to be established.

The export market is riddled with several big issues involving price, volume constraints, licensing terms, contractual rigidities, and transportation inflexibility. With the ability to negotiate export contract terms as granted in July 1984, Canadian gas exporters were able to better compete in the U.S. gas market. However, the constraint that the export price could not be lower than the Toronto City Gate wholesale price (approximately U.S.$3.00/MMBTU) began to create marketing problems as the U.S. price of natural gas declined. If Canadian exporters were to compete, it became clear that this constraint had to be removed. Producers also wanted to pursue the growing short-term export market which has been estimated to be near 25 percent of the U.S. gas market. In order to accomplish this, several things had to be done:

1. an expansion of the short-term export licensing limits,

2. an ability to respond to the short-term spot market without undue regulatory constraints,

3. relaxation of the twenty five-year gas inventory rule for exports, and

4. access to competitively priced transportation for new gas exports.

With both export and domestic issues at a critical juncture, an agreement needed to be made to the satisfaction of both the Alberta producers and domestic consumers. The issues between producers and domestic consumers could be categorized quite simply. Could producers get freer access to the export market in exchange for providing consumers access to direct and more competitive supplies of gas within Canada? In addition, the distributor wished to retain his existing position in the buying, selling and transporting of gas within his franchise area, while TransCanada remained concerned about servicing its take-or-pay liabilities and maintaining a full pipeline system. As well, after having been a virtual monopoly seller in the domestic market, TCPL was reluctant to see its market penetrated by direct sales.

The question for the deregulators, then, was how could these divergent interests be resolved to ensure a vital natural gas industry. This is not to deny the obvious political issues which required competitive gas supplies for eastern Canadian consumers.

DEREGULATION -- THE NEW AGREEMENT

Under the Western Accord of March 28, 1985 on Energy Pricing and Taxation, the signatory governments decided to create a more flexible and market-oriented pricing regime for natural gas. On October 31, 1985, the governments of Canada, Alberta, British Columbia and Saskatchewan signed the A-greement on Natural Gas Markets and Prices. This section highlights important tenets of that agreement.

DOMESTIC SALES

Effective November 1, 1986, the prices of all natural gas in interprovincial trade will be determined by negotiation between buyers and sellers. The twelve-month period prior to that date is to allow for an orderly transition to a fully market-sensitive pricing regime. During the transition, prices will continue to be set by governments but immediate steps have been taken to enable gas consumers to enter into supply arrangements with gas producers at negotiated prices. Effective November 1, 1985 consumers may purchase natural gas from producers at negotiated prices, either directly or under buy-sell arrangements with distributors, provided distributor contract carriage arrangements are available in respect of such purchases. This provision was not to interfere with provincial jurisdiction in regard to regulation of gas distribution utilities. During the transition, consumers who seek release from existing contracts with distributors are eligible to enter into direct sales contracts only if the producers supplying gas under existing contracts agree to such release. Although a distributor may enter into new or renegotiated contracts at market prices, the distributor shall take full volumes of gas committed under existing contracts before accepting delivery of gas under a new contract, up to November 1, 1986.

To enable the market-response pricing system to operate within the intent of this Agreement, the governments requested the NEB to review the following:

1. whether inappropriate duplication of demand charges will result from possible displacement of one volume of gas by another; and

2.   whether the policy regarding the availability of T-Service is still appropriate. (T-Service is the gas transportation tariff offered by a pipeline company or distributor to transport gas
owned by others.)

Effective November 1, 1985, competitive marketing programs (CMP) -- which allows distributors
currently selling system gas to offer discounts on
certain volumes to meet competition in the market
place -- may be renegotiated between distributors,
shippers and the producers. A consumer purchasing
natural gas under a CMP or a direct sale must waive
eligibility for payments for those volumes under
the Natural Gas Market Incentive Program (NGMIP).
The NGMIP is an incentive plan for Alberta natural
gas sold to large-volume users, primarily industrial, in Manitoba, Ontario and Quebec. The plan
provides for rebate of up to C$0.37/MMBTU (C$0.35
/GJ) on eligible volumes and is in effect from May
1, 1984 to April 30, 1986.

For existing sales, the Alberta border price
shall remain frozen at C$3.00/MMBTU (C$2.79804 per
GJ) until October 31, 1986. The governments further froze the Toronto City Gate wholesale price at
its current level of C$4.06/MMBTU (C$3.79 per GJ).
Consumers will not be asked to absorb the increase
of C$0.112 per GJ in TCPL tolls took effect Novem-
ber 1, 1985. In order to maintain the Alberta
border price and the Toronto City Gate wholesale
price at their current levels, the new Transportation Assistance Program (TAP II) will accommodate
the TCPL increase for all domestic zones and for
all domestic TCPL services. The cost of the
program will be funded from an extension of the
Market Development Incentive Program (MDIP) to
October 31, 1986.

In the absence of an Agreement between a
shipper and a distributor, or a producer and a
shipper, on the price to be paid for gas under
existing conracts on November 1, 1986, and thereafter, the price shall be determined through arbitration. Accordingly, the Government of Alberta

intends to amend Section 17 of the Arbitration Act
to permit the arbitrator to arrive at a fair
decision on the price of gas in question.

EXPORT SALES

To improve access to export markets, the
export pricing policy will be amended with respect
to the relationship between domestic and export
prices for natural gas. The Toronto City Gate
wholesale price floor for all exports is replaced
with a regional reference price criterion. Exporters of natural gas must now demonstrate that their
contracts meet the following criteria:

1.   the price of exported gas must cover its
      appropriate share of costs incurred;

2.   the price of exported gas shall not be
      less than the price charged to Canadians
      for similar types of service in the area
      or zone adjacent to the export point;

3.   export contracts must contain provis-
      ions which permit adjustments to reflect
      changing market conditions over the life
      of the contract;

4.   exporters must demonstrate that export
      arrangements provide reasonable assur-
      ance that volumes contracted will be
      taken;

5.   exporters must demonstrate that produc-
      ers supplying gas for an export project
      endorse the terms of the export arrange-
      ment and any subsequent revision there-
      of.

The Government of Canada is to take appropriate steps to amend its existing policy on short-
term export sales. Specifically the "incremental-
ity test" and the "competing fuels test" are to be
eliminated. Further, the NEB shall allow gas
exports without volume limitation for terms not
exceeding twenty four months. The participating
governments anticipate that the review of surplus
tests currently underway by the NEB and soon to be
initiated by the governments of Alberta and British Columbia will result in significantly freer

access for producers to domestic and export markets. Alberta will amend the Gas Resources Preservation Act to ensure that it does not require new sales to be incremental to existing sales prior to November 1, 1986. Saskatchewan, in order to decrease its reliance on non-provincial gas, will permit limited quantities of its gas for sale outside the province and for direct sale within the province to stimulate exploration. So long as Saskatchewan is reliant on extraprovincial gas, the price of gas sold outside the province shall not be less than the price at which gas may be purchased in Saskatchewan.

In the spirit of deregulation, the governments agreed to an early and all-encompassing review of the role and operations of interprovincial and international pipelines engaged in the buying, selling, and transmission of gas. The review is to be completed by June 30, 1986 and submitted to the Minister of Energy, Mines and Resources by the end of July 1986.

The Government of Canada will undertake to ensure that direct sales have equitable and open access to TCPL transmission facilities. It will further ask the NEB to review the pertinent issues regarding access to TCPL's transmission facilities. Equitable access will also be provided for British Columbia gas through the Alberta pipeline system to new markets in the U.S. and eastern Canada.

IMPLICATIONS OF DEREGULATION

The implications of the deregulation package are extensive although it will understandably take time to make the system workable. While we do not intend to explore them in any great detail, the implications are both broad and require further scrutiny and analysis. The major issues are the following:

1. The potential growth in Canadian exports to the U.S. means further aggravation of the U.S. surplus situation.

2. U.S. consumers of gas will now have at least one more direct purchase option which will further help their position,

and thereby worsen the position of the U.S. gas producers.

3. Lower U.S. natural gas prices and increasing Canadian gas supply will create yet further declines in the U.S. drilling effort, and therefore tend to lessen development of new supplies. Consequently, the service industries that support them will also see continued problems.

4. Canadian direct sales will create yet more pressure for common carriage in the U.S.

5. Canadian gas consumers will be able to purchase from several sources thereby breaking up the tightly controlled domestic natural gas market.

6. Marketing will become a central component of a producer's business transforming some production companies into more integrated businesses. However, this does not imply that the traditional gas marketers such as TCLP will have an insignificant role in the marketing of gas in both the United States and Canada.

Most important, deregulation of natural gas in the U.S. and Canada will likely lead to a North American natural gas industry. This continental industry will transform the way in which natural gas is produced, transported, and sold both north and south of the border. It will be critical to all players to understand how this will impact their businesses today and in the future.

10

Mexican Natural Gas: A Lost Opportunity?

Charles K. Ebinger

COMMENTARY

The issues enveloping Mexican gas are unique. Here is a potential major producer of gas for whom the U.S. market is its only large gas export option. But Mexico has to determine whether it can overcome its political concerns about dealing in the U.S. energy market. If it should be able to do that, then, as the author emphasizes, the U.S. gas market is still one in which the larger foreign supplier is Canada. Mexico has to meet the Canadian competition.

There are other aspects to the importance of Mexico which should bear heavily on U.S. perspectives and which go far beyond gas trade itself. While a mutually successful gas trade could benefit both countries, it cannot, probably, be as important to Mexico's prospects as its oil. Nevertheless, U.S. interest in Mexico's well-being is based on very solid considerations of national interest. To the extent that for reasons of a burgeoning growth in Mexican needs for revenue, gas trade with the United States could commence in earnest, the agenda of issues between the two countries would be shorter.

It is not necessarily easy for either government to initiate such a development. The U.S. market is already generally in surplus; Mexican experience in gas negotiations, as Charles K. Ebinger makes clear, has left it with a political distaste for the subject. As Jonathan P. Stern emphasizes in his earlier essay, the role of government in gas trade is unavoidable and likely to increase, regardless of ideology or preference for an altogether commercial market. The requirement to consider gas as a long-term

247

investment is at variance with current U.S. domestic and
imported gas policies which are subject to continuous and
important changes. In this regard, can either Mexico or
Canada regard the U.S. as a reliable buyer?

-- Editor --

In Mexico, petroleum (oil and natural gas) and economic development are inseparable. Since their revolution, Mexicans have viewed oil both as the catalyst for economic growth and as a symbol of national sovereignty. The 1938 expropriation of the petroleum industry was the clearest expression of Mexican nationalism toward its resources. Since 1938 many events have made Mexico apprehensive about the United States and the international energy industry. In the wake of the nationalization, oil companies terminated equipment sales to Pemex (the national oil company), boycotted its petroleum products and lobbied against U.S. loans for Mexican petroleum development. The companies were to a significant extent supported in these actions by U.S. government policies, which then as now, reflected a disturbing failure to understand the realities of Mexican politics; namely, the view prevailing in Mexico that it is better for the country to develop its oil and gas resources slowly, even if the economy suffers, than to compromise its sovereignty over its natural resources.

Even during the Mexican oil and gas boom of the 1970s, when Mexico was vigorously promoting the development of its petroleum sector, Mexican leaders never wavered either from the belief that petroleum is a natural treasure, a scarce resource that should be used to spark economic development or from their long standing position that oil and natural gas export markets should be diverse with no single country receiving more than 50 percent of Mexico's oil and natural gas.

From 1955 until the early 1970s, Mexico had no negotiations with U.S. regulatory authorities responsible for petroleum imports or with the major international oil companies; Mexico in retaliation abrogated existing contracts with a few independent oil companies. In the 1950s and 1960s when Canada was seeking assurances about U.S. markets for oil and natural gas, Mexico was strenuously trying to avoid dependence on foreign markets. Pemex Director Antonio J. Bermudez (1947-58) said:

> "It is illusory, and would be harmful to pretend that petroleum produced and exported in large quantities could become the factotum of Mexico's economy or the panacea for Mexico's economic ills. Mexico does not wish ever to be forced to export such an indispensable energy and chemical resource. Neither does it wish to compete with or join a world oil combine which does not and could not have Mexico's best interest at Heart."[1]

Bermudez's views were supported by all Pemex's Director Generals until the giant oil discoveries of the early 1970s. By then Pemex and the Mexican economy were in serious trouble.

THE REFORMA DISCOVERIES

Before the giant Reforma oil and natural gas reserves were discovered in 1972, total Mexican oil exports in the post-1938 era, which peaked at 38,000 B/D in 1951 were minuscule. Falling reserve/production ratios, increasing oil imports and rising world oil prices precipitated a major economic crisis in the country. Pemex responded by embarking on an aggressive development program that added enough oil and natural gas to Mexico's resource base by the fall of 1974 to restore domestic self-sufficiency and to allow Mexico to resume exports.[2]

Awareness that Mexico might once again become a major petroleum exporter reignited U.S. interest in Mexican production for oil and to a lesser extent, natural gas. As Jonathan P. Stern has noted, recognition of the importance of natural gas to the industrialization and modernization of the Mexican economy lagged behind interest in oil owing to (1) the paucity of data on natural gas reserves and (2) the fact that Mexico lumps oil and gas together owing to the large volume of associated gas in the country.[3] This fact makes it absolutely necessary that any discussion of natural gas production occur in concert with an examination of the oil sector.[4]*

While the utilization of Mexico's natural gas reserves commenced after 1938, it was not until the late 1940s that large-scale production took off. By the early 1960s, Pemex was producing 10 BCM/yr. Although Pemex has signed an agreement with Texas Eastern Transmission Corporation to supply 1-2 BCM/yr beginning in 1957,[7] by the early 1970s, exports had dropped substantially owing to rising internal domestic demand. Even after the Reforma discoveries, rising natural gas production was viewed as a problem area "which had to be faced as a consequence of large scale oil production."[8] Fortunately, the natural gas shortages in the United States during the winters of 1976-77 generated interest both in Mexico and the United States on enhanced gas trade. Before discussing the ensuing 1977 gas negotiations between the U.S. and Mexico, it is first necessary to understand the economic situation prevailing in Mexico between 1974-77.

MEXICAN PETROLEUM SECTOR 1974-77

President Luis Echeverria Alvarez set ambitious goals to overcome problems in education, health care, housing and rural development, while giving impetus to iron and steel, metal working and the petrochemical industries.[9] However, despite the petroleum discoveries at Chiapas and Tabasco, which raised Mexican oil and gas reserves to 6 billion barrels, Echeverria's poor financial management produced a major economic crisis in 1976.

Luis Echeverria's emphasis on vast infrastructure projects required large quantities of imported capital goods. Unable to attract sufficient domestic savings and investment to finance his projects, he relied instead on expansive monetary policies and heavy foreign borrowing. During

*Footnotes 5 & 6 included in table which follows.

Table 10.1

Mexican Crude Oil Production and Associated Gas Availability[5 & 6]

(Oil in MMB/D; Gas in BCM)

| | ACTUAL | | PROJECTIONS | |
	Actual Oil Crude Production	Associated* Gas Production	Crude Oil Production	Associated Gas Production
1978	1.2	18	1.4	17
1979	1.5	21	1.8	22
1980	1.9	28	2.2	26
1981	2.3	33	2.3	30
1982	2.7	42	2.4	34
1983	2.7	45	2.6	39
1984			2.8	45
1985			3.1	53
1986			3.3	59
1987			3.6	68
1988			3.8	76

*Includes flared, reinjected, wastage, assumes 8 BCM per year non-associated production.

his term, the public debt increased fivefold to $20 billion; debt service as a percentage of exports grew from 24 percent in 1970 to 32 percent in 1976. In late 1976 -- as the debt mounted, the balance of payments deteriorated and inflation roared -- investors lost confidence in the overvalued peso and removed their capital from Mexico.[10] As a consequence, he had to devalue the peso twice during 1976, by 46 percent in dollar terms.[11] So severe was the economic crisis that Mexicans speculated about a possible coup d'etat.[12]

Lopez Portillo entered office in late 1976 facing these inauspicious economic conditions. Nevertheless, the peso depreciated and increased energy revenues, and with International Monetary Fund (IMF) assistance, seemed to put Mexico back on a more stable course.[13] The IMF-Mexican agreement, in particular, bode well for Mexico. Under the agreement, Mexico was to implement an austerity program, which included the following objectives: external liberalization, lower inflation, lower wages, and less government expenditure.[14]

The Mexican government never implemented the IMF policies. Instead, President Portillo, like his predecessor, followed expansionary monetary and fiscal policies aimed at rapid economic growth. Actual and future oil revenues served as a base for obtaining loans from commercial bankers, who willingly accommodated Mexico, given the nation's economic potential.[15] By 1977, Mexico's foreign debt had reached $27 billion. What Mexico and the commercial banks did not expect, however, was a declining world oil market and rising interest rates, a combination which sparked another economic crisis in Mexico in 1982. It was against this background of a major deterioration in the Mexican exonomy and a natural gas shortage in the United States that the Mexican-U.S. gas negotiations commenced in 1977.

From the outset, there were deep divisions in the Mexican government as to the wisdom of selling gas to the United States. Some nationalists in the Partido Revolucionario (PRI), Mexico's ruling party, fearful of domination by the "colossus of the north" categorically rejected linking the United States and Mexico by a natural gas pipeline, and argued that Mexican gas should be used domes-

tically. Still others feared that too rapid a
development of the country's hydrocarbon reserves
(oil and gas) was already overheating the economy,
accelerating inflation, speeding up rural-urban
migration, and creating a structural imbalance
between the agricultural and industrial sectors of
the economy by increasing dependency on food imports and exacerbating the maldistribution of income between regions and groups of Mexicans.

In contrast to these voices, the new government of Lopez Portillo, which believed in rapid
industrial expansion and development projects,
financed by energy revenues and foreign borrowing,
saw the export of natural gas to the United States
as financially advantageous. President Portillo
also supported the pipeline because he believed
that the development of a pipeline network would
lead to an expansion in domestic gas demand, especially in the industrial centers in northern Mexico. As Stern notes, however, the primary motiva-
tion behind the project was as an export project.[16]

Clearly President Portillo emphasized petroleum's role in economic development even more than
Luis Echeverria did, viewing oil and gas as a
potential solution to Mexico's problems.[17] A mid-
1978 study by the Mexican National Bank highlights
the high expectations for petroleum.

> "[Petroleum] would generate funds
> for various industries, provide the
> necessary energy for an increase in the
> production of goods and services, create
> demand and employment through Pemex's
> purchases, strengthen Mexico's finan-
> cial stability in foreign markets, and
> promote the industrial capacity to
> achieve new projects."[18]

Reflecting this less cautious approach,
President Portillo chose the aggressive Jorge Diaz
Serrano to be Director of Pemex. An engineer, Diaz
reevaluated the data on Mexican oil and gas deposits and claimed that Mexican proved oil and gas
holdings were 11 billion barrels, not the previously stated amount of 6 billion barrels. During
Diaz Serrano's tenure, that figure continued to
climb. In 1984, Pemex upgraded its assessment to
72.5 billion barrels (69 percent crude, 21 percent

dry gas and 10 percent NGLs). Production climbed as well. In 1973, crude oil production was 47,000 B/D in 1977, production was one MMB/D; and by the early 1980s, the figure was over 2 MMB/D. Mexico jumped to fifth place (from fourteenth) among oil-possessing nations and seventh in gas.

Lopez Portillo and Diaz Serrano were adroit at manipulating the size of Mexico's oil and natural gas reserves to attract the attention of lending institutions, especially commercial banks. Ragei El Mallakh describes the Mexican President's strategy, "Mexico intends not to finance development out of current oil revenues but to borrow funds to finance development expansion, using oil in the ground as collateral to back up debt and using appreciating flows of future oil revenues to retire debt."[19] The commercial banks, which saw oil and gas revenues as a guarantee of future economic success, offered loans to Mexico in 1979 for only .625 points above the London Inter-Bank offering Rate (LIBOR) in contrast to the 1.75 points above LIBOR that Mexico paid in 1976. The willingness of U.S., European, and Japanese banks to lend on easy terms caused Mexico's external debt to rise from $23 billion in 1977 to $85 billion in 1984 and $89 billion in 1985.[20] President Portillo's rush to borrow money using oil and gas as collateral played a major role in moving the gas pipeline negotiations forward since the international bankers placed a high premium on finding a market for Mexico's natural gas.[21]

NATURAL GAS NEGOTIATIONS

In his second state of the nation address to the Mexican Congress, President Jose Lopez Portillo stated, "We have surplus gas. We can sell, consume, or keep it in reserve, but we will never undersell it, which would be equivalent to burning it."[22] Shortly thereafter, however, under the onslaught of Mexico's burgeoning debt crisis, he entered into natural gas negotiations with the United States.

As originally conceived, the natural gas pipeline was designed to move gas from the Reforma fields 685 miles west and north to San Fernando where it would divide into two branches, one going

155 miles west to Monterrey and the other 74 miles
north to Reynosa, with an extension over the border
to McAllen, Texas.[23]

Under the original schedule, construction was
to be completed in 1979; the initial export capacity of the line was one BCF/D to be raised later to
2.2 BCF/D. In August 1977, Pemex signed a letter
of intent with six U.S. companies, specifically
selected by Pemex to ensure the widest possible
distribution of natural gas in the United States to
the east (north and south) and to California.[24] On
October 7, 1977, Mexico commenced building the
pipeline. Then disaster struck. After the U.S.
and international community had shown great interest in financing the line and the U.S. Export-
Import Bank had tentatively approved its first
loan to Pemex ($590 million), the U.S. government,
having shown a few signs of opposing the terms of
the sale during the negotiations, withheld approval.

Secretary of Energy James Schlesinger, supported by the U.S. Department of State, opposed the
sale on the grounds that at $2.60 per thousand
cubic feet (MCF) the price was too high. The U.S.
and Canadian governments had just concluded
lengthy negotiations over a Canadian natural gas
export price of $2.66 MMBTU, and U.S. officials
argued that acceptance of the Mexican price would
reopen the Canadian negotiations. Some officals
also worried that because the Mexican gas was
priced so much higher than price-controlled U.S.
domestic (which was $1.46 MMBTU), the approval of
the deal would worsen U.S. inflation (an argument
not prominently featured in negotiations with Canada). U.S. officials also opposed linking the
price of Mexican gas to the price of No. 2 home
heating fuel, because if Mexican gas prices increased at the same rate as world oil prices they
would be giving de facto parity equivalence to oil
and natural gas prices, a principle the administration was opposing in its negotiations with the
Algerians for supplies of liquefied natural gas.

As if technicalities in both countries' arguments were not complex enough to block an early
agreement, key U.S. Congressmen intervened publicly in the debate and U.S. officials remarked
intemperately that sooner or later Mexico would

have to sell its gas to the United States, since Mexico could earn more that way than by exporting LNG to overseas markets. Nothing could have fueled the flames of Mexican nationalism more effectively.

Despite some merit to the U.S. negotiating position opposing linking the price of Mexican gas to the price of No. 2 residual fuel oil delivered in New York harbor, the Mexican perception that Washington was trying to dictate terms to Mexico and the introduction in Congress of measures designed to punish Mexico for its intransigence made it impossible for Pemex to calm critics of the deal who already feared that the contract represented too much dependence on the United States. Indeed, some Mexicans suspected that if the United States were one day to demand unacceptable terms that Mexico would have to refuse, the United States might intervene militarily. With Mexico bitter about the breakdown of negotiations in 1978, President Portillo reaffirmed the dedication of Mexican gas resources to domestic consumption despite the lost opportunity cost. Natural gas to the Mexican market was sold at $.032 MMBTU. Psychologically, the damage to U.S.-Mexican relations was incalculable.

In an attempt to improve relations, President Carter went to Mexico in February 1979. As a result, the United States and Mexico established a consultative group to study outstanding issues between the two countries related to energy, finance, industrial technology and development, law enforcement, migration, border cooperation, and tourism. To demonstrate the degree of its interest, the United States appointed an ambassador-at-large to coordinate the activities of various U.S. agencies that impinged on Mexican affairs.

The natural gas negotiations that resumed in June 1979 culminated in August in an agreement to export 300 MCF/D at a cost of $3.62 MMBTU, a 38 percent increase over a price U.S. officials had argued a year earlier was too high. The price was to escalate with the price of a basket of five crude oils. Likewise the final volume of gas made available to the United States was only about one seventh the amount Mexico was originally willing to sell.

The issue of who won or lost in the negotiations has been well delineated elsewhere and need not detain us here.[25] What is significant is whether Washington learned anything from this "fiasco" of U.S. policy. It would be comforting to think that the United States had learned something from the natural gas negotiations; apparently it had not. It was difficult, for example, for Mexico to accept the U.S. Department of Commerce's complaint in January 1980 that Mexico was unjustified in increasing oil prices to $32/barrel. Not only did the Commerce Department seem to be implying that the United States had the right to dictate Mexican pricing policy, but shortly thereafter Washington also auctioned off its equity oil from the naval petroleum reserve at Elk Hills at prices over $40/barrel.

In February 1980 in response to Canada's decision to raise the price of its natural gas to $4.47 MMBTU, Mexico demanded that it receive a comparable price. After difficult negotiations, the U.S. Economic Regulatory Administration agreed and the U.S. government stated that competitive fuel pricing would there after govern all imports.[26] Following this change, in March 1980 Mexican natural gas export prices were equivalent to Canadian export gas prices up to November 1984 when exports were suspended in a new pricing dispute with the United States.

Before reviewing the 1984 crisis in U.S.-Mexican gas negotiations, one should review the political and economic events in Mexico between 1980-84 as well as changes in the world petroleum market that worked to Mexico's disadvantage.

THE MEXICAN DEBT

An overreliance on foreign borrowing was one of a number of problems with Lopez Portillo's economic development strategy. Another problem was that the Mexican economy was becoming overheated, with resultant inflation. High inflation caused the peso to grown progressively overvalued, a situation which discouraged tourism and exports of manufactured goods, and forced further reliance on petroleum for export revenues.[27] Whereas hydrocarbon exports were 15 percent of total exports in 1976, they were 75 percent in 1981. In 1985, hydrocarbons accounted for 93 percent of primary energy, a level higher than in 1970. Furthermore, government spending created a huge federal deficit, amounting to 8 percent of GNP in 1980 and 10 percent in 1982. Only with enormous, sustained increases in oil revenues could Mexico maintain such policies, a situation which never materialized.

External and internal difficulties caused the 1982 Mexican debt crisis. The internal problems were described above: an overheated economy (real economic growth of 8 percent in 1979-81, despite long-term capacity growth of 6 percent), high inflation, high budget deficits, and an overvalued exchange rate. The external problems were a weakening oil and gas market and higher interest rates.[28]

A world oil surplus of 2-3 MMB/D occurred in 1981 because of conservation efforts, substitution of other fuels, record Saudi output, expanded sales by Mexico, Great Britain and others, and a worsening world economy.[29] As a result, in 1982 Mexican energy revenues amounted to only $14 billion, instead of the $20 billion that the government had expected.[30] In concert with the oil surplus, a rise in world interest rates occurred. Higher interest rates caused the interest burden to rise from $5.4 billion in 1980 to $8.2 billion in 1981.[31]

It grew increasingly obvious that the Mexican government could no longer maintain the peso at its overvalued level. During the first six weeks of 1982, capital flight reached $2.5 billion (double the 1981 level).[32] With the central bank running out of reserves, Mr. Portillo devalued the peso from 26 to 45 per dollar in February 1982.[33] Unfortunately, the Mexican government, facing an upcoming presidential election, refused to take the tough economic measures necessary to remove the imbalances in the Mexican economy. Inflation continued to rise; Mexicans continued to convert pesos to dollars. By August, Mexico had almost exhausted its foreign exchange reserves.

On August 13, 1982, Finance Director Silva Herzog flew to Washington to request international support to overcome the financial crisis in Mexico. A weekend package of U.S. assistance (SPR purchases of one billion dollars and agricultural credits of one billion dollars) and a Bank of International Settlements bridge loan ($1.8 billion) was put together, with the expectation that the IMF would take further measures to help Mexico.[34] On September 1, Mr. Portillo nationalized the Mexican banks, using them as a scapegoat for the economic crisis. When the banks reopened and the government floated the pesos, the peso went from 70 to 120 per dollar.[35]

After the inauguration of Mexican President Miguel de la Madrid Hurtado in November 1982, Mexico signed an agreement with the IMF. In exchange for a letter of credit of almost $4 billion, Mexico agreed to reduce the budget deficit, raise taxes, and curb imports.[36] Specifically, the 1982 budget deficit of 18 percent of GDP was to be reduced to 8.5 percent in 1983, 5.5 percent in 1984, and 3.5 percent in 1985.[37]

Unlike his predecessor, President de la Madrid has taken the IMF prescriptions very seriously. He has acted to slow the pace of economic growth, lower the rate of monetary expansion and reduce government expenditures to reflect lower oil revenues. With respect to Pemex, he has dramatically altered its overall strategy. Whereas Pemex policy in the 1970s stressed exploration and production, the present strategy focuses instead on greater efficiency. (Because of heavy investment during the last decade, production capacity is sufficient to meet production goals without significant amounts of new investment.) Pemex has cut back its investment projects and operations as well as its salaries and expenditures.[38] In line with this emphasis on efficiency, the Mexican government has reduced Pemex's allocation by 15 percent compared to past budgets. Pemex, the largest publicly owned enterprise in Latin America, presently receives about 30 percent of the public budget. In an effort to diversify the industrial base, the Mexican government has increased the allocation of the agricultural and traditional sectors of the Mexican economy.[39]

The Mexican government has taken other measures to increase energy conservation and to decrease dependency on petroleum as an economic

catalyst. First, the government has implemented a
three-part energy conservation program. Along
with automobile mileage standards and increased
day-light savings time in the Mexican Caribbean,
Mexico has doubled the domestic price of oil. The
"rationalization" of domestic oil prices is the
key element to the conservation program, because
it removes the distortionary effects of subsidized
oil and slows domestic consumption.[40] Second,
Mexico has attempted to reduce overdependence on
petroleum exports by the following measures: (1)
limiting exports to 1.5 MMB/D of oil; (2) prohib-
iting hydrocarbon (oil and gas) exports from earning more than 50 percent of Mexican foreign exchange; (3) diversifying the petroleum export market (not exporting more than 50 percent of total
petroleum exports to one country); (4) maintaining
gas exports only if foreign market conditions seem
favorable and domestic demand is satisfied, and
(5) limiting Mexico's share to no more than 20
percent of a country's total oil imports.[41]

A thorough review of President de la Madrid's
progress in implementing many difficult, painful
measures can only result in praise for the Mexican
leader. In 1983, he reduced government spending
and raised receipts, cutting the budget deficit
from 18 percent to 8.7 percent of GDP. That same
year, he achieved a trade surplus of $23.2 billion
and a current account surplus of $4.9 billion,
resulting in a rise of foreign exchange reserves of
$3 billion.[42] He also reduced inflation by 80
percent. The success, however, has come at the
price of a 4.5 percent drop in GDP and a 30-50
percent fall in purchasing power for Mexican na-
tionals.[43] The PRI, the ruling party in Mexico,
has begun to face heightened opposition from its
much smaller rival, the Partido Accion Nacional
(PAN), a conservative party which opposes the
PRI's statist philosophy. This opposition has
intensified greatly in the wake of the PRI's handling of the 1985 earthquake disaster.

WORLD ENERGY MARKET

The fall in world petroleum prices beginning
in late 1981 sent shock waves through the Mexican
economy. At the same time, the phased decontrol of

natural gas prices in the United States begun under the Natural Gas Policy Act of 1978 led to a surge in new drilling activity and the discovery of major new reserves. Furthermore, in response to Canada's completion of the southern portion of the Alaskan Natural Gas Transportation System, significant new gas supplies were discovered that led to a major reassessment of Canada's export policies in Ottawa. Natural gas supplies were also demand constrained by law in the United States. Under the Power Plant and Industrial Fuel Use Act, the combination of all these factors led to a collapse in U.S. natural gas prices, and thus derivatively in Mexico's export revenue. In response to these developments, Border Gas in October 1984 demanded that Mexico reduce its gas export price from $4.40 to $3.86 MMBTU. Mexico refused, announcing that at this price it was more profitable to use the gas domestically. All exports to the U.S. were curtailed effective November 1, 1984.

From the available evidence, it appears that Mexico's decision was a political one not an economic one. As Stern notes, while it is clear that Mexico over time can utilize more gas domestically, perhaps even all its production, at prices above $3.00 MMBTU it is difficult to argue that it is more economic to use the gas domestically.[44] However, with average natural gas prices in the United States in the summer and fall of 1985 dropping to about $2.10 MMBTU, the Mexican decision might be justified if flaring were no longer occurring. The problem of natural gas flaring remains owing to both the lack of key facilities and the inefficiency of the equipment used for natural gas compression and transportation. Whereas in 1982 about 15 percent of natural gas production was flared, by 1985 this had dropped to about 3 percent. Under the National Energy Program of 1984-88, it is estimated that gas flaring will be further reduced as a result of the installaion of new equipment. By 1988, only 2 percent of Mexican gas will be flared.

Whereas domestic sales of natural gas were estimated to be 1.26 BCF/D in 1984, this represented a 10 percent reduction over 1983. Between 1984-88, it is estimated that Pemex will consume about 40-45 percent of total Mexican gas production. The industrial sector uses about 41.8 percent. Mexico subsidizes natural gas prices to reduce fuel oil consumption, which is perceived to be a more valuable commodity.

With the Mexican decision of November 1984, natural gas vanished as a major issue in U.S.-Mexican relations. It appears unlikely that there will be renewed interest in Mexican natural gas until the current gas "glut" in the United States vanishes sometime in the late 1980s or early 1990s.

MEXICO AT THE CROSSROADS

On August 18, 1984 President Miguel de la Madrid approved the 1984-1988 National Energy Program. Among the National Energy Program's goals are "improvement of productivity, energy conservation, energy source diversification....and a responsible behavior in the world oil market."[45] To achieve these goals, the Energy Program sets a number of policy guidelines:

1.   To increase productivity, the National Energy Program seeks the elimination of bottlenecks affecting the hydrocarbon and electrical sectors.

2.   To encourage energy conservation, prices and tariffs of government produced goods and services will continue to be adjusted. Prices of refined products will be set taking into account supply and demand, consumption patterns, and their relative benefits to the consuming sector. Owing to Mexico's comparative advantage over importing nations, domestic prices will remain below world market levels.

3.   The electric subsector will be the leader in the diversification effort. The use of nuclear energy, hydropower and coal to generate electricity will be implemented. Geothermal energy is also expected to play a role in the diversification process.

4.   ...The National Energy Program calls for the contributions of the (energy) sector to economic development by redirecting its purchasing power to the domestic market.

5.   In the world oil market, Mexico will maintain an open dialogue with producing and consuming nations in order to contribute to price stabilization. Pemex will keep its exports at 1.5 MMB/D; this level will be adjusted adjusted according to market conditions. Pemex will continue to sell crude oil only under contracts, and will not participate in the spot market. Gas exports will only be made after all Mexico's internal needs are met and prices justify exports.

6.   Crude oil sales will be limited to 50 percent of total exports to any single country.[46]

By following the policy guidelines, the Mexican government hopes to overcome structural problems such as over-consumption of energy and bottlenecks in the energy industry.

Another plan, the Program for Industrial Development and Foreign Trade 1984-1988, sets guidelines to promote Mexican industrial development. Included in the plan is a diagnosis of past barriers to economic development:

1.   ...[T]he major restriction to Mexico's economic growth in the last four decades has been an external disequilibrium caused by deficits in the foreign trade balance of manufactured goods. The availability of different sources to finance the external deficits set the path for economic growth. In the 1950s and 1960s, the major financing sources were agricultural exports and tourism. In the 1970s, the external deficit was financed by external debt and hydrocarbon exports.

2.   Facing the current limitations of these financial resources, imports will be primarily financed with resources generated by the national industry. For that purpose, a more efficient and competitive industrialization process is required.   The strategy will be directed to increase productivity and efficiency in the industrial sector.

The program defines future industrial and foreign trade goals:
1.   The creation of new industrialization and foreign trade patterns that increase competitiveness. Double growth rates in industrial sec-

tors with export potential. Increased growth rates in sectors producing basic and intermediate inputs, and reductions in sectors that depend strongly on imports.

2. To develop technologies consistent with Mexico's endowment of natural resources and provide training for the work force to promote efficiency in the production process.

3. A better industrial integration to take advantage of economies of scale. [47]

To finance the Program for Industrial Development and Foreign Trade, the Mexican government will attempt to increase domestic savings and strengthen domestic capital markets.

In addition to the Energy Program and the Program for Industrial Development and Foreign Trade, Pemex has published its own five-year plan. Given Pemex's importance in the Mexican economy, the Pemex five-year plan is very significant. According to President de la Madrid, what happens to Pemex "will determine what happens in the rest of Mexican society." [48]

Recent statistics highlight Pemex's crucial role in the Mexican economy. Joaquin Munoz Izquierdo, Pemex Assistant Director for Finance, summarizes these statistics:

1. Pemex revenues represent 43 percent of total revenues of the public sector.

2. Pemex contributes ... 46.5 percent of the federal government fiscal revenues ... .

3. Since 1983, Pemex has contributed to the reduction in the deficit of the public sector. This year, Pemex will generate savings of 150 billion pesos with respect to its authorized budget.

4. Exports from [the] petroleum industry represent 75 percent of total exports from Mexico. [49]

As the figures demonstrate, Pemex still plays a dominant role in the Mexican economy, in spite of a weak oil market.

At the January 1985 meeting of its governors, Pemex released its five-year plan. The plan states the following goals: more drilling; less natural gas flaring; substitution of Mexican oil field supplies and equipment for imports; increased development of drilling and offshore production; and improvement in its efficiency, management, and financial position.[50] At the meeting, President de la Madrid told the Pemex governors that they had made substantial progress in meeting Pemex's "mandate to recondition [itself] administratively, financially, technically, and morally."[51] He cautioned the Pemex officials, however, to remain alert for the future, when even more strategic thinking and planning will be needed -- given uncertainties in the world energy market.[52]

In the face of market uncertainties, Mexican plans for the development of energy, trade, and industry are ambitious, but necessary. In spite of President de la Madrid's success in 1983-84, the future will hold many obstacles to prevent economic progress. One major obstacle could be falling oil prices which in July 1985 became a reality as Mexico cut its light and heavy crude oil prices between $.83-$1.25/barrel.[53]

Realizing that the future of the world energy market may not be bright, Mexico appears to be toughening its policies for the rough road ahead. The Mexican decision to drop its light crude prices below OPEC's is just one example. Another is the new austerity package announced in February 1985. President de la Madrid ordered $465 million in additional budget cuts, to be achieved by reducing subsidies and investments, disposing of the 236 state-run companies, and placing a partial freeze on new hiring.[54] Given the precarious state of the world oil market and the possibility of interest rate hikes, Mexico is bracing itself for the future.

MEXICAN OIL AND GAS: A MIXED BLESSING

Clearly, petroleum has been a mixed blessing for Mexico. On the one hand, petroleum has raised Mexico's international standing and has provided economic benefits for Mexicans employed by the petroleum industry. On the other hand, petroleum has caused massive economic imbalances in Mexico: hyperinflation, stagnation of non-oil exports, huge external debts, and a reduction of real purchasing power for "ordinary" Mexicans.[55] Additionally, petroleum has aggravated corruption and polluted the Mexican environment. In short, Mexican petroleum is a source of both despair and hope.

On the negative side, the Mexican government's overreliance on petroleum has led to many problems, the most important of which is the damage done to other industries. The subsidization of domestic petroleum has resulted in a bias toward energy-intensive technology and industry,[56] a bias which has harmed traditional agricultural and manufacturing sectors. As oil and natural gas production rose several years ago, agricultural exports fell in proportion to imports, making Mexico a net importer of agricultural products. In 1984, the Mexican deficit in agricultural trade climbed to near $1 billion. Manufactured exports have also fallen.

The biases in Mexican policy toward energy and capital-intensive machinery and production methods and the resultant detrimental effects on the agricultural and manufacturing sectors, have exacerbated the severe unemployment problem in Mexico. According to the 1980 census, Mexico had a population of 67.4 million, though experts place it closer to 76 million. With an annual population growth rate of 2.5 percent, Mexico must create 800,000 new jobs each year just to prevent a rise in unemployment. Since the debt crisis, approximately one half of the working population has been either unemployed or under employed. The problem is serious and blame goes not only to capital-intensive biases but also to excessive population growth and the recent debt crisis. In conjunction with more effective population control, greater attention to labor-intensive sectors would help solve the Mexican unemployment problem.

Aside from contributing to unemployment, petroleum has damaged the Mexican environment, as anyone who travels through Villahermosa, Tabasco (in the center of the Reforma petroleum zone) will say. According to a December 1980 report by the

National Research Institute on Biotic Resources
(cited by Millor), "the tropical states of Tabasco, Chiapas, Oaxaca, Campeche, and Quintana Roo
are under ecological siege, and Mexico is in danger
of becoming an extensive desert.[57]   In terms of
agriculture, the noxious effects of gas burning
are destroying crops (corn, cacao, and bananas)
and grasslands.[58] Regarding underwater life, oil
spills -- most notably the Ixtoc spill in Campeche
Bay in 1979 -- have harmed some of the richest
fishing zones in Mexico.[59] The ecological damage
inflicted by Mexican petroleum development has
been substantial.

On the positive side, petroleum (both oil and
gas) provides Mexico with certain advantages over
other nations.   First, unlike most countries,
Mexico does not have to divert foreign exchange to
purchase petroleum imports.   Furthermore, Mexico
can use its oil wealth to promote economic development.   Though there were many shortcomings to
previous Mexican attempts to channel oil and natural gas earnings into the economy, many Mexicans
did benefit (although they were a minority). The
challenge for the future will be to funnel oil
earnings into industries and projects that will
benefit Mexico as a whole.

NOTES

[1]David Ronfeldt, Richard Nehring and Arturo
Gandara, Mexico's Petroleum and U.S. Policy: Im-
plications for the 1980s, RAND, Santa Monica,
California, June 1980, p.55.

[2]Charles K. Ebinger, et al., The Critical
Link: Energy and National Security in the 1980s
(Ballinger, Cambridge, Massachusetts 1982), p.
219.

[3]Jonathan P. Stern, Natural Gas Trade in
North America and Asia (Gower: Brookfield, Ver-
mont, 1985), pp.67-68.

[4]For a detailed discussion of this phenomenon
see Ibid. p.87; also Gary J. Pagliano and David M.

Lindahl, "Mexico's Oil and Gas Export Policy to 1988" in Mexico's Oil and Gas Policy: An Analysis, Washington, Government Printing Office, December 1978 (Committee on Foreign Relations and Joint Economic Committee, U.S. Congress), p.33.

[5]Ibid.

[6]Under the 1984-88 Energy Plan announced in October 1984, domestic gas consumption is expected to rise from 17 BCF/D to 16 BCF/D in 1988. It is anticipated that gas exports curtailed in November 1984 may not resume in this period.

[7]Stern, op.cit., p.68; see also Fredda Jean Ballard, Mexico's Natural Gas: The Beginning of an Industry, Bureau of Business Research (University of Texas, Austin, Texas, 1968), p.197.

[8]Stern, op.cit., p.69.

[9]Victor L. Urquidi, "Not by Oil Alone: The Outlook for Mexico," Current History Vol. 81, No. 472, February 1982, pp.78-81.

[10]George Grayson, The Politics of Mexican Oil (Pittsburgh, Pennsylvania, University of Pittsburgh Press, 1980), p.55.

[11]Urquidi, op.cit., p.79.

[12]Francisco Jose Paoli, "Petroleum and Political Change in Mexico," Latin American Perspectives, Vol. 9, No. 1, Winter 1982, p.68.

[13]Charles K. Ebinger and Penelope Hartland-Thunberg, "Mexico's Economic Anguish" Banks, Petrodollars and Sovereign Debtors: Blood from a Stone? (Lexington Books: forthcoming, 1985), p.11.

[14]Ragaei El Mallakh, Oystein, Barry Paulson, Petroleum and Economic Development: The Cases of Mexico and Norway, p.43.

[15]Ibid., p.44.

[16]Stern, op.cit., p.6.

[17]Grayson, op.cit., p.56.

[18]Manuel R. Millor, Mexico's Oil: Catalyst for a New Relationship with the United States? (Boulder, Colorado, Westview Press, 1982), p.125.

[19] El Mallakh, op.cit., p.56.

[20] George W. Grayson, The United States and Mexico: Patterns of Influence (New York, Praeger Press, 1984) p.61.

[21] Interviews Chase Manhattan Bank, July 1985.

[22] M. Edgar Barrett and Mary Pat Cormack, Management Strategy in the Oil and Gas Industries: Cases and Readings (Gulf Publishing Co., Houston, Texas, 1983), p.297.

[23] Stern, op.cit. p.69.

[24] Ronfeldt, op.cit. p.59.

[25] Stern, op.cit., pp.76-77.

[26] Robert S. Price, "U.S. Policy on the Importation of Natural Gas," in Harry M. Trebing, ed., Challenges for Public Utility Regulation in the 1980s (East Lansing, Michigan, Michigan State University 1981) pp.582-94.

[27] Grayson, The United States and Mexico, p. 61.

[28] William R. Cline, "Mexico's Crisis, the World's Peril," Foreign Policy, No. 49, Winter 1982-83, pp.107-108.

[29] Grayson, The United States and Mexico, op. cit., p.175.

[30] Cline, op cit., p.107.

[31] Ibid, pp.107-108.

[32] Grayson, The United States and Mexico, op. cit., p.179.

[33] Cline, op.cit., p.108.

[34] Ibid, p.109.

[35] Ibid.

[36] Robert L. Looner, "Mexican Policy Dilemmas: During the De La Madrid Presidency," Inter-American Economic Affairs, Vol. 337, No. 1, Summer 1983, p.31.

[37] Ebinger and Thunberg, op.cit., p.20.

[38] El Mallakh, op.cit., pp.50-51.

270

[39] Ibid, p.46.

[40] El Mallakh, op.cit., p.49.

[41] Ibid.

[42] Ebinger and Thunberg, op.cit., p.41.

[43] Ibid, p.41.

[44] Stern, op.cit., p.79.

[45] PEMEX Newsletter, September 1984, p.2.

[46] Ibid.

[47] Ibid.

[48] Excelsior, December 19, 1984.

[49] PEMEX Newsletter, September 1984, p.7.

[50] Oil and Gas Journal, January 28, 1985, p.83.

[51] Ibid.

[52] Ibid.

[53] The Wall Street Journal, July 12, 1981.

[54] The New York Times, February 10, 1985.

[55] Jahangir Amuzegard, "Oil Wealth: A Very Mixed Blessing," Foreign Affairs, Vol. 60, Spring 1982, pp.820-821.

[56] El Mallakh, op.cit., p.20.

[57] Millor, op.cit., p.163.

[58] Ibid, p.162.

[59] Ibid.

11

Beyond the Rainbow: Gas in the Twenty-First Century

Paul Tempest

COMMENTARY

This final essay broadens our perspective on natural gas from the confines of present economic constraints; it does so without ignoring the very real market forces which impinge upon gas and gas pricing. We are reminded also that politico-security issues affecting gas will be of permanent concern.

The author also does what no other contributor suggests: That in comparatively low-scale gas projects, countries of the developing world could find a fuel which could be the means through which their energy needs are met. Do not be misled into thinking his views are akin to fantasy or even science fiction. He is telling us the gas revolution has really just begun.

-- Editor --

Oil, we can assume with some certainty, will not run out in the twenty first century. Yet the geological evidence of the industry, based on a decade of feverish search, indicates that beyond the current "rainbow of plenty," there will be much less produced than at present. Oil, therefore, will be increasingly reserved for high value uses and its real price appears to be bound inexorably, if as hitherto unevenly, upward.

Gas, on the other hand, shows every indication of abundance. Proven gas reserves are already over two thirds of proven oil reserves and are

271

overhauling oil steadily. Not only is the reserves/production ratio for gas rising steadily, the finds are widely distributed. Almost a hundred countries have proven reserves adequate for commercial exploitation. This is welcome news indeed to the many, whose economy is hobbled and security threatened by dependence on high cost and vulnerable oil imports. What is more, there is hope for the rest. Gas exploration -- as opposed to <u>oil and gas</u> exploration, where gas has frequently been regarded as a marginally useful (or if flared or too much trouble to develop, an embarrasing) byproduct -- is still in its infancy.

This concluding paper looks first at the conventional wisdoms regarding gas development -- in particular, economies of scale, base-load priorities, premium use and the perceived need for public sector regulation. It then offers a single scenario of accelerated gas use through the twenty first century as a means of high lighting how these conventional wisdoms may have to change. An important component must be rapid technological progress in the more efficient utilization of natural gas. Given that the large scale mobilization of finance for gas megaprojects looks doubtful while the availability of oil at current prices persists, we must look to those areas where commercial forces are likely to exert most pressure. These are, in my view, likely to be <u>first</u>, Western Europe, and <u>second</u>, the sixty or so developing countries with already proven gas reserves. The conclusion is that whereas Western Europe is likely to be able to look after itself, drawing largely on experience and techniques already evolving in the United States, the developing world will be very dependent on the evolution of standard investment packages and an international climate which can rescue gas development there from the inertia into which it is rapidly falling.

AN OUT-DATED TECHNOLOGY OF SUPPLY

In taking such a broad worldwide, long-term sweep, one has to assume that the technology of gas production and use will, on the evidence of coal in the nineteenth century and oil in the first half of

the twentieth century, be rapid. Indeed, technological advance in the world gas industry has been
remarkably slow: high-pressure gas line technology dates back over forty years in the United
States, as does the use of liquefied natural gas
(LNG). Much of the technology of low-pressure
natural gas use derives from a much older industry,
that of gas manufactured from coal or naphtha. It
would be a waste of time to speculate[1] just which
form this technological progress will take, but it
is prudent to look carefully where the commercial
and economic pressures are likely to force the pace
of change, and where the example of large scale
substitution of gas for other fuels presents least
technical difficulties.

ECONOMIES (SO-CALLED) OF SCALE

Outside a handful of industrialized countries, gas development, production, and transmission has not yet been given much serious
thought. The popular view tends to assume that
only vast multi-billion dollar mammoth schemes,
whether by dedicated LNG routes or large-diameter
pipelines to very large markets, can produce adequate economies of scale. By comparison with oil
projects, which produce an easily divisible, stor-
able, transportable, and tradable product, the
economics of gas projects have to include the
largely uncertain cost of delivery year in, year
out to the same burner-tips. The financing of gas
projects by long (fifteen to twenty five year
supply contract) is therefore quite different from
that required for oil. All the capital requirement
is front-end and once the gas flows, it has to flow
at maximum throughput to recover cost. The pricing
of gas thus differs fundamentally from that of oil
in that it has to seek to secure base-load, premium
use, and interruptible contracts to optimize
throughput.

The cost of gas megaprojects is horrendous.
Statfjord in the Norwegian sector of the North Sea
is said to be in the $8-$10 billion bracket; the
Yemal line from Siberia to Western Europe and the
Saudi Master Gas System are at about twice that
level and the Alaska-mid West, West Africa-West

Europe, Gulf-West Europe routes almost beyond meaningful computation at present. Equally, the new LNG projects in the Atlantic Basin, Mediterranean, and Arabian Gulf appear to have come to a halt and the development of Pacific LNG supply to Japan, Korea, and possibly Taiwan, Philippines, and Hong Kong is now proceeding cautiously. Some of the great dreams of the past -- Iran to Europe via southern U.S.S.R., Arabian Gulf to northern India, Venezuela/Trinidad by pipe up the Caribbean chain to mainland U.S. -- have faded into oblivion.

The U.S.S.R. is perfectly positioned to mount a major acceleration of gas use in Western Europe. The full capacity of the West Siberian line is 40-50 BCF/D; current contracts amount to about 21 BCF/D. Further, the additional compression and loopline to carry throughput even higher can be achieved at an incremental cost per unit of gas delivered far below that of gas from almost any other alternative source except the Netherlands where reserves are limited.

This high degree of dependence on a single energy source, should, in the end, force the issue of developing alternative large-scale supplies from first North (and later West) Africa, and second from the greatest almost untapped source of oil, the Arabian Gulf and Iranian gas. Given the ten to fifteen year lead times of megaproject development, it might then be too late.

I will leave others to speculate on the geopolitics of gas. One economic aspect, however, seems clear: Apart from the rapid development of Russian gas, it is going to be very hard to launch brand new gas megaprojects while alternative energy is available and remains relatively cheap.

PREMIUM (SO-CALLED) USE AND BASE-LOAD NEEDS

We are only just escaping from the fictitious myth of the 1970s concerning natural gas -- that this relatively pollution-free "noble" fuel deserved at least pricing parity on equivalent calorific terms with oil. Its implications in terms of pricing gas out of electricity generation in many industrialized countries, excluding it from many valuable industrial markets and bringing many major schemes to collapse with considerable waste of resources and investment are only now being fully felt. As a result the consensus view is that this abundant resource of gas is expected to lose much of its share of the global energy market over the next fifteen years -- say from 16 percent in 1984-90 to 12 percent in 1990-2000.

One of the major anomalies at present is the division of approach between the industrialized world and the developing world. In the developing world, which has highly diverse potential markets for gas, it is easier for planners and bureaucrats to dream up schemes with limited outlets, notably for electricity generation and one or two selected industries than to face up to the much more complex and costly task of securing penetration of the existing oil product market. The national control of the marketing of oil products also represents an entrenched vested interest in many cases. Equally, in the industrialized world, opinion is colored by the very stable patterns of gas utilization, notably, as recently analyzed by the International Energy Agency:

1. The mix of large volume high-load factor and residential space-heating for principal premium use (e.g., Germany, Italy, Japan, and Belgium);

2. The emphasis of premium use offered by the availability of large old low- pressure distribution systems (e.g., U.K. and France);

3. A balanced use deriving from the availability of very large volumes of very cheap indigenous gas (e.g., U.S. and the Netherlands).

So much of the dialogue on technology transfer between the industrialized world and the developing world is a dialogue of the deaf. It is, I think, a major tragedy of our day that the industrialized world -- particularly the United States -- has produced a whole generation of experts in gas utilization, flexible contracting, computerized flexible tariff formulation to match fluctuating demand, a generation which, now with the

flattening of gas penetration is largely under-
employed, and which has not yet had the wit to use
that technology and expertise where it is so very
badly needed -- in the developing world. Coordination of what effort is made at present, is still
hopelessly inadequate.

THE PUBLIC/PRIVATE SECTOR INTERFACE

One of the main obstacles to technology
transfer in the gas industry is the conventional
wisdom that gas is very largely, at the exploration
and development and production stage, a matter for
the international oil industry which responds essentially to world market stimuli and disciplines,
while the utilization of gas is the responsibility
of public utilities more or less under the direct
control of government. In the developing world,
most of the time, one is discussing the formation
of new government controlled bodies to handle the
monopoly distribution of gas with all the risks and
uncertainties of untried management under bureau-
cratic direction which are thereby implied. The
relationship between the gas producers and the
government is often already determined largely by
that build-up in the production and sale of oil.
Gas contracting is so often the poor cousin of the
oil contracting business. Again here, the underlying assumption -- which may in the long-term be
proved false -- is that the vast scale of a megaproject in gas will inevitably require the participation of government at all stages.

A TRIPLE SURPRISE SCENARIO

So much for the conventional current wisdoms
of the international gas industry. When reviewed
against the prospect of an ample oil supply for
quite some years to come -- say up to a decade --
they amount to a fairly widespread block on gas
megaproject development for some time. One exception springs immediately to mind and there the
investment is largely in place, the accelerated
penetration of Russian gas into Western Europe.
One could sketch a purely hypothetical triple
surprise scenario to explain why, in my view,
developments in Western Europe may be the most

significant globally in breaking down the conventional wisdoms on gas and setting a more flexible and sensitive framework for small-scale gas development worldwide.

The first of the three surprises is, of course, that, with ample current oil supply and a falling real price, increasing demand for oil and inadequate incentives for exploration and investment eventually, as in 1973-74 and 1979-80, produces another major oil price discontinuity. With global energy supply bottlenecks of a political character such as the Straits of Hormuz, the Bab al Mandab, the Cape route and Gibraltar and the explosive character of some of the oil producer regimes, there must, on the evidence of the last twenty years, be some unpleasant surprises ahead, which might accelerate the almost inevitable third oil price discontinuity.

The second of the three surprises is the flip-over when gas (and possibly internationally traded coal) becomes the principal energy price-setter. This might occur in Europe when Western Europe is taking three times the present throughput of Russian gas. This will only occur if the Russians continue their policy of marketing incremental gas at a price which cuts out competing higher cost supplies, notably new Norwegian gas and Algerian LNG, seeking every extension of the market (as recently in Turkey and offers to other smaller European countries) and above all, seeking to carve the market up so that it is selling direct to the main industrial and electricity generating consumers and cutting down the bargaining power of the main transmission consortia.

The third surprise is that this penetration is so effective that it gives Europe major relative energy cost advantages that are reflected in trade competitivity and a very sharp surge in economic growth rates. As principal beneficiaries in terms of increased hard currency earnings from these gas sales, it would be prudent to assume parallel developments in terms of growth in the U.S.S.R. and probably the Eastern Bloc in general. Growing mutual economic interdependence may or may not be a stabilizing political factor.

THE TECHNOLOGICAL BREAKTHROUGHS

Where then, in the next fifteen years, are the likely breakthroughs in gas technology likely to occur? Not, I would argue from the above review, in the megaproject league and not particularly in the production and transmission of gas. The opportunities lie, I think, in the utilization of gas, particularly in the small scale multiplication of standard planning/finance/marketing packages which can be applied with low cost and low risk worldwide. We have to look at each of the main utilization sectors in turn: electricity generation, petrochemical feedstock use, other large scale industrial use, small scale industrial use, commercial use, transportation, and residential use for space heating and cooling, hot water and cooking. This is not intended to be a comprehensive list, but simply one where I have something I want to say.

ELECTRICITY GENERATION

As oil security continues to play a large political role in Western Europe, the attractions of reversing the trend and moving more gas on special flexible tariffs into electricity generation to compete with coal and nuclear are very strong. Above all, the dual firing of a wide range of power stations with the use of gas only when its deep valley price makes it particularly attractive or where it has a premium value (e.g., for environmental reasons on days of low cloud cover or high precipitation or when the wind is in a particular direction) is likely to give major economies to the electricity industry, which have not yet been fully explored.

PETROCHEMICAL FEEDSTOCK

Most base-load feedstock contracts are extremely simplistic and clumsy. Again here there may be scope for dual-firing (e.g., mixing or alternating with naphtha for ammonia production as relative input prices and market values shift). Substitution of gas for oil products may be increasingly seen as commercial prudence as the gas/oil price relationship changes. The indexation of gas to fuel oil, gas oil, crude or particular product/crude mixes may increasingly be seen as a device to keep gas out of the market as long as possible.

LARGE-SCALE INDUSTRIAL USE

The United States is currently undergoing a gas supply and marketing revolution as large consumers and utilities led by large scale industrial users increasingly seek to secure their own supply from source and then to use the transmission companies as utilities whose fees are negotiable. As mentioned above, I would expect the same phenomenon to occur in Western Europe as the penetration of Russian gas begins to hot up.

SMALL SCALE INDUSTRIAL AND COMMERCIAL USE

My last four years travelling the world on international gas prospects have convinced me that there is no effective clearing house of information on small scale industrial use and very little creative thinking, except here and there at the local level. One of the main stimuli are cities where gas is being introduced -- and has to be used intensively -- for the first time. In Europe, the leaders are Copenhagen, Helsinki, Milan, and Madrid. In Southeast Asia, the development of local distribution networks based on LPG in Korea, Taiwan, and Hong Kong, for example, is preparing the way for link-ups to permanent natural gas supply.

TRANSPORTATION

Although there are many pilot projects in compressed natural gas and LNG transportation systems for rail, road, sea, and even air transport, they do not add up to anything in terms of a total share in global gas demand. Yet the potential, as the oil/gas price relationship changes, is considerable. The development of a standard planning/development/finance package with standardized equipment, operational expertise and training would be of particular value.

RESIDENTIAL SECTOR

It is still a widespread misunderstanding, particularly in the developing world, that cooking with its premium value per unit of gas consumed holds the key to premium use of gas resources. The unit hook-up cost for residential cooking purposes is, however, frequently so high that the economics of the development are undermined. In a Southeast Asia-type environment with fast precooked foods, residential demand for two million households, maybe ten million people, for gas cooking can be satisfied by as little as half a million tons of LNG per annum. Moreover, this shows up as a sharply needle-point demand twice or maybe once each day. Lacking the requirements of North America and Western Europe for gas for space heating, much of the African, Asian, and South American developing world may have to wait for competitively priced and fuel-efficient gas-fired air-conditioning for the residential sector to increase its share of over-all gas demand. Again, LPG and naphtha reformed gas distribution systems serving new apartment complexes and new industrial areas can begin to prepare the way to bigger natural gas systems.

CONCLUSIONS

As the World Bank has been at pains to point out[2] over the last two years, the potential for gas development in the developing world is consider-able with major import substitution and, in some case, hard currency export earning effects. One of their most important conclusions is that the costs of gas development can be reduced below what was previously considered possible, making gas fully competitive with oil and even coal. Yet the institutional, financial, and contractual hurdles remain considerable. There are two areas, I think where the World Bank may be able to help:

(1) On the supply side the development of a standard development contract would win widespread recognition. There is, at present, far too much relearning the wheel each time a new project comes up. One possible development in the long term, might be the elaboration of a new form of inter-

national development contract on standard lines
backed by rather strong guarantees from the international agencies. A start might be made on those
areas where there is a commerical argument for
joint national exploitation, e.g., Trinidad/Ven-
ezuela, Nigeria/Cameroon, Qatar/Saudi Arabia or
even given an improvement in the political climate, Qatar/Iran or Libya/Sudan.

(2)   On the demand side, as indicated above,
there is a pressing need for the industrialized
world to put its act together and with simple
computer software and standardized market surveys,
all of which are commonplace in Western Europe and
North America, sweep through the developing world
looking for all the small scale gas marketing
opportunities. Much of this activity would be
essentially private sector in origin: It can be
relied upon to generate a wide variety of private
sector solutions in the developing world, which
may have beneficial reverberations far beyond the
gas sector itself.

                              NOTES

[1]Nonetheless, as an amateur sailor, I am
always struck by the fact that, while oil and gas
are frequently produced simultaneously, the world
finds oil a heavy cargo to move by sea and gas too
light to be lifted by sea without very expensive
liquefaction. A glance at the old commercial
sailing clipper routes sets the imagination going.
Twin oil tankers or freighters tethered to water-
ballasted gas balloons slung between them -- thun-
dering up the trades under wind power with gas
engines for docking and calm. The balloons de-
flated for the return trip, of course, the same on
skids over the Arctic ice cap (surely cheaper than
General Atomic's nuclear submarine LNG carriers or
Dome Petroleum's Ice Scale 10 ice-crushing LNG
carriers). Just look at the wind patterns. And

what routes!   Seasonal peak gas from Chile and
Argentina to Europe.   North West Shelf gas from
Australia to India; Alaska to California.   More
practically, it must eventually be possible to
come up with an immense metal or fabric gas cylin-
der with a powerful gas engine and thrusters for
maneuverability and some device to put it directly
-- and slowly -- from the field into space for
space-shuttle and orbiting space station use,
where one of the greatest problems in developing
non-gravitational industry is the constraint of
large scale energy supply.

[2] Energy in Transition, World Bank, 1984.

Final Note

Our discussions in The World Gas Trade *have ranged from consideration of the size of the gas resource, and the changing conditions for the obtaining of supply. We have given attention to the great gas markets. Our last essay was an effort to suggest a gas future which reaches out to new consumers in industrial and developing societies with technological advances in how gas is found, developed, and employed. Paul Tempest's vision is not unlike that of the Editor.*

He -- and all the other contributors -- put special stress on the absolute need for gas to be priced below its competition. If it is not for reasons of confusion (or greed) on the part of suppliers, abetted by governments, then buyers will go elsewhere. From an American viewpoint, the greater latitude given market forces in shaping competition between fuels, the better, eventually, for all gas interests. And perhaps the most exciting aspect of gas is that for various reasons and in many places, the obtaining of natural gas is moving out into the market place. That single development can accomplish more than anything else in assuring a greater future for gas.

-- Editor --

Selected Gas Readings

BP Review of World Gas, and the BP Statistical
    Review of World Energy, 1985 available from
    the British Petroleum Company, Britannic
    House, Moor Lane, London EC2Y 9 BU, England.
    These two surveys are considered to be the
    most useful compendia on energy.
World Petroleum Resources: A Perspective
    by Charles D. Masters, U.S. Geological Sur-
    vey, Reston, Virginia, 1985. An important
    look at the underlying resource base with
    unusual maps.
U.S. Conventional Oil and Gas Production:
    Prospects to the Year 2000 by Joseph P. Riva.,
    Jr., John J. Schanz, Jr., and John G. Ellis,
    Westview Press, Boulder, Colorado, 1985. The
    latest and authoritative review of a vital
    subject.
World Petroleum Resources and Reserves by Joseph
    P. Riva, Jr., Westview Press, Boulder, Colo-
    rado, 1983. An essential companion study to
    U.S. Conventional Oil and Gas Production.
Blue Gold: The Political Economy of Natural
    Gas by J.D. Davis, George Allen and Unwin,
    London, England, 1984. An indispensable,
    thorough review and analysis of natural gas,
    its uses, the policy context in which it is
    available, case studies.
International Gas Trade in Europe, 1984; Gas's

Contribution to U.K. Self-Sufficiency, 1984 and Natural Gas Trade in North America and Asia, 1985 by Jonathan P. Stern (all published by Gower Publishing Company, Hants GU11 3HR, England). These three studies are lucid, analytical accounts of major aspects of contemporary natural gas.

Soviet Natural Gas Development to 1990 by Jonathan P. Stern, D.C. Heath/Lexington Books, Cambridge, Massachusetts, 1980. A key appraisal by a leading expert.

The Natural Gas Revolution of 1985 by Stephen F. Williams, American Enterprise Institute, Washington, D.C., 1985. An excellent review and analysis of the natural gas "revolution" in the United States.

Oil and Gas Journal, published Tulsa, Oklahoma; monthly, authoritative; covers worldwide petroleum events.

Petroleum Economist, published London, England; monthly and essential.

Gas Energy Review, publication of the American Gas Association, Arlington, Virginia. An important resource; other reports issued by the AGA on gas trends worldwide.

International Energy Agency, OECD, Paris, France. Energy reports.

List of Contributors

Balint Balkay, Senior Research Fellow, Institute for World Economics of the Hungarian Academy of Sciences (fuels, energy, and raw materials); Editor, Trends in World Economy; author, numerous articles in learned journals. B.A. (1953); PhD. (1958) both from Eotvoes University, Budapest.

Simon A. Blakey is a specialist in natural gas currently working with the International Energy Agency in Paris. Prior to this he was a consultant with the Energy Economics group of Arthur D. Little, where he had assignments at various times with most of the major suppliers and some potential suppliers of pipeline and liquefied natural gas to Western Europe. Mr. Blakey has an M.A. in Economics from Cambridge University, and has lectured to candidates for final bankers' examinations in the United Kingdom.

Melvin A. Conant, Editor and Publisher of Geopolitics of Energy and President, Conant and Associates, Ltd., Washington, D.C. Editor, Oil Strategy and Politics 1941-1981 (Selected papers of Walter J. Levy); The Oil Factor in U.S. Foreign Policy, Council on Foreign Relations.

Previously, Professor, International Security Affairs, U.S. National War College; Directing Staff, Council on Foreign Relations, Senior Government Relations Counselor EXXON Corporation and Assistant Administrator (International Energy) U.S. Federal Energy Administration.

286

Charles K. Ebinger is a graduate of Williams College and of the Fletcher School of Law and Diplomacy. He is currently Director, Energy and Strategic Resources Program, Center for Strategic and International Studies/Georgetown University. From 1976-79, he was Vice President and a director of Conant and Associates, Ltd. From 1975-76 he was Foreign Affairs Officer, Federal Energy Administration, Office of International Energy Affairs, Washington, D.C. responsible for analysis of political and economic forces affecting energy market trends first in the Far East and, subsequently, in the Caribbean and Latin America.

Daniel E. Gibson is Vice President, Fuel Resources of the Pacific Gas and Electric Company. He is a graduate of the University of California (Berkeley) and the Harvard Law School. His prior service included the Federal Power Commission, 1965-68. From 1969 to the present he has been with PGandE in several legal capacities becoming Assistant General Counsel and then Vice President in 1983. He is a director of a number of gas companies.

Gerald B. Greenwald is a partner in the Washington law firm of Arent, Fox, Kintner, Plotkin & Kahn and acts as legal advisor to U.S. and foreign companies engaged in international energy projects. Mr. Greenwald is a specialist in transactions for the purpose and sale of natural gas, LNG and LPG, and its transportation by pipelines and ships. He serves as Chairman, Oil and Gas Law Committee of the International Bar Association's Section on Energy and Natural Resources Law, and as a member of the Maritime Law Association's Committee on the Transportation of Hazardous Substances.

Toyoaki Ikuta is President of The Institute of Energy Economics of Japan. A graduate of Tokyo University, he served in the Ministry of International Trade and Industry, the Economic Planning Agency, Defense Agency, and the Embassy of Japan in the Philippines. He retired from government service as Director General of Atomic Energy Bureau of the Science and Technology Agency.

Arnold J. Lowenstein, Manager, Energy Marketing and Planning, CHEM SYSTEMS, Inc., Tarrytown, New York. Previously, Supervisor, Economics, Alberta Energy Company, Calgary. Has an M.A. (Economics) from University of British Columbia. Member, Natural Gas Committee for the Independent Petroleum Association of Canada involved in formulating industry recommendations to government on the deregulation of natural gas.

Janne Haaland Matlary has an M.A. degree from the University of Minnesota in political science and modern European history, 1980; the degree of magister artium from the University of Oslo in political science in 1983 with thesis on interest groups participation in decision-making in Western democracies. From 1981-84, she was Executive Officer in the Ministry of Petroleum and Energy, Oslo, concentrating on energy planning and the European gas market. On leave 1985-86 to complete study of "The Organization of the Gas Sector in Western European Countries," at the Norwegian Institute of International Affairs. The study will be published in the fall of 1986.

Sandor Sipos, Research Fellow, Institute for World Economics of the Hungarian Academy of Sciences (analysis of energy policies in East and West, fuels, petrochemicals and development economics.) Author, numerous articles on CMEA energy and Third World. M.A., Economics (1981) and PhD., Economics (1984) Karl Marx University of Economics, Budapest.

Jonathan P. Stern is the Head of the Joint Energy Program based at the Royal Institute of International Affairs in London. He has an undergraduate degree in Soviet Studies from the University of Birmingham and a Masters Degree in International Relations from the University of Virginia. Mr. Stern has worked as a consultant on international energy issues on both sides of the Atlantic and has published extensively on Soviet and East European energy problems and international gas trade. His major publications include: Soviet Natural Gas Development to 1990, (D.C.

Heath/Lexington Books, 1980), <u>International Gas Trade in Europe</u>, and <u>Gas's Contribution to U.K. Self-Sufficiency</u>, (Gower Publishing Company, 1984), and <u>Natural Gas Trade in North America and Asia</u>, (Gower, 1985).

<u>Shane S. Streifel</u>, Senior Economist, Canadian Energy Research Institute (CERI). He has a Masters Degree (Economics) from the University of Calgary. He was with Richardson Securities and after joining CERI served as Coordinating Editor of the World Oil Market Analysis and Director of Conferences.

<u>Norio Tanaka</u> is Chief Coordinator and Manager, Oil and Gas Group of the Institute of Energy Economics. A graduate of Keio University, he joined Osakaya Securities Co., then the Petroleum Association of Japan before joining the Institute. In 1984 he received the Energy Forum Prize for his study of crude oil prices.

<u>Paul Tempest</u> has just completed twenty five years in and out of the Bank of England, the last fifteen on energy or energy-related matters. Since 1981, he has spent two years on secondment to the British Gas Corporation and two with the Energy Department of the World Bank. In October 1985, he became Head of International Energy Policies in the Group Public Affairs Division of Shell International, London. He was Chairman of the British Institute of Energy Economics in 1980-82 and President of the International Association of Energy Economists for the year 1984.

<u>Mason Willrich</u> is Senior Vice President of Corporate Planning for Pacific Gas and Electric Company and a member of the Company's Management Committee. Prior to joining PGandE in 1979, Mr. Willrich was Director for International Relations at the Rockefeller Foundation, New York. Previous to that he was John C. Stennis Professor of Law at the University of Virginia, and from 1968-73 he also served as Director of the University's Center for the Study of Science, Technology and Public Policy. Mr. Willrich was Assistant General Counsel of the U.S. Arms Control and Disarmament Agency from 1962-65. He was in private law practice with

Pillsbury, Madison, and Sutro in San Francisco 1960-62. Mr. Willrich served in the U.S. Air Force 1955-57 and was a pilot in Strategic Air Command.

Mr. Willrich's books include Radioactive Waste Management and Regulation (with R.K. Lester), 1977; Administration of Energy Shortages: Natural Gas and Petroleum, 1976; Energy and World Politics, 1975; Nuclear Theft: Risks and Safeguards (with T.B. Taylor), 1974; SALT: The Moscow Agreements and Beyond (with J.B. Rhinelander), 1974; and Global Politics of Nuclear Energy, 1971. He is also author of numerous journal articles on energy policy matters and national security issues.